The Revels Plays
COMPANION LIBRARY

E. A. J. HONIGMANN, J. R. MULRYNE
and R. L. SMALLWOOD
general editors

The court masque

THE REVELS PLAYS COMPANION LIBRARY

The
court masque

edited by DAVID LINDLEY

Manchester University Press

© MANCHESTER UNIVERSITY PRESS 1984

published by
MANCHESTER UNIVERSITY PRESS
Oxford Road, Manchester M13 9PL
and 51 Washington Street, Dover,
New Hampshire 03820, USA

BRITISH LIBRARY CATALOGUING IN PUBLICATION DATA

The court masque.
1. Masques—History and criticism
I. Lindley, David
822′.3   PN6120.M3

ISBN 0 7190 0961 8
ISBN 0 7190 0982 0 pbk

LIBRARY OF CONGRESS CATALOGING IN PUBLICATION DATA

The court masque.
(The Revels plays companion library)
Bibliography: p. 184
1. English drama—17th century—History and criticism—Addresses, essays, lectures. 2. Masques—History and criticism—Addresses, essays, lectures. 3. Great Britain—Court and courtiers—Addresses, essays, lectures. 4. Theater—Great Britain—History—17th century—Addresses, essays, lectures. 5. Theater and state—Great Britain—Addresses, essays, lectures. 6. Platonists—Addresses, essays, lectures. I. Lindley, David, 1948-. II. Series.

PR678.M3C68 1984   822′.3′09   83-24820

ISBN 0-7190-0961-8
ISBN 0-7190-0982-0 pbk

Printed in Great Britain by
Butler & Tanner Ltd, Frome and London

CONTENTS

*Illustrated by 12 pages of plates at the end of the chapter   *between* 168/9

SINCE THE LATE 1950S the series known as the Revels Plays has provided for students of the English Renaissance drama carefully edited texts of the major Elizabethan and Jacobean plays. The series now includes some of the best known drama of the period and has continued to expand, both within its original field and, to a lesser extent, beyond it, to include some important plays from the earlier Tudor and from the Restoration periods. The Revels Plays Companion Library is intended to further this expansion and to allow for new developments.

The aim of the Companion Library is to provide students of the Elizabethan and Jacobean drama with a fuller sense of its background and context. The series includes volumes of a variety of kinds. Small collections of plays, by a single author or concerned with a single theme and edited in accordance with the principles of textual modernisation of the Revels Plays, offer a wider range of drama than the main series can include. Together with editions of masques, pageants, and the non-dramatic work of Elizabethan and Jacobean playwrights, these volumes make it possible, within the overall Revels enterprise, to examine the achievement of the major dramatists from a broader perspective. Other volumes provide a fuller context for the plays of the period by offering new collections of documentary evidence on Elizabethan theatrical conditions and on the performance of plays during that period and later. A third aim of the series is to offer modern critical interpretation, in the form of collections of essays or of monographs, of the dramatic achievement of the English Renaissance.

So wide a range of material necessarily precludes the standard format and uniform general editorial control which is possible in the original series of Revels Plays. To a considerable extent, therefore, treatment and approach is determined by the needs and intentions of individual volume editors. Within this rather ampler area, however, we hope that the Companion Library maintains the standards of scholarship which have for so long characterised the Revels Plays, and that it offers a useful enlargement of the work of the series in preserving, illuminating, and celebrating the drama of Elizabethan and Jacobean England.

E. A. J. HONIGMANN
J. R. MULRYNE
R. L. SMALLWOOD

D A V I D   L I N D L E Y

Introduction

❧∘❧

IN MOST SURVEYS of English Renaissance literature, and most under-graduate courses, the court masque occupies at best a peripheral place. The reasons are not far to seek. Masques, by their very nature ephemeral works, written for a specific occasion and rarely performed more than once, appear to lack the solidity of the poetry or drama that is the customary target of the literary critic. Confronted by a few pages of text which is often chiefly concerned to describe scenery and costume, contains lyrics that have no music, and is frequently opaquely allegorical or nakedly flattering, the commentator is bewildered. It is not surprising, therefore, that despite a thin trickle of significant scholarly studies, the masque should have been largely neglected or lightly dismissed. Such indifference can only be supported by comments such as Francis Bacon's peremptory observation 'these things are but toys'.[1]

The underlying purpose of this book is to take issue with this attitude, and to demonstrate that the masque can be a fascinating and valuable object of study from a variety of points of view. The aim of this intro-duction is to map out the territory and indicate the place of individual essays within it.

The majority of the essays here assembled are concerned with the court masques of the Jacobean and Caroline periods, when, out of a very mixed ancestry, the genre evolved into a fairly fixed form. The sequence *poetic induction/antimasque(s)/masque/revels/epilogue* is common to most of the works of this kind, and, as Alastair Fowler observes, it means that 'Renaissance masque ... is very readily identified'.[2] Its heart is the appear-ance of a group of noble personages dressed in elaborate disguise to celebrate a particular occasion and to honour their monarch. They per-form some specially designed (and well-rehearsed) masque dances, and then take out the members of the court audience in the communal dance of the revels. The fundamental job of the masque writer was to provide a fiction to explain the disguised arrival, and the basic symbolic assertion of all court masques derived from the moment of the dissolution of the masque's fiction into the social reality of the court. The antimasque (also called the ante-masque, or antic masque) became a fixed part of the masque's pattern after 1609, when Ben Jonson, in answer to Queen Anne's request for 'some Daunce, or shew, that might praecede hers, and have the place of a foyle, or false-Masque' responded with the presentation of twelve witches 'not as a *Masque*, but a spectacle of strangenesse, producing multiplicity of Gesture'.[3] The antimasque was therefore clearly distinguished from the main device, and usually performed by professional actors. It satisfied the Renaissance appetite for 'variety' as an aesthetic desideratum, and offered the writer an opportunity for excercising his wit to establish a symbolic appropriateness for the contrastive pattern this form offered him.

Most frequently, of course, the formal pattern of the masque became an image of harmony and order, and an idealisation of the court by whom and for whom it was performed. Discord threatens in the antimasque, but is inevitably overturned by the epiphany of the masquers' arrival. As Stephen Orgel says: 'the masque presents the triumph of an aristocratic community; at its center is a belief in the hierarchy and a faith in the power of idealisation'.[4] But for all the security of its form and its self-confident assertion of courtly values, the masque was, throughout its history, a genre vulnerable to attack from those who did not share its values or refused to accept the serious claims for its potential that Jonson and others advanced. At the same time its very form contained within itself tensions that threatened its firmly maintained harmony.

The 'canonic' masque of the Jacobean and Caroline period grew from a fusion of diverse elements. Alastair Fowler comments:

> The Elizabethan masque combined mummery, masquerade, pageant, and entertainment: discrete kinds that were to some extent recognised as such and referred to by their separate names. Subsequently, however, a successful combination will come to be regarded as a single repertoire. We are no longer much aware which features of masque derive from which contributory kind.[5]

Enid Welsford has traced the evolution of the masque, and for Stephen Orgel it is precisely the process of fusing the 'discrete kinds' that constitutes the triumph of the artist (specifically, Ben Jonson).[6] But this triumph is bought at some cost, and without reduplicating the details of the form's ancestry, it is possible to see some of the problematic features of the later masques as resulting from the effort to yoke together kinds that are significantly dissimilar.

In the first place the court masque sits rather uneasily between two basic postures—those of celebration and offering. When Henry VIII burst in, disguised, upon the ladies in 1513 he may have been initiating the history of the masque, but basically he was doing no more than play a courtly game, provide an excuse for a party. While it was true that his own place as monarch had to be respected (which, as Orgel observes, generated problems for the masque writer who had to 'create a figure that will serve as an adequate representation of the monarch beneath the mask'[7]) the involvement of the sovereign as masquer, from Henry VIII to Charles and Henrietta Maria, emphasises the sense of the court masque as ceremonious play.[8]

But many Tudor pageants, progress shows, and entertainments were quite clearly offerings *to* the monarch, the privileged spectator, by University, city, acting company or grateful courtier. (The difference is that between the entry of the lords in *Love's Labour's Lost* disguised as Muscovites and the pageant of the Nine Worthies presented to them by Holofernes—in both cases the failure of the projects results from the wilful failure of the audience to recognise the nature of the enterprise.) Some later entertainments preserved these characteristics. Campion's *Caversham Entertainment* and Jonson's two late entertainments at Welbeck and Bolsover have something in common with the progress entertainments offered to Queen Elizabeth. Some were actually pageants at which gifts were offered, such as the disastrous entertainment Robert Cecil mounted at Theobalds for Christian IV, or the elegant piece Jonson designed for the same nobleman when he surrendered the house at Theobalds to the King in 1607. Very many more later masques were offerings by the Inns of Court or by courtiers anxious to display their readiness to serve the monarch. (Bacon's financial support for the Inns of Court masques presented in 1613 and 1614 is but one obvious example.) In such cases it may well be that the patrons of the masques used the opportunity to express a particular view of events before their sovereign. I have argued elsewhere that such was the case with Campion's *Lord Hay's Masque*,[9] and the motivation of the Inns of Court masque, *The Triumph of Peace*, seems to have included a wish to draw abuses to the attention of Charles I. Nor must it be forgotten that outside the court the City pageants (often written by dramatists) continued throughout the period to give voice to a political point of view often at variance with that of official policy.[10] Furthermore, the posture of offering was frequently maintained in masques which used as their basic fiction a narrative of masquers coming from distant parts to honour the monarch.

The point here is that though such an offering may be panegyric in intent, it retains an independence from its recipient that the masque as courtly celebration must find difficult. So, for example, Queen Elizabeth's fierce reaction to the Earl of Leicester's Kenilworth entertainments persuading her to marry could scarcely be expressed in a masque where the sovereign performed.[11] The fusion of celebration and offering inevitably increases the risk of the masque becoming mere self-confirming narcissism, a risk that, it might be argued, became increasingly difficult to avoid when both Charles and Henrietta Maria took part in masques, however it might be circumvented before King James who did not himself dance as a masquer.

The court masque, as we have seen, embodies a kind of contest in the opposition of antimasque and masque. Such a pattern has strong links with the characteristic inclusion of debate in many kinds of Tudor entertainment, which provided, as Altman suggests, 'the opportunity to entertain opposing ideas and to discover how they might be defended'.[12] In many such debates open-endedness rather than conclusion was the goal, and in Sidney's *Lady of May*, for example, a dispute between Therion and Espilus was offered to the Queen for adjudication. In some of the moral interludes, however, the aim was to secure a reconciliation of opposed views, as was the case in the 1527 entertainment *Riches and Love*, where the dispute was articulated, maintained by a fight at barriers, and resolved by the entry of an old man who declared that 'both be necessarie to princes'.[13]

A debate pattern was obviously very suitable surround for a tilt, and though the Elizabethan enthusiasm for tilting was somewhat attenuated in Jacobean times, Jonson supplied texts for three such events, including the 1613/14 *A Challenge at Tilt*, where two Cupids dispute which of them is the 'true' god of love, summon nobles to fight on each side, but are finally reconciled when told by Hymen that they are both true and necessary embodiments of love, representing Eros and Anteros. But the pattern could also be employed in masques like *Pleasure Reconciled to Virtue* which celebrated the uniting of these opposed qualities in an interwoven dance.

In general, however, the court masque form inhibits such humanist debate. The antimasque, by its grotesque nature, and because it was performed by professional actors, is no equal for the noble presence of the silent masquers. Characteristically the masque does not debate, but asserts, for all that its form appears to offer a dialectical possibility. The Jacobean and Caroline form in general represents a distinct narrowing, even anaesthetising, of the possibilities that were open to the earlier entertainments.

Helen Cooper's essay argues that such narrowing is evidenced also in the representation of place in the court masque, where illusionist settings confine and contain the symbolic fluidity of the stage world in morality play or drama. Thomas Nashe's show, *Summer's Last Will*, incorporates many of the features of Elizabethan entertainments in its idiosyncratic style, and Elizabeth Cook demonstrates how the active exploration of that variety deliberately resists the kind of ordering the Jacobean masque required.

But however tempting it might be to see the court masque of the seventeenth century as containing and suppressing the potentially uncomfortable aspects of the traditions it fused, and however seductive it would be to explain this narrowing as the inevitable symptom of the attempt to concentrate political power in the hands of the sovereign that reached its climax in the period of Charles's 'personal rule', to do so would be a gross oversimplification.

Jonson, in reducing to order the disparate elements of court entertainment, did so to make possible something serious. In the lengthy preface to *Hymenaei* he speaks of the way he wishes to convert the conventional demands upon the masque into something altogether more purposeful. Familiar though it may be, it is worth quoting at length:

> It is a noble and just advantage, that the things subjected to *understanding* have of those which are objected to *sense*, that the one sort are but momentarie, and meerely taking; the other impressing, and lasting: Else the glorie of all these *solemnities* had perish'd like a blaze, and gone out, in the *beholders* eyes. So short-liv'd are the *bodies* of all things, in comparison of their *soules*. And, though *bodies* oft-times have the ill luck to be sensually preferr'd, they find afterwards, the good fortune (when *soules* live) to be utterly forgotten. This it is hath made the most royall *Princes*, and the greatests *persons* (who are commonly the *personaters* of these *actions*) not onely studious of riches, and magnificence in the outward celebration, or shew; (which rightly becomes them) but curious after the most high, and heartie *inventions*, to furnish the inward parts: (and those grounded upon *antiquitie*, and solid *learnings*) which, though their *voyce* be taught to sound to present occasions, their *sense*, or doth or should alwayes lay hold on more remov'd *mysteries*.[14]

This richly suggestive passage will provide, as it were, the text for much of the ensuing discussion, but the core of Jonson's claim for the potential of the masque is its capacity to 'lay hold on more remov'd mysteries'.

Underlying this statement is a neo-Platonic conception of the possibilities of art. Images are shadows of the 'truth' that lies behind and beyond them. The myths which masques enact provide for their spectators access to the significances they adumbrate. To this end Jonson fashioned his masques from the repositories of allegorised myths by authorities such as Cartari, Comes, Giraldi, and Ripa. At the same time the images of the scene designer, also secured by their scholarship, were imbued with significance as a making visible of hidden truth.[15] Similarly, the music of the masque enacted the Orphic power of the art to stir, calm, and order the passions by its imitation of the cosmic harmony, and dance was seen as an analogue of the cosmic dance as it traced out the ground in signifying patterns.

Such ambitious aspiration for the masque was not, of course, peculiar to Jonson. Indeed the most thoroughgoing attempts to produce entertainments on neo-Platonic principles were probably those associated with the French court. Frances Yates has amply demonstrated the way in which the *Ballet Comique de la Reine* fulfilled the theories of Baïf's neo-Platonic Academy in its plot (based on the Circe myth and later echoed in *Tempe Restored*), in its music, composed in a style (*musique mesurée*) which endeavoured to recreate the classical unification of word and tune, and in its dancing which traced geometrical patterns derived from the Academy's belief that 'all things are related to number, both in the outer world of nature and in the inner world of man's soul'.[16] Neo-Platonism is everywhere apparent in the English court masque, and has been discussed by Frances Yates, D.J. Gordon, Stephen Orgel, and others. But Jonson's confidence in his power to make something 'impressing and lasting' out of the transitory show was not without its difficulties and its critics.

In the first place the hermetic allusiveness of the iconography of the masque, though in theory it should 'work its end upon the senses' of the beholders whether they comprehend it or not, just as Spenser's *Faerie Queene* should 'fashion a gentleman' even if he only responds to the outer rind of the allegory, was not necessarily received perceptively by its aristocratic audience. Jonson complained at the end of the *Hymenaei* preface 'It is not my fault, if I fill them out *Nectar*, and they runne to Metheglin', and with some relief dedicated *The Masque of Queens*, with all its copious annotation, to the judicious understanding of Prince Henry. Chapman complained of insensitive and uncomprehending auditors in the preface to his *Memorable Masque*, and Campion, in *The Lords' Masque*, berated those who could not 'taste them in their dignitie'.[17] The schoolmasterly tone of these rebukes can scarcely conceal the writers' uneasy awareness that the court audience was not, on the whole, 'studious' or sensitive to the aspect of the masque genre that later literary critics find most amenable to discussion. It is indeed symptomatic that there is scarcely any contemporary comment on the iconology of masques, but abundant testimony to the splendour of the 'outward show'.

The educative ambition of Jonson's masque ideal was, however, vulnerable to more than the ignorance of his audience. For though the masquers bear the weight of the masque's affirmative symbolism, they are never fully absorbed into the roles they play. For, as Orgel puts it, 'a masquer's disguise is a representation of the courtier beneath. He retains his personality and hence his position in the social hierarchy.'[18] Such identification of the role with the performer inevitably renders the educative purpose of the masque precarious. Though Campion, at the end of *The Lords' Masque*, adjures the masquers who had been introduced as heavenly stars to 'remember the fires that shined in you of late', the tendency must always be for the role to authenticate and validate the courtier's sense of his own importance, rather than to persuade him to aspiration and effort. As Jonas Barish suggests, the masque 'represents a society not so much aspiring after, as joyfully contemplating its own well-being'.[19] Such an attitude must be largely impervious to any educative stimulus.

Samuel Daniel probed a further weakness in Jonson's high claim for the masque's capacity to outlive its brief moment of display. Since all its mythology and symbolism are constructs made by an artist, they are all subject to time. Just as Prospero turns the dissolved masque for Ferdinand and Miranda into an image of our little life, rounded with a sleep, so, John Pitcher here argues in defence of the neglected *Tethys' Festival*, Daniel insists upon the vital importance of the court recognising its own impermanence as figured in the transitory harmonies of his masque. (A position strikingly, and surprisingly, similar to Nashe's in *Summer's Last Will*.)

But perhaps the most vigorous abuse of the masque emanated from the King's opponents, those outside the court, or disaffected by the direction of royal policy. Lumped together as 'Puritans' they have usually been characterised as mistrustful of the image-making of the masque. David Norbrook challenges this standard picture in his essay. The Puritans, he argues, were often not opposed to the philosophy of the masque itself, though conscious of a need to redirect and reform it to serve their religious and political beliefs. Milton's *Comus* is seen here (as in Helen Cooper's and Jennifer Chibnall's essays) as radical and innovative, but fundamentally a direct heir of the earlier tradition. The relationship of Milton's masque to its tradition is more fully worked out in John Creaser's study.

In the end, however, the ambitions of Jonson, Campion, Chapman, and others were undermined by the erosion of confidence and belief in their whole way of thinking about art. By the time of the Restoration such idealism was in decay. It would be far beyond the scope of this introduction to suggest the complex interplay of factors that generated this change, but the symptoms are displayed by Paul Hammond in his essay on Dryden's *Albion and Albanius*. This work contains many conscious echoes of pre-Civil War masques, but yet, he argues, fails to cohere as different fashions, aesthetic assumptions, and political circumstances render insubstantial its inherited neo-Platonic imagery. For though the description 'Masque' survives in the later seventeenth century, it is applied very randomly to entertainments whose connection with the earlier genre is at the level of theatrical ingenuity and splendour, of an operatic musical style (though here the direct link with the earlier declamatory air is almost certainly less than was once thought), and of the employment of classical myth (though usually in a far more decorative and enhumanised form). Blow's opera *Venus and Adonis* is an exquisite and moving work, but though called a masque, it has really very little in common with Jonson's ambitious educative project.

For the critic it is vital that he recognise and respect Jonson's claim for the masque's capability to 'lay hold on some more remov'd mystery'. Much work remains to be done in the detailed analysis of the iconology of specific masques. But at the same time the dominating presence of Jonson should not blind us to the fact that his enterprise was not universally applauded or even comprehended, and his energetic neo-Platonism, far from making 'the beholders wise' could seem, as Arthur Wilson saw it, to 'wrap up' the King's spirit 'and keep it from descending towards earthly things'.[20]

Jonson himself was, of course, aware of the danger, and suggests that the anchor is the masques' requirement to 'sound to present occasions'. Later, in his 1630 masque *Loves Triumph through Callipolis*, he asserts that 'publique Spectacles, eyther have bene, or ought to be the mirrors of mans life'.[21] If the mirror thus offered is bound to be a secular version of Herbert's 'thankfull glasse That mends the lookers eyes', 'the well that washes what it shows',[22] rather than the satiric reflector of the plays, nonetheless the image suggests that Jonson saw the connection of the court masque with the political and social realities out of which it grew as vitally significant.

It has, indeed, always been recognised that the masque was necessarily involved with court politics. Both in general terms and more specifically, critics have attempted to relate individual masques to the particular occasions for which they were composed. But, as Leah Marcus rightly observes: 'Having noted such correspondences, we have tended to set them gently aside as curiosities for the antiquarians, less than central to our consideration of the masque as art.' She goes on to argue that this is mistaken since:

> In a good masque by Jonsonian standards, 'present occasions' are not merely 'named' but divided into component elements, rearranged and rebuilt so that the form taken by the masque becomes an original and often sturdily independent statement about the situation it commemorates. The masque's occasion is the key to its unity and to its autonomy as art.[23]

It is in this belief, or some variant of it, that a number of recent discussions of the masques have been written, and from it that several of the essays in this volume take their starting point. For if the neo-Platonic aspiration of the masque threatens to take it and its participants into a comfortably enclosed never-never land, it is the focus on the specific occasion that allows the masque writer and his patrons to preserve something of the hortatory directness of the older pageants and progress entertainments, and attention to particular participants and precise political context that allows the critic to comprehend fully the subtlety and sophistication of the form.

Few masques, perhaps, offer very direct criticism of the monarch or his policies—though Campion's *Lord Hay's Masque* implies a somewhat critical attitude to James's conduct of the project to unite England and Scotland,[24] and Shirley's *Triumph of Peace* points, however tentatively, to abuses that the king should rectify. But, as Leah Marcus points out, the later masques of Jonson, where the antimasques frequently centre around the life of the court itself, often characterise abuses that the King at least tolerated, so that the restoration of order in the masque itself takes on a positive, hortatory function.

Though in many cases close study of contexts will reveal an attitude or statement that is explicitly supportive of royal policy, it is still true that many of the opacities of meaning or apparent randomness of form are only to be understood after such enquiry. Sara Pearl's essay shows how Jonson's late Jacobean masques, hitherto largely neglected by his apologists as imperfectly controlled in comparison to earlier works, emerge with a fresh pointedness when placed against the background of the discussion of news and the reporting of news at the time. I myself have elsewhere attempted to rescue Campion's masques from their unjustified neglect by stressing their sensitive response to the occasions for which they were commissioned;[25] John Pitcher here performs the same service for Samuel Daniel, so often assumed to be a sad throwback to a pre-Jonsonian age. Jennifer Chibnall argues that the Caroline masques are not a decline from some Jacobean ideal, and John Creaser explores the enriched understanding of Milton's *Comus* that results from proper attention to the detailed circumstances of its presentation.

It is not perhaps surprising that this should be a direction that masque criticism in general is taking at the present. Apart from the stimulus to literary critics offered by Marxist or sociological approaches, the work of historians too has undergone significant redirection in recent years. The old Whig contempt for monarchical vanities has been supplanted and, perhaps more significantly, the teleological approach which mined the period 1603-40 only for signs and portents of the civil war to come, with its consequent tendency to divide the realm into conveniently opposed camps—court and country, Laudian and Puritan—is giving way to a 'revisionist' history that maps out the intricacies and complexities of factional politics, revealing a much more fluid and variable pattern of affiliation than was convenient for the older history. David Norbrook's essay bears witness to the new awareness that results from an attention to the facts about Puritan attitudes to the masque that is not conditioned by a simplistic wish to divide the Stuart world into two incompatible camps, while John Creaser maps out the way the Puritan Milton could, in all conscience, write *Comus* for a 'royalist' occasion.

The implication of this kind of study is to broaden significantly the *kind* of interest the masque might properly have, both for students of literature and for historians. For the historical detail is not merely a 'background' which the literary student has to recover in order to footnote his text before turning back to aesthetic judgement; instead, the masques themselves encode and express a particular historical moment in a complex and often revealing way, as Jennifer Chibnall's essay demonstrates.

Preoccupation with detailed exegesis should not, however, obscure the simple political gesture that every court masque was expected to make.

David Lindley

Jonson in *Hymenaei* speaks of the royal princes and greatest persons being 'studious of riches, and magnificence in the outward celebration, or shew; (which rightly became them)'. The aim was simply to declare the magnanimity of the monarch and promote the reputation of his court in the eyes of the world—especially the foreign ambassadors whose invitation occasioned so many bitter wrangles about precedence.[26] The response of the Venetian ambassador to the *Masque of Beauty* was exactly what was desired:

> The apparatus and the cunning of the stage machinery was a miracle, the abundance and beauty of the lights immense, the music and dance most sumptuous. But what beggared all else and possibly exceeded the public expectation was the wealth of pearls and jewels that adorned the Queen and her ladies, so abundant and splendid that in everyone's opinion no other court could have displayed such pomp.[27]

From this positive response many would have dissented, both the financial advisers within the court, and the many outside who saw such display as typifying the extravagance and gilded corruption which they so hated. (Such ambivalent response still persists in attenuated form today when approving reports of crowds gasping at the diamonds worn by the Queen or the Princess of Wales are balanced by the censorious rumblings that attend the annual publication of the Civil List.) In the end it probably scarcely matters whether the court masques were in truth inordinately expensive, or the occasions of drunkenness and dissipation; the point is only that for many people they provided a convenient image for aspects of the court from which they felt increasingly alienated.

Certainly for many dramatists the masque provided a powerful metaphor for the concealed villainy of courtly society, nowhere more successfully than in the double masque of revengers which brings to grotesque conclusion *The Revenger's Tragedy*, summing up the play's obsessive employment of images of disguise and superficial vanity. The romance mode is much less hostile to the masque, but Shakespeare's *Tempest*, I argue, is a work which analyses with considerable subtlety the ambiguities and problematic features of the masque genre. Certainly students of drama in this period should be aware of the way the form and strategy of the court masque provided a generic 'set' that dramatists could exploit and audiences respond to.[28]

The Tempest, I suggest, uses musical symbolism and gesture to focus its interrogation of the masque. That it should do so is symptomatic of the vital place that music held in the court masque's display. A fanfare often announced the arrival of the monarch; songs meditated upon the action and its significance or, more importantly perhaps, were the vehicles of the charms which transformed or freed the noble masquers. These court shows, like Prospero's island, were full of noises, sounds, and sweet airs. It has already been remarked how the conventional neo-Platonic significance afforded to music supported and enacted the idealising purposes of the masque. But at the same time the conditions under which music was performed in the masque had considerable significance for the evolution of musical style itself.

In the first place, Renaissance instruments were, in the main, much quieter than their modern counterparts. Composers and masque designers were compelled to take this into account. It is not surprising that Thomas Campion, himself a composer, should have left one of the most detailed accounts of musical arrangements in his description of *The Lord Hay's Masque*:

> The upper part, where the cloth and chaire of State were plac't, had scaffoldes and seates on eyther side continued to the skreene; right before it was made a partition for the dancing place; on the right hand whereof were consorted ten Musitions, with Basse and Meane lutes, a Bandora, double Sackbott and an Harpsichord, with two treble Violins; on the other side somewhat neerer the skreene were plac't 9 Violins and three lutes; and to answere both Consorts (as it were in a triangle) sixe Cornets, and six Chappell voyces, were seated almost right against them, in a place raised higher in respect of the pearcing sound of those Instruments.[29]

This polychoral arrangement is used dramatically throughout the masque, and, symbolically, the first time all the consorts play together is at the moment when the praises of King James are sung.

An account of a similar sort of arrangement in the records of the Merchant Taylors' Company indicates that this was not atypical, and also suggests the practical reason for it:

> And upon either side of the Hall in the windowe neere the upper end were galleries or seates made for musique in either of which were seaven singuler choice musitions playing on their lutes. And in the shipp which did hang aloft in the Hall three men and very skilful who sang to his Majesty. And over the skreene cornettes and lowd musique, wherein it is to be remembered that the multitute and noyse was so great that the lutes nor songs could hardly be heard or understood.[30]

The spatial placement of the musicians was some sort of guarantee that the music would be heard, at least by the most privileged spectators. But the demands of audibility also mean that a polyphonic style of composition with overlapping voice parts would be inappropriate. The massed bands of lutes prohibit the intricate harmonic texture of Dowland's inward-looking song. What therefore evolves is a declamatory style, where slow-moving chords support a flexible, heroic declamation of the words by the singer, or else a clear part-song texture where the voices move from syllable to syllable simultaneously. The practical necessities of the masque were probably at least as important a stimulus to composers like Ferrabosco, Lanier, and Lawes as their desire to imitate continental, especially Italian, composers.

The specific demands of masque music, and the consequent stylistic evolution have their own importance in musical history, not least in the fact that the performative art needed to do justice to declamatory song made it an increasingly professional preserve. But for the student of the masque itself the significance of the music lies in part in the way it indicates how the masque in its later stages moves away from a court function whose focus is entirely upon the noble personages taking part, to an increasingly performative art form. The increasing elaboration of antimasques, and the ingenious inventions of Inigo Jones, similarly testify to the way the genre tended to become an entertainment presented *to* a passive audience, rather than a ritual game which involved them.

Salmacida Spolia, the last masque performed before the civil war, is made up of an elaborate series of antimasques articulating the discord that threatens the crown. The climax is the successive entries of King and Queen as masquers. While the work does celebrate the power of the monarchs to image and engender order, its aim is much more polemic. It is a performance designed to demonstrate to an audience the monarch's awareness of discontent, and determination to control it. But the irony and pathos of the masque is that it was a performance aimed at an audience who would never see it—and who would scarcely have been satisfied by its message.

Upon this last masque Inigo Jones exerted all the art he had acquired during the last thirty years or so. It contains successive elaborate transformations of the scene, descents upon clouds, carefully contrived effects of coloured candlelight reflecting off costume jewellery, and costumes rich and strange.

It has always been recognised that the court masque, largely because of Inigo Jones, represented a significant period in the evolution of the theatre. He achieved magnificent scenic effects, first through the employment of the *machina versatilis* or turning machine, later through his adoption of the *scena ductilis*, or series of shutters, that were successively parted to reveal further scenes in fluid transformation. Lighting effects were generated by shining candles through coloured liquid. More significantly, perhaps, he played a major part in introducing the perspective, illusionist stage to England, with enormous consequence for later theatrical history.[31] Some of the implications of these developments are discussed by Helen Cooper.

But Jones was not merely a theatrical showman, despite Jonson's bitter opinion of him in the last years of their collaboration. His art, as Gordon, and Orgel and Strong, have demonstrated, was put to the service of a coherent and seriously-held philosophical position.[32] Furthermore it is too simple to dismiss the wonderful and surprising effects upon which contemporaries commented as mere sensation. The amazement that devices like the massive mountain of *Coelum Britannicum* provoked, as it rose out of a mere six feet of under-stage space, expressed 'the age's wonder at the infinite possibilities of machinery, scenic or otherwise'. As Orgel rightly observes, Inigo Jones's mastery is a demonstration of the 'essential divinity of the human mind' in its capacity to 'overcome gravity, control the natural world, reveal the operation of the heavenly spheres'.[33]

John Peacock's essay stresses another aspect of Jones's achievement, and one that it is all too easy for the literary student to overlook. By giving attention to Jones's manipulation of continental models he not only reminds us of the significant, but often forgotten, fact that the English court masque exists in a European context, but demonstrates that for Jones the court masque was in a very significant sense a part of a larger effort of learning, the attempt to capture and represent the classical past. Jonson in the *Hymenaei* preface insisted that the 'most high and heartie *inventions*' must be 'grounded upon *antiquitie*, and solid *learnings*'. For both artists the court masques must be seen as having equal significance with their other enterprises.

The court masque, then, is a genre full of implication and significance. It is at once the last expression of a full-blown Renaissance idealism in the service of a hierarchical and ordered view of the world and a form which permitted the evolution of musical and theatrical techniques that look forward to the post-Restoration era. It is at the same time an art which aspires to translate its participants into an ideal contemplative vision and a kind intimately related to the flux of political reality. Its confident celebration and triumphant assertion are couched in a literary form that is full of inner tension. It is a kind open to a wide variety of attention, from literary critic, theatre historian, political and cultural analyst alike. Indeed it is entirely right at a time when the business of literary study has become more varied in approach than ever before that the court masque should be brought in from the margins of critical activity to a substantial and more central place.

NOTES

1 *Essays* (London, 1625), No. 37. For a modern version of this attitude see Glynne Wickham 'The Stuart Mask' in *Shakespeare's Dramatic Heritage* (London, 1969), pp. 103-18.

2 *Kinds of Literature* (Oxford, 1982), pp. 60-1. It is, of course, true that there were many entertainments throughout the period both at court, in the city streets, or in private households that are generically ambiguous, but the basic point still holds.

3 *Ben Jonson*, ed. C.H. Herford and Percy and Evelyn Simpson, 11 vols (Oxford, 1925-1952), 7, p. 282. (Further references to this edition, throughout this collection, are to 'Herford and Simpson', with volume and page numbers.) Some sort of anticipatory dances had been employed in

David Lindley

earlier entertainments, but it is Jonson who ensures the antimasque's firm place and contrastive character.

4 *The Illusion of Power* (Berkeley, Los Angeles, and London, 1975), p. 40.

5 *Kinds of Literature*, p. 171.

6 Enid Welsford, *The Court Masque* (Cambridge, 1927); Stephen Orgel, *The Jonsonian Masque* (Cambridge, Mass., 1965).

7 *The Jonsonian Masque*, p. 22.

8 For a fascinating study of the place of role-playing in courtly life, see Daniel Javitch, *Poetry and Courtliness* (Princeton, N.J., 1978).

9 David Lindley, 'Who Paid for Campion's *Lord Hay's Masque*?', *Notes and Queries*, N.S. 26 (1979), pp. 144–5.

10 See David Bergeron, *English Civic Pageantry* (London, 1971) and Margot Heinemann, *Puritanism and Theatre* (London, 1980).

11 See Helen Cooper's essay.

12 Joel B. Altman, *The Tudor Play of Mind* (Berkeley, Los Angeles, and London, 1978), p. 107.

13 Orgel, *Jonsonian Masque*, p. 30. For Elizabethan tilts see Roy Strong, *The Cult of Elizabeth* (London, 1977), Part Two.

14 Herford and Simpson, 7, p. 209.

15 For a useful discussion of the theory see D.J. Gordon, 'Roles and Mysteries', in *The Renaissance Imagination*, ed. Stephen Orgel (Berkeley, Los Angeles, and London, 1975), pp. 3–23.

16 Frances Yates, *The French Academies of the Sixteenth Century* (London, 1947), pp. 236–74. For French court masques in general see Margaret M. McGowan, *L'Art du Ballet de Cour* (Paris, 1963). Jonson echoed this theory of the significance of dance in *Pleasure Reconciled to Virtue*:

> For Dauncing is an excercise
> not only shews the movers wit,
> but maketh the beholder wise,
> as he hath power to rise to it.
>
> (Herford and Simpson, 7, p. 489).

17 Herford and Simpson, 7, pp. 280–1; *The Plays of George Chapman: The Comedies*, ed. Allan Holaday and Michael Kiernana (Urbana, Ill., 1970), pp. 569–70; *The Works of Thomas Campion*, ed. W.R. Davis (London, 1969), p. 251.

18 *The Jonsonian Masque*, p. 117. For a confirmation see Trumbull's description of *Oberon* where all the masquers' costumes included 'a very rich blue band across the body, except that of the prince, whose band was scarlet to distinguish him from the rest' (Herford and Simpson, 10, p. 522).

19 *Ben Jonson and the Language of Prose Comedy* (Cambridge, Mass., 1960), p. 244.

20 *The History of Great Britain* (London, 1653), reprinted in W. Kennet, *A Complete History of England*, 3 vols (London, 1706), 2, p. 694.

21 Herford and Simpson, 7, p. 735.

22 'The Holy Scriptures I', ll. 8–10.

23 Leah Sinanoglou Marcus, 'Masquing Occasions and Masque Structure', *Research Opportunities in Renaissance Drama*, 24 (1981), p. 7.

24 David Lindley, 'Campion's *Lord Hay's Masque* and Anglo-Scottish Union', *Huntington Library Quarterly*, 43 (1979/80), pp. 1–11.

25 In *Thomas Campion* (Leiden, forthcoming), Chapter 4.

26 For an amusing account of efforts to pacify the wounded pride of ambassadors see John Finett, *Finetti Philoxenis* (London, 1656).

27 Herford and Simpson, 10, p. 457.

28 See Inga-Stina Ewbank, ' "These Pretty Devices": A Study of Masques in Plays', in *A Book of Masques*, ed. T.J.B. Spencer and Stanley Wells (Cambridge, 1967), pp. 407-48 for a useful survey, and consult select bibliography for other studies.

29 *Works*, ed. Davis, p. 211.

30 Quoted in N.E. McLure, *The Letters and Epigrams of Sir John Harington* (Philadelphia, 1930), p. 99.

31 See the works by Campbell, Nicoll, Wickham, and Southern in the select biliography.

32 D.J. Gordon, 'Poet and Architect: The Intellectual Setting of the Quarrel between Ben Jonson and Inigo Jones', in *The Renaissance Imagination*, pp. 77-101; Orgel and Strong, *Inigo Jones* (New York and London, 1973; hereafter referred to as Orgel and Strong).

33 *The Illusion of Power*, pp. 57-8.

ELIZABETH COOK

'Death proves them all but toyes': Nashe's unidealising show

THE FIRST SCENE of Caryl Churchill's play *Top Girls* presents a dinner party in a contemporary London restaurant. The hostess, Marlene, is a fictional but credible modern woman who is celebrating her promotion to the position of Managing Director of the Top Girls employment agency. Her guests are a mixed bunch. They are all women of admirable fortitude, but there the similarity stops. The last to arrive is Patient Griselda, heroine of Chaucer's *Clerke's Tale*. Marlene introduces her to the others:

> This is Joan who was Pope in the ninth century, and Isabella Bird, the Victorian traveller, and Lady Nijo from Japan, Emperor's concubine and Buddhist nun, thirteenth century, nearer your own time, and Gret who was painted by Breughel. Griselda's in Boccaccio and Petrarch and Chaucer because of her extraordinary marriage.[1]

Here is an enormous range of status: not just of social status—with a pope, a peasant, and a company director—but of ontological status. Here at one table are two documented historical figures (Lady Nijo and Isabella Bird), one apocryphal historical figure (Pope Joan), and three fictional figures of whom one is a symbol (Dull Gret), one an *exemplum* (Patient Griselda), and one a verisimilar figure from contemporary life (Marlene). But these distinctions seem to break down in the very act of being applied, just as the barriers between the characters are dissolved and connections established in the course of their conversation. They are united in the fictional world of the play and that fictional world has itself been enlarged by the incorporation of historical figures and of previously established fictions. The inclusion of historical figures in a contemporary fiction has the effect of authenticating that fiction whilst simultaneously releasing the historical figures from the restraints of contingency so that they are invested with the power of fictions. The realms of nature and of fancy are seen as mutually enlarging—as in Cleopatra's experience of a world which has included Antony: 'Nature wants stuff / To vie strange forms with fancy; yet, to imagine / An Antony, were Nature's piece 'gainst fancy, / Condemning shadows quite.'[2]

A Renaissance audience might have found Caryl Churchill's juxtaposition of characters rather less *avant garde* than a modern audience finds it. An Elizabethan would have been used to, and not confused by, such differences in ontological status. The magnificent street shows of the Renaissance assumed of their spectators an easy ability to interpret and distinguish between real and allegorical figures, to relate symbolic dumb-show to historical narrative, to understand and 'read' symbolic as well as naturalistic modes of representation. The three-tiered triumphal arches which were used to stage spectacles at royal entries would combine carving, painting, dumb-show, and dialogue[3]. The elaborate configuration of the whole must have resembled the allegorical title-pages of so many Renaissance books.[4] But whilst one tends to associate the interpretative sophistication needed to read the many levels of these title-pages with the learned literate for whom these books were produced, we should remember that very similar skills were being assumed and drawn upon in the most popular and spectacular forms of entertainment.

The court masque was hardly the most popular (in the precise sense) of Renaissance dramatic forms.[5] Its wonderful mechanisms were costly as well as elaborate. The glory of the English court masque, as developed by two men of rare technical and intellectual prowess, Inigo Jones and Ben Jonson, would not have been seen had it not been for court patronage and a budgeting capacity understandably resented by Parliamentarians.[6] While Jones and Jonson argued bitterly over who had contributed the 'soul' and who the 'body' to their (just) co-operative enterprise, it remains true that without liberal funding no soul would have been made visible enough to argue about.[7] Whilst the guilds who produced civic pageants were often prosperous and capable of sumptuous display on their moveable pageant waggons, the splendour of the court masque, which had the benefits of a roof and a fixed audience, was on a different scale. But more than the cost, the rationale of the court masque made it intrinsically élitist. The culminating moment to which the court masque moved was the moment of the dance: a moment at which the spectators, having witnessed the Ideal versions of themselves on the stage, are joined by the masquers. The barriers between spectators and wonderful spectacle are broken down at this moment and the real is assimilated into the Ideal. The spectators are, symbolically, perfected, and the ease of their perfectibility has to do with an hierarchical conception of the natural order which has God at the summit and earthly kings as God's deputies. The higher up you are socially, the less far you have to go to be perfect. Such a rationale underlay the use of masque by the Stuart court as a reaffirmation of political power.[8] But the reaffirmation became increasingly narcissistic, preaching only to those desperate to be converted.

The extraordinary way in which the real figure of Elizabeth I was dramatised and allegorised in her lifetime so that she became a living fiction, has also a lot to do with political affirmation.[9] But the movement between the world of real historical particulars and the symbolic world to which those particulars were expected to aspire, seems to have been more a two-way one in the Elizabethan than in the Jacobean era. The relative informality of the Elizabethan masque must have facilitated this. The literary and scenic complexity and fixity of the Stuart masque would probably have prohibited the kind of intervention of which Elizabeth was fond. Whatever the reasons, Elizabeth seems to have been better than James at accommodating the unexpected, and the impromptu nature of her responses at the receptions and entertainments arranged for and around her must have sharpened the sense of reciprocation between the actual world and the world of desirable fiction.[10]

Thomas Nashe's show *Summer's Last Will and Testament*, which dramatises the turning of the year, was devised on the occasion of a royal visit to Archbishop Whitgift's palace at Croydon late in the summer of 1592.[11] The allegorical figure of Summer, whose first appearance is an emblematic one, leaning wearily on the shoulders of his successors, Autumn and Winter, announces that he is more than ready to depart:

> This month have I layne languishing a bed,
> Looking eche houre to yeeld my life and throne;
> And dyde I had in deed unto the earth,
> But that *Eliza*, Englands beauteous Queene,
> On whom all seasons prosperously attend,
> Forbad the execution of my fate,
> Untill her joyfull progresse was expir'd.
> For her doth Summer live, and linger here. (ll. 130–8)[12]

It is the obvious weariness that makes this compliment so back-handed. We are reminded, with a humour that is less dangerous than resentment, of the tyranny which demands that even nature co-operate in the syco-phancy.[13] Summer's last speech, his 'last will', contains a more gracious address to Elizabeth. Having dedicated his withered flowers to corpses, his 'pleasant open ayre' to Croydon, his short nights 'to young married soules', and his fruits to his heir, Autumn, he bequeaths to Elizabeth

> All my faire dayes remaining. . . .
> To waite upon her till she be returnd.
> Autumne, I charge thee, when that I am dead,
> Be prest and serviceable at her beck,
> Present her with thy goodliest ripened fruites,
> Unclothe no Arbors where she ever sate,
> Touch not a tree thou thinkst she may passe by.
> And, Winter, with thy wrythen frostie face,
> Smoothe up thy visage, when thou lookst on her;
> Thou never lookst on such bright majestie:
> A charmed circle draw about her court,
> Wherein warme dayes may daunce, & no cold come.
>   (ll. 1843–54)

The poignancy of this address, which is similar in effect to Puck's protective speech after the wedding of Theseus and Hippolyta, derives from the way in which it reminds us that winter will indeed strip the trees and chill the ground. The jussive voice reminds us that even queens are subject to certain laws.

The specific setting and occasion of this show have a lot to do with its tone. Whitgift's palace must have been a safer place than most to remind the sovereign of her own mortality. Elizabeth called Whitgift her 'little black husband' and it was to him that she turned for spiritual guidance. He was also the best patron that Nashe could possibly have had at this time. Not only was Whitgift renowned as a lover of learning; more significantly it was he who had power over stage censorship. An almost palpably anxious letter from the Lord Mayor of London in February 1592, begs Whitgift to exercise his powers to rid the City of London of its plays and players whereby the youth of London 'is greatly corrupted & their manners infected with many evill & ungodly qualities'. He asks Whitgift to 'vouchsafe us your good favour & help for the refourming & banishing of so great evill out of this Citie'. He concedes that 'the Q. Maiestie is & must be served at certen times by this sort of people' but beseeches his Grace to consult the Queen's Master of Revels to see 'if by any means it may bee devised that hir Majestie may bee served with these recreations as hath ben accoustomed (which in our opinions may easily bee don by the privat exercise of hir Majesties own players in convenient place) & the Citie freed from these continuall disorders'.[14] Whitgift complied with the request of this obsequious kill-joy, but the fact that he welcomed players under his own roof at Croydon indicates a greater tolerance on his part.[15] The comment of Will Summer—the figure whom Nashe uses as presenter of *Summer's Last Will and Testament*—that ''tis no Play neyther, but a shewe' (l. 75) might be a sly allusion to the current disfavour in which plays were held.

While Elizabeth's arrival at Croydon may in some sense be taken as the occasion of this show, the narrative of the work as a whole is less concerned with this unique occasion than with the annual cycle of the seasons: historical time is placed within a context of cyclical time. Harvest makes his appearance 'with a sythe on his neck, & all his reapers with siccles, and a great black bowle with a posset in it borne before him'. Their song

> Hooky, hooky, we have shorne,
>   And we have bound,
>   And we have brought Harvest
>   Home to towne.   (ll. 808–11)

is precisely the sort of song that might have been sung with the hocky cart which carried home the last load of corn to mark the end of the harvest.[16] We are reminded at this moment of how thin the boundaries are between scripted 'drama' and popular celebration. One of the differences between a 'play' or 'show' and a popular festival is the idea of the spectator. Festival customs may involve some kind of annually repeated performance (for which there may be no script but all know their lines) but no separable spectators. The very act of placing such a song and its singers on a stage— even if, as is conceivable, the participants were the same as those who brought the real harvest home—frames it and makes it into a 'show'. One should not forget that all the artlessness and spontaneity of Nashe's work is carefully scripted. Nevertheless, this harvest festival group, appearing on stage at the appropriate season, must have had the effect of thinning the barriers between spectacle and spectator in a rather different way than occurs at the end of a masque.

The appearance of Harvest on stage at harvest time, anchors Nashe's show in its particular moment. The reference to Elizabeth's visit provides a more specific anchor. The show as a whole is very localised: full of topographical as well as topical references. One of the most pressing topical references which the show makes is to the plague. The Prologue tells us that 'because the plague reignes in most places in this latter end of summer, Summer must come in sicke' (ll. 80-2). J.B. Steane, in his introduction to the Penguin selection of Nashe's work, writes that '*Summer's Last Will and Testament* has a great deal of charm and happiness in it, and critical discussion is always in danger of misrepresenting it because it finds the sombre backdrop the most interesting thing to discuss'.[17] The observation is just, but the sombre backdrop is something to which the show repeatedly returns us.

The figure of Harvest with his scythe should remind us—and could not have failed to remind spectators used to reading emblems—of the Great Reaper.[18] Andrew Marvell's mower, Damon, concludes that only death can heal his wounded heart 'For Death thou art a Mower too'.[19] Damon is both individual and type: an individual reaper and an emblem of the Great Reaper to whom as individual he is subject. Nashe's Harvest has many different modes of being: that of individual harvester transformed for a day; that of allegorical figure—a personification of all harvest; lastly, and in a way that subsumes the previous two, he is an emblem of time and death. When Summer asks Harvest 'hadst thou a good crop this yeare?' (l. 891) Harvest replies 'Hay, Gods plenty' (l. 892). The knowledge that around eighteen thousand died of the plague of 1592 gives the lines a chilling equivocation.[20] The church's celebration of harvest festival— indeed the framework within which the early church managed to accommodate pagan harvest rites—makes a very close connnection between the nourishing fruitfulness-in-death of the autumn harvest, and the consummation that is human death: 'Lift up your eyes and looke on the regions:

for they are white already unto harvest. / And he that reapeth, receiveth wages, and gathereth fruits unto life eternall, that both hee that soweth, & he that reapeth, might rejoyce together' (John iv. 35-6, Geneva Bible).

The connection between seasonal passage, for which there are the consolations of fruitfulness and repetition, and the loss of a unique human life is made in Shakespeare's Sonnet 12:

> When I do count the clock that tells the time,
> And see the brave day sunk in hideous night,
> When I behold the violet past prime,
> And sable curls all silvered o'er with white,
> When lofty trees I see barren of leaves,
> Which erst from heat did canopy the herd,
> And summer's green all girded up in sheaves
> Borne on the bier with white and bristly beard;
> Then of thy beauty do I question make
> That thou among the wastes of time must go,
> Since sweets and beauties do themselves forsake,
> And die as fast as they see others grow,
> And nothing 'gainst time's scythe can make defence
> Save breed to brave him when he takes thee hence.

The wagon which bears the harvest home—perhaps the hocky cart itself— is seen as a bier bearing a corpse. The anthropomorphic 'beard'—usually a dead metaphor when applied to corn—beautifully brings together the worlds of vegetable and human death. The death of summer's green—the grass that all flesh is—works both as an image of human death and as a contrast to it. The clock that tells the time is the world of history in which the consolations of cyclical renewal are not to be found: its moments and its individuals are perishable and fleeting.

The elision of white hair and corn pale before the harvest is made by Nashe's Summer: 'Harvest and age have whit'ned my greene head' (l. 125). C. L. Barber gives this as an example of the 'poised two-sidedness' of the work.[21] This two-sidedness is integral to Barber's understanding of 'festive comedy' by which the individual is assumed into a larger communal life. I would like to suggest that there is another kind of two-sidedness operating in this work by Nashe: a two-sidedness represented by the antagonistic modes of existence of the stage's personnel.

The establishment of the antimasque as a companion to the court masque proper seems to have been a comparatively late development. Jonson, who perhaps devised the first antimasque to accompany the masque for the Ramsay-Radcliffe wedding of 1608, describes the antimasque as 'a foil, or false masque'.[22] What the antimasque suggested, with its grotesque dances, its images of madness and deformity, was the obverse of the Ideal perfection to which the masque aspired. It acted as a form of negative definition. The madmen in *The Changeling* who are called upon to perform at the nuptials of Beatrice-Joanna and Alsemero would have been performing in this tradition of negative definition (though of course in that play their suggestions are rather more positive). Their passionate disorder would have been seen as a representation of what the confines of marriage hoped to re-order and contain. On a more basic level, which has little to do with its philosophic rationale, the antimasque must have satisfied a craving for variety and light relief.[23]

Nashe's *Summer's Last Will and Testament*—though not properly either a masque or an antimasque—combines in one work the idealising and the anti-idealising elements of both. The show, having opened with the dignified and melancholy spectacle and speech of the dying Summer, leaning on the shoulders of Autumn and Winter and attended by Vertumnus, is disrupted by the advent of Ver who soon brings on a hobby horse and initiates a Morris dance (l. 193). Ver refuses to attend to the purpose of his summons: to give an account of how he has employed Summer's wealth. He is relentlessly and undeflectably boisterous. The sickly Summer is overwhelmed by this jarring presence:

> SUMMER Nay, nay, no more; for this is all too much.
> VER Content your selfe, we'le have variety.   (ll. 210–11)

And with that '3 *Clownes, & 3. maids*' come on to the stage, singing and dancing. The 'variety' which an antimasque contributes to a masque's spectators is built into the single show of *Summer's Last Will and Testament*.

Nashe was a master of stylistic variety. His prose narrative, *The Unfortunate Traveller*, is a show cabinet of the various stylistic possibilities then available and, having shown himself capable of these, Nashe uses them to set off an idiom of his own: an idiom which is precise, lively, and indecorous. The idioms employed by the characters in *Summer's Last Will and Testament* are similarly various.[24] The most obvious contrast is that between the deflating vitality of Will Summer and the stately melancholy of his namesake, Summer. And this show, which contains so many elements derived from popular festivities—Morris dancers, the hocky cart, and numerous references to games[25]—also contains many examples of learned literary modes. For example, the mock *encomium* (the rhetorical praise of self-evidently unworthy objects): Orion's lengthy and resourceful defence of dogs (self-evidently unworthy objects at a time when current medical opinion held dogs to be bearers of the plague[26]) (ll. 669–741); Bacchus's marvellously sophistical praise of drink, garnished with supporting quotations from Plato and Aristotle (ll. 978–99). The classical myth of Proserpina, whose annual descent into Pluto's court marks the end of summer and lightness, is as much behind the show as are popular, folk ways of making sense of harvest and passage:

> Goe not yet away, bright soule of the sad yeare;
> The earth is hell when thou leav'st to appeare.   (ll. 109–10)

and later, as Summer ends the recitation of his last will:

> Slow marching thus, discend I to the feends,
> Weepe, heavens, mourne, earth, here Summer ends.   (ll. 1870–1)

And in addition to this calling upon established myth, the show includes many examples of new explanatory myths—examples of what Elizabeth Donno has called 'the aetiological conceit'.[27] One of the finest is Winter's moralizing explanation of the hardship of his season. Here precise horticultural understanding is given the extra dimension of moral explanation:

> Youth ne're aspires to vertues perfect growth,
> Till his wilde oates be sowne: and so the earth,
> Untill his weeds be rotted with my frosts,
> Is not for any seede or tillage fit.
> He must be purged that hath surfeited:
> The fields have surfeited with Summers fruites;
> They must be purg'd, made poore, opprest with snow,
> Ere they recover their decayed pride.   (ll. 1547–54)

What is remarkable is that Nashe, employing so many different idioms and drawing on such a wide range of popular and learned experience, should allow no single mode a monopoly of the truth. Each idiom both complements and undermines each other, so that we get a cumulative sense of how various are the ways of making sense of the world.

But whilst we have a cumulative impression of variety, this variety does not at any time add up to or get assumed into a single understanding. Whilst the masque proper, philosophically working between the polarities of real and Ideal, works towards the moment at which the real is assumed into the Ideal, the spectators momentarily at one in the dance with the Ideal selves they have witnessed, in Nashe's show the Ideal world of allegorical figures and the real world of historical individuality resist one another. The relative statuses of Damon the Mower and Death the Great Reaper in Marvell's poem are comparable to those of the historical figure of Will Summer (who is nevertheless in some sense fictional here since he is played by an actor—the real Will Summer, Henry VIII's fool, being long dead) and the eponymous, but allegorical, figure of Summer.

The court masque, in its Stuart and Caroline development, was a very illusionistic affair. The careful perspective of the settings would have ensured that the spectators could fully participate in the wonderful spectacle. Heavy illusionism is something we associate very much with the baroque in art. The vertiginous perspectives of baroque ceiling paintings where we see the soles of saintly feet on their way to heaven have the effect of making heaven accessible to the senses. The carefully scripted spontaneity with which Nashe's show opens—'Enter Will Summers in his fooles coate but halfe on, comming out'—has a similar effect to those baroque portraits in which the sitter appears to be resting his arm on the picture base, transgressing the limits which divide the fiction of the painting from the world of the spectator. The part of Will Summer clearly demands a professional actor's skills in order that the illusion of spontaneity and informality be sustained. But dramatically Will Summer's most consistent function is as shatterer of illusions, and that shattering in turn has the effect of making the figure of Will Summer himself seem more 'realistic'.[28] Will Summer allows Nashe both to employ and to distance himself from a variety of modes and idioms. In his first speech, as he struggles to get dressed, he tells us that he speaks to us 'in the person of the Idiot our Playmaker' (ll. 21-2) and promises to show us 'what a scurvy *Prologue* he had made [him], in an old vayne of similitudes' (ll. 26-7). With Will Summer as commentator—a verisimilar historical character who seems to participate in the same kind of reality as the audience—we are forced to think about the various modes which the show employs. A dead fool—alas poor Yorick—Will Summer is himself an ambivalent figure: a *memento mori* at a time when people would not have needed much reminding, or an image of triumphant empty-headedness (a fool may not be changed in death). Will Summer's world is a world of play as opposed to plays, of games rather than drama:

> who would be a Scholler? not I, I promise you: my minde alwayes gave me this learning was such a filthy thing, which made me hate it so as I did: when I should have beene at schoole, construing *Batte, mi fili, mi fili, mi Batte*, I was close under a hedge, or under a barne wall, playing at spanne Counter, or Jacke in a boxe ... Here, before all this companie, I professe my selfe an open enemy to Inke and paper ... Hang copies; flye out, phrase books; let pennes be turnd to picktooths: bowles, cards, and dice, you are the true liberal sciences; Ile ne're be Goosequil, gentlemen, while I live. (ll. 1462-8; 1473-5; 1480-3)

Such a figure both undermines and enriches a show. The glimpse that Will Summer gives us of the persistent world of game is like a glimpse of the skull beneath the skin of sophisticated drama: from this thou camest, to this must thou return. Nashe, for all his learned articulacy, knew the limits of that articulacy ('Wit with his wantonnesse / Tasteth deaths bitternesse', ll. 1602-3).

Will Summer is the figure who breaks through the invisible wall dividing spectator from spectacle, bringing what is learned and general into the specific world of immediate experience. After the tableau, song, and dance of Summer's entry, it is Will Summer who brings us back to the biographical realities of the players who had, momentarily perhaps, transcended those identities:

Elizabeth Cook

The Satyrs and wood-Nymphs goe out singing, and leave Summer and Winter and Autumne, with Vertumnus, on the stage.
WILL SUMMER A couple of pratty boyes, if they would wash their faces, and were well breecht an houre or two.   (ll. 117-18)

When the figure of Sol accounts for himself and defends himself against the accusations of Autumn, Winter, and Summer, we enter into this world of personifications to such an extent that Sol can refer to '*Diana*, whom our fables call the moone' (l. 559). Our usual understanding of mythological figures as fictional personifications is inverted. It becomes fabulous and fictional to deny Diana's personal identity by making her into an inanimate planet. But Will Summer soon brings us back to earth and to the earthly way of looking at things:

I thinke the Sunne is not so long in passing through the twelve signs, as the sonne of a foole hath bin disputing here about had I wist. Out of doubt, the Poet is bribde of some that have a messe of creame to eate, before my Lord goe to bed yet, to hold him halfe the night . . . To be sententious, not superfluous, *Sol* should have bene beholding to the Barbour, and not the beard-master. Is it pride that is shadowed under this two-leg'd Sunne, that never came neerer heaven then *Dubbers* hill?   (ll. 583-8; 617-21)

Will Summer brings us back to Croydon—Duppa's Hill—and to the physical here and now in which a local biped is struggling to overcome the limitations of his particular identity and to persuade us that he is a planet—or rather, Sol, whom our fables call the Sun.

Quite consistently, throughout the show, Will Summer wrenches us back from the world of allegorical beings—a world of explanatory mythology—to the world and milieu of that particular performance:

The truth is, this fellow hath bin a tapster in his daies.   (l. 193)

You, friend with the Hobby-horse, goe too fast, for feare of waring out my Lords tyle-stones with your hob-nayles.   (ll. 204-6)

The combined effect of the mythological pageant and Will Summer's wilfully literalistic commentary, is of a double way of looking at things. The way in which the figure of Sol both is and is not the London lad that 'never came neerer heaven than *Dubbers* hill' resembles what must have been the experience of those who watched the mystery cycles performed by their neighbours and fellow citizens. The figures of Herod, John the Baptist, Christ, and the Magdalene both were and were not the familiar local citizens who took on these parts for a spell. In that case the familiarity of the actors would in no way have undermined the consistent truth of the story they re-enacted: rather it would have reinforced the sense that Christ's story should engage with every moment of life in a way which should redeem and transform the particular.

The double and simultaneous sense of both actor and role need not be an undermining one. It was something that the post-Renaissance theatre gradually lost and which Brecht had programmatically to reintroduce to his theatre. This double vision which takes in both fiction and the constituents of that fiction in an awareness of fictiveness, does not just transform a naively participating audience into one which is intelligently self-conscious. It enlarges our understanding of the possibilities of the natural, historical world to which it persistently brings us back so that, as in Caryl Churchill's *Top Girls*, nature and fancy reciprocate.

So this habit of confronting an audience with the fallible individuality of the actors, the here and now of performance, need not be reductive. It is not reductive in *Summer's Last Will and Testament*. But it does create a dialectic which is very different from and less resolved than the idealising dialectic of the court masque. In the court masque the real spectators overcome the limitations of their biographical identities when they are assumed into the Ideal vision which they have witnessed. *Summer's Last Will and Testament* does not grow to this kind of resolution. There is no moment at which the barriers between show and spectators are physically broken down: the show's dances and songs only symbolically include the audience in their mood of communality. But within the limits of the show itself barriers are occasionally dissolved.

I began this essay with some comments about the varieties of ontological status—the different modes of existence—which a Renaissance spectator might have been expected to shift between and accommodate. In *Summer's Last Will and Testament* there is a spectrum which ranges between historical identities (Will Summer, who in turn refers us to the identities of the actors who take the other parts), allegorical figures (Summer, Autumnus, Harvest), mythological figures (Bacchus, Orion). The allegorical personifications and the figures from mythology do not differ from each other to the point of mutual incomprehension; they both derive from a poetic impulse to make sense through embodiment. This mythologising impulse is actually discussed in the course of Winter's invective against poets:

> They vomited in verse all that they knew,
> Found causes and beginnings of the world,
> Fetcht pedegrees of mountaines and of flouds
> From men and women whom the Gods transform'd.   (ll. 1271–4)

A fine one he is to talk, allegorical personification that he is.

But it is not at all clear whether the allegorical figures that move pageant-wise across the stage are actually aware of Will Summer's commenting presence. Like the figures of Revenge and Andrea's Ghost who flank the stage throughout Kyd's *Spanish Tragedy*, Will Summer's presence is something the spectators cannot forget but which the other figures on the stage seem to ignore because they partake of a different kind of reality. Unlike the figures of Andrea and Revenge, however, Will Summer's status is *more* realistic, *more* historically specific, than that of the stage's other occupants. If one looks, for example, at the passage involving the Morris dance initiated by the boisterous Ver to Summer's dismay (ll. 193–276) it seems that neither Ver nor Summer are aware of Will Summer's additional commentary. The realistic Will Summer can understand the mythological mode, but the allegorical figures cannot focus on Will Summer's kind of unabstracted particularity. They cannot hear him.

There are only two moments in the show when the two levels of existence—the historically realistic and the mythological—clearly meet and come together. Those moments are significant. The first is when Bacchus, who as drinker and gamester has more in common with Will Summer than any of the other mythological figures, is urging the resisting Summer to drink:

BACCHUS   ... Summer, wilt thou have a demy calvering, that shall cry husty tusty, and make thy cup flye fine meale in the Element?

SUMMER   No, Keepe thy drinke, I pray thee, to thy selfe.

BACCHUS   This *Pupillonian* in the fooles coate shall have a cast of martins and a whiffe. To the health of Captaine *Rhinocerotry*: looke to it, let him have weight and measure.

WILL SUMMER   What an asse is this! I cannot drinke so much, though I should burst.

BACCHUS   Foole, doe not refuse your moyst sustenance; come, come, dogs head in the pot, doe what you are borne to.

WILL SUMMER   If you will needs make me a drunkard against my will, so it is; ile try what burthen my belly is of.

BACCHUS   Crouch, crouch on your knees, foole, when you pledge god *Bacchus*.

Here Will Summer drinks, and they sing about him. Bacchus begins

ALL   Monsieur Mingo for quaffing did surpasse,
           In Cup, in Can, or glasse.

BACCHUS   Ho, wel shot, a tutcher, a tutcher: for quaffing *Toy* doth passe, in cup, in canne, or glasse.

ALL   God Bacchus doe him right,
           And dub him knight.

Here he dubs Will Summer with the black Jacke

BAC   Rise up, Sir Robert Tospot.

SUM   No more of this, I hate it to the death.   (ll. 1047–72)

It is a moment of rare unanimity. Characters of diverse status attend to the real act of drinking and it is significant that, for once, the role of illusion-puncturer should be taken away from Will Summer. Bacchus refers, not to Summer, but to *Toy*—the actor who took Summer's role. When Will Summer drinks, it is Toy who drinks. Certain gestures or states of an actor's body can have the effect of confronting the spectator with the actor's physical identity, making us aware of the fact that it is his or her sentient body that is enacting this 'fiction' and that this fiction is evoked through real muscular actions. The nakedness of the actor in the modern theatre has this effect—an effect which should carry over to our understanding of all the clothed and acted gestures on the stage. Eating and drinking on stage have a similar effect. When Will Summer drinks, Toy drinks too and the barriers between the various levels of being which the show contains are momentarily broken down in this communal act. That this act should be drinking—an act which is not just bodily but social—is also significant. It is an inclusive moment which symbolically (and possibly actually if they join in the song) reaches out to the spectators. The mock knighting inverts and parodies the usual process of knighting by which one individual is raised above the common order. This knighting admits Will Summer into a more communal world.

Comparably, in *Top Girls*, it is the communality of drinking that provides the most unanimous moments in the first scene, forging a corporeal link between the extraordinarily diverse characters. But the moment of most complete unanimity—which the audience shares—is the silence that follows Pope Joan's description of her death. It comes at the end of a hilarious account of going into labour during a Rogation Day procession:

> JOAN   One of the cardinals said, 'The Antichrist!' and fell over in a faint.
> *They all laugh*
> MARLENE   So what did they do? They weren't best pleased.
> JOAN   They took me by the feet and dragged me out of town and stoned me to death.
> *They stop laughing*
> MARLENE   Joan, how horrible.
> JOAN   I don't really remember.
> NIJO   And the child died too?
> JOAN   Oh yes, I think so, yes.
> *Pause*[30]

The moments of connection, in both Nashe's work and Caryl Churchill's, are significantly moments that focus on the materiality of the body: celebrating its pleasures or mourning its transience. The other moment in *Summer's Last Will and Testament* at which the different ontological levels represented by Will Summer and Summer meet, is a moment of sorrow. It is after the wonderful song for which the show is best known. I shall quote it all since the cumulative effect of the song's steady pace is so much part of its meaning:

> Adieu, farewell earths blisse,
> This world uncertaine is,

Fond are lifes lustfull joyes,
Death proves them all but toyes,
None from his darts can flye;
I am sick, I must dye:
    Lord, have mercy on us.

Rich men, trust not in wealth,
Gold cannot buy you health;
Phisick himselfe must fade,
All things to end are made,
The plague full swift goes bye;
I am sick, I must dye:
    Lord, have mercy on us.

Beauty is but a flowre,
Which wrinckles will devoure,
Brightnesse falls from the ayre,
Queenes have died yong and faire,
Dust hath closde *Helens* eye.
I am sick, I must dye:
    Lord, have mercy on us.

Strength stoops unto the grave,
Wormes feed on *Hector* brave,
Swords may not fight with fate,
Earth still holds ope her gate.
Come, come, the bells do crye.
I am sick, I must dye:
    Lord, have mercy on us.

Wit with his wantonnesse
Tasteth deaths bitternesse:
Hels executioner
Hath no ears for to heare
What vaine art can reply.
I am sick, I must dye:
    Lord, have mercy on us.

Haste therefore eche degree,
To welcome destiny:
Heaven is our heritage,
Earth but a players stage,
Mount wee unto the sky,
I am sick, I must dye:
    Lord, have mercy on us.

SUMMER   Beshrew mee, but thy song hath moved mee.
WILL SUMMER   Lord, have mercy on us, how lamentable 'tis!

(ll. 1574–618)

The unanimity of response from the two Summers derives from the song's reminder that 'death doth with degree dispense'. 'Death proves them all but toyes' in the song's first stanza may be another reference to the name of the actor who played Will Summer. If it is, it is an ironic one, since all such individuality is perishable—the song forces this meaning home. The refrain, 'I am sick, I must dye: / Lord, have mercy on us', anchors the song's message of transience in the dangerous and melancholy present. The phrase 'Lord have mercy upon us' would have been grimly familiar to those beseiged in Croydon by plague. It was the phrase written on the doors of plague-stricken houses: a warning to the as yet uninfected to pass by, for none but the Lord would have mercy on those within.[31]

This acute, and often grievous sense of the present and the particular, is never long absent from Nashe's show. And when the more idealised, allegorical or mythical level confronts the level of particular reality, it confronts it as a challenge. It is not able to absorb it. The death of known individuals resists such consolations.

NOTES

1 Caryl Churchill, *Top Girls* (London, 1982), p. 13.
2 *Antony and Cleopatra* V.ii.97-101.
3 See Alice Venezky, *Pageantry on the Shakespearean Stage* (New York, 1951), p. 95 and David Bergeron, *English Civic Pageantry 1558-1642* (London, 1971), Chapter 1.
4 For the fullest description of the allegorical title-page see M. Corbett and R. W. Lightbaum, *The Comely Frontispiece: The Emblematic Title Page in England, 1550-1660* (London, 1979); Frances Yates also discusses them in relation to the Renaissance emblem in 'The Emblematic Conceit in Giordano Bruno's *De Gli Eroici Furori* and in the Elizabethan Sonnet Sequences', *Journal of the Warburg and Courtauld Institutes*, 6 (1943), pp. 101-21.
5 Nevertheless E. K. Chambers has traced its roots in the Mummers' play (*The English Folk Play* (Oxford, 1933)). But he notes that despite this popular and indigenous connection, the masque came to England (from Italy and France) 'under the rather unjustifiable colour of a novelty' (*The Elizabethan Stage*, 4 vols. (Oxford, 1951), 1, p. 152).
6 See Glynne Wickham, *Early English Stages 1300-1600*, vol. 2, part 1 (London, 1963), p. 239.
7 For an account of their quarrel and an explanation of the theories that underlay it see D. J. Gordon, 'Poet and Architect: The Intellectual Setting of the Quarrel between Ben Jonson and Inigo Jones', *Journal of the Warburg and Courtauld Institutes*, 12 (1949), pp. 152-78.
8 See Stephen Orgel, *The Illusion of Power: Political Theater in the English Renaissance* (Los Angeles, 1975).
9 For the fictionalising of Elizabeth see Frances Yates, *Astraea: The Imperial Theme in the Sixteenth Century* (London, 1975).
10 See Venezky, p. 146; E. K. Chambers (*The Elizabethan Stage*, 1, p. 112) writes of Elizabeth's indecision and changeability. This may have been a factor determining a certain fluidity in the spectacles prepared for her.
11 The time, place, and occasion of this work have all been inferred from the text; see *The Works Of Thomas Nashe*, ed. Ronald B. McKerrow, revised by F. P. Wilson, 5 vols (Oxford, 1958), 4, pp. 416-19.

Elizabeth Cook

12 All references will be to McKerrow's edition; *Summer's Last Will and Testament* is printed in Volume 3, pp. 231-95.

13 The conceit of Elizabeth 'soothing' and 'taming' a wild nature was a commonplace one at her receptions. At Kenilworth, in 1575, a porter who had been railing at the gates was 'soothed' at her arrival. On the entry into Bisham in 1592 a wild man came from the woods and proclaimed himself 'tamed': 'Thus Vertue tameth fierceness; Beauty, madnesse' (John Nichols, *The Progresses and Public Processions of Queen Elizabeth*, 3 vols (London, 1823), 3, p. 108); see also E. K. Chambers, *The Medieval Stage*, 2 vols (Oxford, 1903), 1, p. 185, for the folk origins of the 'wild man'.

14 E. K. Chambers, *The Elizabethan Stage*, 4, pp. 307-8.

15 Muriel Bradbrook sees the piece as an offering on the part of Paul's Boys to atone for the dissolution of plays at St Paul's (*The Rise of the Common Player* (London, 1962), p. 219). Harold Newcomb Hillebrand argues in greater detail that Paul's Boys performed the show and finds a reference in the Prologue to the banning of the company in 1590 or mid 1591. Some of the parts in the show were clearly played by boys and it was usual for the choir master and possibly one or two other grown men from the choir to act with the boys; see 'The Child Actors: A Chapter in Elizabethan Stage History', *University of Illinois Studies in Language and Literature*, 11 (1926), p. 148 n.

16 See A. R. Wright, *British Calendar Customs: England*, 3 vols (London, 1936-40), 1, p. 182.

17 Thomas Nashe, *The Unfortunate Traveller and Other Works*, ed. J. B. Steane (Harmondsworth, 1972), p. 36.

18 It is also an emblem of Time, described by Henry Peacham (in *The Gentleman's Exercise* (London, 1612) p. 112) as 'commonly drawne upon tombes in Gardens, and other places an olde man bald, winged with a Sith and an hower glasse'.

19 'Damon the Mower', l. 88.

20 McKerrow, 4, p. 422 gives the figure 17,890.

21 C. L. Barber, *Shakespeare's Festive Comedy* (Princeton, N. J., 1972), p. 61.

22 E. K. Chambers, *The Elizabethan Stage*, 1, p. 193.

23 Jonson, describing his *Mask of Queens* (1609), writes that 'her majesty (best knowing that a principle part of life in these spectacles lay in their variety) had commanded me to think on some dance, or shew, that might precede hers, and have the place of a foil, or false masque' (Chambers, 1, p. 293).

24 Stanley Wells, in his edition of selected writings of Nashe (London, 1964), observes that the debate form of *Summer's Last Will* 'admirably suits [Nashe's] chameleon-like literary personality' (p. 10).

25 For example, Jacks (l. 1040 s.d.); 'spanne Counter' (l. 1467 & 1950); 'poutch' (l. 1898).

26 F. P. Wilson, *The Plague in Shakespeare's London* (Oxford, 1927), pp. 37-8.

27 In her essay 'The Epyllion' in *English Poetry and Prose 1540-1674*, ed. Christopher Ricks (London, 1970), p. 88.

28 The figure of Rafe in Beaumont's *The Knight of the Burning Pestle* is a comparably illusionistic shatterer of illusions.

29 Other instances are ll. 232-6; 422-40; 776-840; 941-61; 1567-70; 1621-2; 1805-21; 1886-900.

30 *Top Girls*, p. 12.

31 *The Plague in Shakespeare's London*, p. 63.

JOHN PITCHER

'In those figures which they seeme': Samuel Daniel's *Tethys' Festival*

And I can not but wonder at the strange presumption of some men that dare so audaciously adventure to introduce any whatsoever forraine wordes, be they never so strange; and of themselves as it were, without a Parliament, without any consent, or allowance, establish them as Free-denizens in our language. But this is but a Character of that perpetuall revolution which wee see to be in all things that never remaine the same, and we must heerein be content to submit our selves to the law of time, which in few yeeres wil make al that, for which we now contend, *Nothing*.[1]

T HIS PASSAGE was published less than a month after James I arrived in London to take the English throne. It is the final passage in a collection of poems and prose addressed to the new Scots King and his English aristocracy by the court poet Samuel Daniel. The immediate subject of the passage is the conclusion of a literary debate with another poet, Thomas Campion, but this should not distract us from the terms of conflict and effacement with which Daniel has chosen to end his first Jacobean publication. Figured here, in an essay defending rhyme, are parliaments and lawless innovators; foreign intruders who have been naturalised; a perpetual revolution; an inexorable law; a few years; and *Nothing*. In this conclusion, words, arguments, debates, and even bodies are all to be funnelled down into a circle, a nought, an O for Oblivion. Daniel had begun the volume with a panegyric to the King, prophesying and predicating the new completeness, the new (and here the shape is important) orb of England. The nation could never, before the accession of James, be thus blest at home 'nor ever come to grow / To be intire in her full Orbe till now'.[2]

So at the beginning of the volume Daniel figures in verse the globe of regal authority, and the *orbis*, or ring of statehood; and at the end, in prose, a circle of history perpetually turning, reducing all endeavour to *Nothing*, itself the noun of extinction *and* the irreducible cipher of nought. At the beginning, when a reign is about to commence, there is a sphere newly fulfilled; at the end, merely a character, a circular line marking how every reign, and every thing, is revolved into the past. And it is these figures of celebration, conflict, and replacement, strangely proleptic of the fortunes of the next Stuart King, which are to be found again and again in the verse Daniel wrote for the Jacobean court. What begins in this collection of 1603, in a greeting to the new King, manifests itself in the next decade in Daniel's verse essays on, among other things, the achievement of Montaigne, the patronage of the Pembroke family, the founding of the Bodleian Library, and (in contrast) the time-servers, graft and back-sliding at court, and the sheer irresponsibility and greed of great ones. But the play of accession against succession, and of past and present authority against future oblivion, is most acutely, and most appropriately, Daniel's concern in *Tethys' Festival*, a masque written in 1610 to celebrate the investiture of King James's elder son, Henry, as Prince of Wales.

The festivities for the investiture began on Thursday 31 May when Prince Henry's barge sailed down the Thames towards the City from the Palace at Richmond. The night before, the Prince had left St James's by water, accompanied by his household and 'divers young lords and gentlemen of speciall mark', and he had landed at Richmond where 'he supped and reposed himself for that night'. This journey downstream towards Chelsea where a fleet of City barges awaited him made Henry, for one day at least, the centre of royal symbolism. It linked him, in the usual modes of Jacobean panegyric and typology, to his predecessor, the first Henry of the House of Tudor. Coming by water from Richmond with only a few followers, this Jacobean Prince of Wales was the typological as well as the dynastic successor of Henry VII, that other prince who in 1485 had landed in Wales as Earl of Richmond, accompanied by only a small number of men. And just as the Tudor Henry of Wales drew support as he moved inland, so in 1610 his Stuart namesake attracted crowds of Londoners who packed the river banks to acknowledge the succession. Soon 'the Thames began ... to flote with Botes and Barges, hasting from all parts to meete him, and the shores on eyther side, where conveniency of place would give way to their desires, swarmed with multitudes of people, which stood wayting with greedy eyes to beholde his triumphant passage.'[3] As he journeyed down river to meet the City's flotilla, Prince Henry was in 1610 re-enacting, or more precisely reformulating, the beginnings of the Tudor dynasty: he was another Henry of Richmond arriving by water to become Prince of Wales. When the Prince finally reached the water pageant at Chelsea, his arrival completed yet a further typological figure. Riding the waters in front of and behind the City boats were artificial sea-monsters, fashioned in the likenesses of a huge whale and of a dolphin. In other circumstances the appearance of a whale up river beyond London Bridge might have portended a tempest, or even danger to the state,[4] but here, as a contemporary observer, Anthony Munday, explained, the two creatures had been sent by Neptune, who not only kept the waters glassily calm but who 'by the power of his commanding trident, had seated two of his choicest Trytons on them, altring their deformed sea-shapes, bestowing on them the borrowed bodies of two absolute actors, even the verie best our instant time can yeeld; and personating in them the severall Genii of Corinea the beautifull Queene of Cornewall, and Amphion, the Father of Hermonie or Musick'.[5]

The appearance of a whale and a dolphin, and even Amphion, is entirely predictable in a water pageant, but the significance of the Tritons is much less commonplace. Munday, who may well have written up his account for the City Fathers, declares that in 'these two well-seeming and richelye appointed persons the Dukedome of Cornewall and the Principalitie of Wales (*by order of Neptune's prophet, or poet, call him whither ye will*), carried some tipe or figure, and not improperly to them so applyed'[6] (my italics). The Tritons were thus 'tipes', or typological figures, who presented Henry with the City's speech of greeting and then its farewell (as he passed on through the barges towards Whitehall), but who also brought to him, from Neptune, his future British titles. The equation of Neptune with Henry's father, King James, is obvious, and if we return to Munday's explanation, that these two 'tipes' were devised *by order of Neptune's prophet or poet*, we can readily perceive through the wordplay on his name that this *prophet* was none other than Daniel. There is evidence that Munday wrote the speeches for the Tritons and that he was paid by the City,[7] but it looks as though he had only a small part in the arrangements for Henry's reception. Given that in *Tethys' Festival* Daniel returns to and elaborates the chief elements in these river triumphs— arrival from Richmond, the origins of the Tudor dynasty, the principality of Wales, and the two Tritons come from a sea-god—it seems quite possible that the total design for the masque, pageant, and symbolic journey down river was in Daniel's hands. Whoever devised these entertainments, one thing is sure: when Henry landed at Whitehall, late in the afternoon, to a salute of guns and tumultuous cheering, he had been acknowledged by two of the estates, the People and the City. Parliament and the Court would follow a few days later.

On Monday 4 June, in the presence of both Houses of Parliament, Henry was created Prince of Wales. *Tethys' Festival* or *The Queen's Wake*, written and devised by Daniel and Inigo Jones, was performed before James and Henry on the following evening in the Banqueting Room at Whitehall. The fiction of the masque, which conveys Queen Anne's public congratulations to her husband and to her son, is that Tethys, Queen of the Ocean, has sent her messenger Zephyrus to greet the British Prince (Meliades), and the Ocean King. Entering Britain through Milford Haven, Zephyrus brings gifts for Meliades and the King (a sword of justice, a scarf of love and friendship, and a trident) and then withdraws. The scene changes to an underwater cavern where Tethys and her river-nymphs are celebrating the glory of the Ocean King. After songs and dancing, Tethys and her attendants proceed to a mountain top on which grows Apollo's tree of victory and there they offer the flowers of the sea-bed. Her oblations completed, Tethys returns to the sea, followed some way behind by Zephyrus and his two Tritons. Before Zephyrus can leave, however, he is stayed by a flash of Jove's lightning, and the arrival of Mercury. Zephyrus is instructed to bring back Tethys and her river-nymphs, and he departs to perform his task. The scene changes once more, this time to a pleasant grove, and Tethys and Zephyrus (now miraculously transformed into their real identities, Queen Anne and Prince Charles) return with their attendants. The whole company of noblemen and ladies process up the hall towards King James and Prince Henry (formerly the King of the Ocean and Meliades).[8]

The first scene, in which the mythic characters, Zephyrus, Meliades, and the Ocean King meet at Milford Haven, resumes the symbolism begun out on the Thames a week earlier: 'The Scene itselfe was a Port or Haven, with Bulworkes at the entrance, and the figure of a Castle commaunding a fortified towne: within this Port were many Ships, small and great, seeming to lie at Anchor, some neerer, and some further off, according to perspective' (E3r).[9] This view across the harbour is framed by a proscenium of two pillars and a frieze, and in front of each pillar there is a statue of a sea-god, one representing Neptune, the other Nereus:

> *Neptune* holding a Trident, with an Anchor made to it, and this Mot. *His artibus*: that is, *Regendo, & retinendo*, alluding to this verse of *Virgill*, He [sic] *tibi erunt artes, & c. Nereus* holding out a golden fish in a net, with this word *Industria*: the reason whereof is delivered after, in the speech uttered by *Triton*. These Sea-gods stood on pedestals and were al of gold. Behinde them were two pillasters, on which hung compartments with other devises: and these bore up a rich Freeze, wherein were figures of tenne foote long, of flouds, and Nymphes.   (E2v-E3r)

As Stephen Orgel has remarked,[10] the Renaissance proscenium did not merely enclose the action, but defined the worlds of both patrons and their dramatic fictions, and this is certainly the case with this first scene in *Tethys' Festival*. The view of Milford Haven, drawn according to perspective, once more sets the investiture of Wales's own Stuart prince in the perspective of the Tudor dynasty—the dynasty, with King James as its successor, which began at Milford, both a Welsh harbour and the port at which Henry VII (then Earl of Richmond) landed in 1485. This return to origins would have been brought into even closer proximity by the mottoes and symbolic furniture of the sea-gods proscenium. The audience would have had to wait for the precise meaning of the golden fish in a net, and the trident and anchor, but they would have known well enough that tag from Virgil. In the Jacobean court, the poets had repeatedly quoted, translated, and adapted the motto King James had chosen to complement his title of *Pacificus*:

tu regere imperio populos, Romane, memento
(hae tibi erunt artes) pacique imponere morem,
parcere subiectis et debellare superbos.[11]

Thus the proscenium related the Milford view, with its associations of strong Tudor peace and Welsh principality, to James's own avowal, 'parcere subiectis et debellare superbos', to spare the humbled and tame the proud. When the young Prince Charles, as Zephyrus, emerged from the same harbour (*through* the proscenium, presumably), the Court audience would have recognised the structure of allusions to past, present, and future princes of peace and glory in Britain. The other devices held by the sea-gods were to be explicated in a speech by one of Zephyrus's attendants, a Triton. Milford Haven, so he declares, is the

> happy Port of Union, which gave way
> To that great Heros H E N R Y, and his fleete,
> To make the blest conjunction that begat
> A greater, and more glorious far then that.

The Triton explains that Tethys has sent Zephyrus through this port to present a trident to the Ocean King (James), and also to greet Meliades, the Prince of the Isles,

> with this sword
> Which she unto Astraea sacred found,
> And not to be unsheath'd but on just ground.
> Herewith, sayes she, deliver him from mee
> This skarffe, the zone of love and Amitie,
> T'ingird the same; wherein he may survay,
> Infigur'd all the spacious Emperie
> That he is borne unto another day.
> Which, tell him, will be world enough to yeeld
> All workes of glory ever can be wrought.
> Let him not passe the circle of that field,
> But thinke *Alcides* pillars are the knot
> For there will be within the large extent
> Of these my waves, and watry Governement
> More treasure, and more certaine riches got
> Then all the Indies to *Iberus* brought,
> For *Nereus* will by industry unfold
> A Chimicke secret, and turne fish to gold.   (E[4]v-F1r)

One aspect of the masque, its counsel against imperialism, is made clear here. Meliades is presented with a scarf on which the British Isles have been *infigur'd*, and he is advised that these will be enough of an *Emperie* when he inherits them. He should not try to extend his frontiers beyond them, and he should regard the pillars of Hercules as his limits. From her waves, Tethys can offer him a treasure that is certain, for with the trident and net, with *industry* (hence Nereus' motto in the proscenium), fish can be taken from her waters and turned into more wealth than all the Indies brought to Spain. The advice to Henry is straightforward: be satisfied with an empire of the British Isles, keep within its political frontiers, and prosper from fishing home waters.[12] In the second and third scenes of the masque, this advice and its outcome are given physical form. From out of a cavern beneath the ocean, come the beauty and riches of English and Welsh river-nymphs (the court ladies) and the Queen of the Ocean (Anne), so generous to Britain and its princes. Before Apollo's laurel tree, the tree of victors and scholars, they place a tribute of flowers in golden urns, and there sacrifice

> their vowes,
> And wish an everlasting spring
> Of glory, to the Oceans King. (F3r)

Represented as Oceanus, King James receives the wealth and beauty of British waters, and the promise of youth—the only true resources of an empire of Britain. In the final scene, the prosperity and order of this *Emperie* is realised in the pleasant grove and formal procession of courtiers. The extent of such divine blessing for James's reign is registered in the flash of Jove's lightning which transforms, or rather reveals, the mythological deities—Tethys, Meliades, and all—as the British royal family.

It is of special importance that Daniel's advice to Prince Henry is once more, as in the 1603 volume addressed to King James, figured in a set of circles. The prime mover of the masque, Tethys, is described as the 'intelligence which moves the Sphere/Of circling waves', while one of her gifts, the scarf, is said to be a zone (*Greek*, circle) which girdles or encircles the other gift, the sword of justice. And the advice itself, infigured on the scarf, is that the young Prince should not 'passe the circle of that field, / But thinke *Alcides* pillars are the knot'. These circles of power, or more properly its rightful circumscription, are concentric with the circles of art. At the end of the first scene, when the view of Milford Haven was replaced by the ocean cave, there was 'the sound of a loud and fuller musique', and 'at the opening of the heavens appeared 3. circles of lights and glasses, one within another, and came downe in a straight motion five foote, and then began to moove circularly; which lights and motion so occupied the eyes of the spectators, that the manner of altering the Scene was scarcely discerned' (F1r). If they scarcely discerned how Jones shifted scenes, the spectators could hardly have appreciated the significance of these minutely specified figures. The three circles of lights moving within a descent of five feet pointed to an exact equation in time: five within itself three times *equals* five to the power of three *equals* 125, or the numbers of years, 1485-1610, separating Henry VII at Milford and the investiture of Prince Henry in London. The artfulness of *Tethys' Festival* has been grossly underestimated by historians of the masque, but in no area more than in this circle of exchange between the art of power and the power of art. Just as Daniel's 1603 volume opened with the new shape of the kingdom and concluded with a debate about the shapes of verse, so in *Tethys' Festival* the political limits suggested to a royal heir correspond to the limits inherent, as Daniel sees it, in the poetry of praise:

> If joy had other figure
>   Then soundes, and wordes, and motion,
> To intimate the measure,
>   And height of our devotion:
>   This day it had beene show'd
>   But what it can, it doth performe,
> Since nature hath bestowd
>   No other letter,
>   To express it better,
>   Then in this forme;
> Our motions, soundes, and wordes,
>   Tun'd to accordes,
> Must shew the well-set partes,
> Of our affections and our harts.   (F3r)

The figure with which joy does intimate its devotion for the monarchy is circumscribed in the exclamation *Oh*! or the letter O—since 'nature hath bestowd / No other letter, / To express it better, / Then in this forme'. This nought, this circle of words, music and movement, defines the limits of praise: even at the very height of devotion, or celebration of power, the poet's achievement is rounded down to Nothing.

It is well known that the literary debate in *Tethys' Festival* was conducted against Ben Jonson, and if we go by current critical estimate Jonson has certainly had the better of Daniel on all counts. This is not all that surprising when we consider that while Jonson claimed everything for the masque, Daniel could render what he took to be its limits in this ambiguous figure of nought. This ambiguity—ignored by his critics and, more surprisingly, his apologists—is at the very heart of Daniel's preface to *Tethys' Festival*, and his postscript of Latin verses:

> And thus have I delivered the whole forme of this shew, and expose it to the censure of those who make it their best show, to seeme to know: with this Postscript:
>> Pretulerim scriptor delirus inersque videri
>> Dum mea delectant mala me, vel denique fallant,
>> Quam sapere & ringi.   (E[4]v)

These last lines are from Horace's Epistle to Florus (*Epistles*, II. ii. 126–28), and they are used as a deliberate swipe at Jonson's pretensions and character:

> I should prefer to be thought a foolish and clumsy scribbler,
> if only my failings please, or at least escape me,
> rather than be wise and unhappy.[13]

Quam sapere & ringi—rather be a contented, even self-complacent poet, with failings, than be a knowing, self-critical one with a snarl. This was obviously a hit at Jonson, who had snarled at everything Daniel had written since around 1600, and who had appropriated Horace as his chief precursor from about the same date. A quotation from the Epistle to Florus, written when Horace was in his mid-forties, must have seemed especially appropriate to Daniel, in both his life and letters. In 1610 he too was in his mid-forties, and like Horace in the Epistle he had decided to give up lyric poetry and withdraw from the squabbles of literary rivalry. Instead of seeking rhythms in lines of verse, he would follow Horace's advice (given only a few lines later than those quoted at the end of *Tethys' Festival*):

> to cast aside toys and to learn wisdom;
> to leave to lads the sport that fits their age
> and not to search out words that will fit the music of the Latin lyre,
> but to master the rhythms and measures of a genuine life.[14]

In the Epistle to Florus this genuine life is depicted as one in which a man accepts that he is mortal, that he will be replaced by others, and that his wealth, so striven for, will be dispersed in the inevitable cycle of succession:

> since to none is granted lasting use, and heir
> follows another's heir as wave follows wave,
> what avail estates or granaries?[15]

This corresponds closely to Daniel's circles of succession and oblivion— ones which erase art as well as each prince's rule— and the resemblances may invite us, perhaps as Daniel intended, to read the postscript to *Tethys' Festival* as a part representing the whole, as a fragment from the Epistle to Florus which invokes the totality of that poem, as well as pointing up (as Daniel saw it) the preposterous claims Jonson was making for the masque. The postscript may lead us back to the heart of Horace's Epistle, and in turn to the heart of *Tethys' Festival*: 'verae numerosque modosque ediscere vitae'. Master the rhythms and measures of the true life: advice which is given figural and tangible reality in Daniel's masque.

The numbers and modes (or figures) in *Tethys' Festival* are at once allusive and elusive. In the first scene, after Zephyrus has presented the gifts to Meliades, and the Triton's speech has ended, the eight attendant naiads dance around their young prince of the spring. The figure of nine thus formed alludes to Henry's future kingship—had he lived he would have been Henry IX—but this promise of his future can last no longer, at least within the masque, than the dance itself. So it is with the song in which Zephyrus, newly arrived at Milford Haven, is asked to breathe out:

> new flowers, which yet were never knowne
> Unto the Spring, nor blowne
> Before this time, to bewtifie the earth,
> And as this day gives birth
> Unto new types of State,
> So let it blisse create.   (E3v–E[4]r)

This is the second of three stanzas, in each of which the metrical lengths 535333, accommodated in three rhymed couplets, anticipate both the numbers of those circles of light (three within a descent of five feet) but also the five niches cut into Tethys' underwater cavern. These are not fortuitous arithmetical patterns: the allusions here are to the five members of the royal family, and the three nations of Britain promised to Prince Henry. Yet once more as the song ends, and the lights disappear, and the cavern is replaced by the garden of Jove, these patterns of numbers and what they signify are also erased. Within the fiction, Zephyrus may create flowers which have never before blossomed or withered, as a celebration of new types of state, but for Daniel art cannot in an equivalent way break into the circle of birth, death and replacement. Like the numbers and the allusions, Zephyrus is only a figure in a masque, which must end within Time.

The filigree of number throughout *Tethys' Festival* shows just how complicated and perturbing this conception of the masque (and for Daniel all political art) must be. We begin, in the first scene, with one song, one dance, and one speech of presentation; in Scene 2, there are three songs, three dances, and three speeches; but in the final scene there is silence—no song, dance, or words. Conversely in the first two scenes there is a conspicuous irregularity of line, metrical length, and rhyme-pattern in most of the songs and speeches, and several odd numbers of participants,[16] but in the final scene where Prince Charles and the six young lords join Queen Anne, Princess Elizabeth, and twelve ladies of Court, these disharmonies of number are resolved into a political tribute. As the procession of twenty-one figures approaches the throne, all the earlier discordant figures in the masque (in stanzas, syllables, and choreography)—5 against 3, set against 7 against 18 and so on—are brought into sudden harmony in seven ranks of three, in each a lord flanked by two ladies. Allusion is distributed along every file: the three nations of Britain, Henry VII, the three royal children, the seven years of James's reign (in total), the twenty-one years of marriage for the King and Queen, and even, separating Anne, Elizabeth, and Charles, the royal rank, from the other six (of aristocrats), James VI of Scotland and James I of England. This figure, made up of figures, not only recapitulates the entire allusiveness of the masque but compels us to ask what it is to figure in such a way:

And for these figures of mine, if they come not drawn in all proportions to the life of antiquity (from whose tyrannie, I see no reason why we may not emancipate our inventions, and be as free as they, to use our owne images) yet I know them such as were proper to the busines, and discharged those parts for which they served, with as good correspondencie, as our appointed limitations would permit.   (E2r)

This passage, from the preface to *Tethys' Festival*, is normally interpreted as an excuse for ineptitude, or (at best) a failure to appreciate how the appointed limits of a masque—the exigencies of the form, in other words—may be where a poet begins, not ends. This was almost certainly Ben Jonson's view, and it is one supported vigorously by Stephen Orgel,[17] but perhaps we should read again Daniel's phrase 'these figures of mine', and notice that the figures in *Tethys' Festival* do indeed go beyond the dimensions of antiquity and establish a 'good correspondencie', or internal coherence. What may be unpalatable is that Daniel's figures modulate down (or up) a scale through space, music, mythical and biographical identity, and tropes, until they arrive at pure number. There is nothing unusual about a Renaissance masque which has figures of speech, dance figures, classical deities revealed as royal figures, and arrangements of musical notes (or *figures*, in the language of 1610): what is unusual in *Tethys' Festival* is that these figural elements, despite temporary alignments and harmonies between them, eventually cede primacy to number. The masque begins with music, poetry, and the dance around Zephyrus: it modulates through irregularity of song, metre, and ratio: and it ends in a court procession excluding not only the spectators, but words, sounds, and rhythmic motion (for it is a march rather than a dance).

In that configuration of twenty-one members of court, even real identities are subordinate to the pure 'proportions', the enclosing dimensions of the procession. The thinking behind this is related ultimately to Plato's theories of number and ratio as the irreducible reality, although for Daniel, who seems not to have known Greek, it is probably Plato out of Seneca.[18] The fictional impurities of a court at play, albeit the play of power, give way in the course of the masque to the purity of number. So one might argue, in platonic terms, but this is too neat, and (one might say) too trite for a poet of Daniel's seriousness. The number twenty-one, and the ratio 3 to 7 are themselves flawed, for they allude to a royal dynasty within Time, to the Stuarts' indebtedness to the Tudor past, whatever their future. And it is only within the masque that the procession can maintain its figural integrity before the monarch. Both the art which contrived the procession, and the significance thereby assumed, must vanish when the march is completed, or at least at the moment when the courtiers step out of their ranks, breaking up the rectangle of allusion. For Daniel it seems that such primary numbers and proportions are indeed reducible: *Nothing* again, although in this case there is not even the nought, the circle of succession left revolving into the future. It is the final regression towards an art extinguished by its own limits. Earlier in the masque, in one song in particular, the platonic ideal had seemed much closer:

> Are they shadowes that we see?
> And can shadowes pleasure give?
>   Pleasures onely shadowes bee
>   Cast by bodies we conceive,
>   And are made the thinges we deeme,
>   In those figures which they seeme.
> But these pleasures vanish fast,
> Which by shadows are exprest
>   Pleasures are not, if they last,
>   In their passing, is their best.
>   Glory is most bright and gay
>   In a flash, and so away.
> Feed apace then greedy eyes
> On the wonder you behold.
>   Take it sodaine as it flies
>   Though you take it not to hold:
>   When your eyes have done their part,
>   Thought must length it in the hart.   (F3v)

As ever with Daniel, the most severe insight into the limits of art is figured in the most artful (and here, regular) of ways. This is one of his most successful (and celebrated) lyrics, yet it testifies that pleasure, and the art which brings it, is only possible within Time—pleasures are not, if they last—and when the fiction and the audience are divided. The work of *greedy eyes*, eagerly pursuing the evanescent irregularities of the masque, can only be completed away from (or after) the action. Then, in their hearts, the spectators, separated from the lights, music, and the fiction, may lengthen the wonder, or make whole the half-understood and seemingly erratic distribution of number and order in the art. But by the end of *Tethys' Festival*, and that march into silence, number and order are no longer immutable or irreducible.

A masque in which poetry surrenders priority to number, itself an unstable authority; in which the court and its art are subject to Time; in which, by design, the audience and the fiction remain separate—plainly, nothing could be further from nor more hostile to Jonson's theory of the masque in which, as Stephen Orgel explains, the central problem was to establish the court dramatically within the symbolic world of the spectacle.[19] A corollary to this, at least as Daniel might have perceived it, is that when and if the court is integrated into the fiction, through the agency of Jonson's poetry, the Prince being celebrated then rules in a Golden Age of No-Time: James or Anne or Prince Henry are monarchs of an imaginary court from which Time has been excluded. So, at the end of *The*

Masque of Queens, performed the year before *Tethys' Festival*, Daniel would have seen Jonson's eternal House of Fame, in which Queen Anne was revealed, complimented, and then enshrined. The pride of Persia, Greece and Rome might pass away, but Fame, with its patron Anne, would continue for ever in a glorified and timeless stasis. Jonson would probably have welcomed such an interpretation if we judge by what, on other occasions, he praises in certain aristocrats—their unmoving, static virtue which resists the flux of mutability.[20] To Daniel this would have been a detestable and mendacious notion. Only by restoring Time, not eliminating it, could the celebration of a prince also contribute to his education. At the moment of his accession, he must accept that he will be replaced. And only by maintaining the distinction between the court and its fictional better selves, or its masques, could the prince acknowledge the mutability of all reigns: an Ideal Court was, after all, only an Ideal.

Such subtleties are a long way from the simpler entertainments provided for Prince Henry out on the Thames in June 1610, and the argument advanced here, that *Tethys' Festival* is a highly sophisticated piece, masque and counter-masque, affirmation and denial, is an equally long way from the received opinion of this work. What has been emphasised here is just how alert we must be to nuances in Daniel's rhetoric of simplicity. When, for example, he describes himself and other masque-makers as 'poore Inginers for shadowes ... [who] frame onely images of no result'(E1v), can we discount the possiblity, after so many circles of nought, that such *images of no result* refer to the end of that figural progression to number, and the ultimate Nothing? So too with the description of the proscenium, and the view of Milford Haven and so forth, which were written by Jones and inserted into the text. Can we ignore the differences between, say, Daniel's repeated use of the word *figure* and its modulations, and the way Jones uses it to describe costumes and settings? Such a question does not attempt to rescue Daniel from his own ideas, but to interpret his dismissiveness about the masque in terms of the highly wrought artifice *Tethys' Festival* can be shown to be. This problem is most acute at the end of the Preface when he writes that 'in these things wherein the onely life consists in shew: the arte and invention of the Architect gives the greatest grace, and is of most importance: ours, the least part and of least note in the time of the performance thereof' (E2r). By now it should be possible to ask new questions about such a passage, even if the answers are not as readily available. What of Time here? Is it really confined to the duration of a performance, or is it related to the title of the masque, a *festival* in which Time is suspended for celebration and yet renewed to educate the Prince? Are the spectators so oblivious to all but non-verbal splendour in an entertainment? Such questions may not be answered here, but they were real issues for a poet who had spent much of his creative ability praising self-indulgent, careless but yet clever courtiers. To read this passage any longer as unambiguous in tone and a straightforward capitulation to Jones is, indirectly and unintentionally perhaps, to allow Ben Jonson his most undeserved Triumph: a Jacobean Dunciad in which Daniel and other rivals are the antimasque driven out of court by Jonson's own Masque of Himself. If we see things in this way, then there is now no place, and perhaps in 1610 there *was* no place in the Jacobean court, for a writer with doubts as well as talent. Yet even against such a Jonsonian prejudice, of one thing we may be sure: Horace's description of the self-complacent blockhead of a poet—*scriptor delirus inersque*—no more fits Daniel in *Tethys' Festival* than it fits Horace himself.

NOTES

1 Quoted from *A Defence of Ryme*, ll. 1025-36, in *Samuel Daniel: Poems and A Defence of Ryme*, ed. A. C. Sprague, corrected impression (London, 1965), p. 158.

2 'A Panegyrike Congratulatorie to His Majestie', ll. 7-8, quoted from the 1603 folio with the same title, 2nd issue (STC 6259), A1r.

3 Quoted from *The Order and Solemnitie of the Creation of . . . Prince Henrie*, 1610, A[4]r. This anonymous account of the festivities and ceremony was published with *Tethys' Festival*.

4 See Peregrine's jokes about a whale at Woolwich and 'three porpoises seen above the bridge' in *Volpone*, II. i. 35-53.

5 Anthony Munday, *London's Love to the Royal Prince Henrie*, 1610 (quoted here from the reprint in John Nichols, *Progresses of James the First*, 4 vols, (London, 1828), 2, p. 319).

6 Nichols, 2, pp. 319-20.

7 For further details of the pageant, and for Munday's payment by the City, see David M. Bergeron, *English Civic Pageantry* (London, 1971), pp. 94-6.

8 This and the next paragraph have appeared, with some differences, in my *Samuel Daniel: The Brotherton Manuscript: A Study in Authorship* (Leeds, 1981), pp. 28-30. I am grateful to the editors of Leeds Studies in English for permission to use this material.

9 References throughout the essay are to the 1610 edition of *Tethys' Festival*. In verse quoted from this edition, italic is rendered as roman, and vice-versa.

10 *The Illusion of Power: Political Theater in the English Renaissance* (Berkeley, Los Angeles and London, 1975), pp. 21-4.

11 *Aeneid*, VI. 851-3 (Loeb text and translation): 'Remember thou, O Roman, to rule the nations with thy sway—these shall be thine arts—to crown Peace with Law, to spare the humbled, and to tame in war the proud!' Quoted from *Virgil*, ed. and translated by H. Rushton Fairclough, 2 vols (London, 1974), 1, pp. 566-67.

12 In 1610 Daniel also wrote a verse epistle urging Prince Henry to disregard the advice of those counsellors who wanted a foreign war and a more active colonial policy. The poem is printed in *Samuel Daniel: The Brotherton Manuscript* (see above, Note 8). For a note of a payment Daniel received from the Prince in 1609, see *New Poems by James I of England*, ed. Allan F. Westcott (New York, 1911), pp. lxx and lxxv.

John Pitcher

13 Quoted from the Loeb translation, *Horace: Satires, Epistles and Ars Poetica*, ed. and translated by H. Rushton Fairclough (London, reprinted 1970), p. 435.

14 *Horace*, p. 437 (ll. 141-4).

15 *Horace*, p. 439 (ll. 175-7).

16 One example of this contrived irregularity is in the song beginning 'Was ever houre brought more delight' on F3r, in which there are thirteen lines and a metrical distribution: 4253233333344. On stage, as this is sung in twelve voices to twelve lutes, there are twelve ladies *and* Princess Elizabeth and Queen Anne. The rhymes are: *delight / sight; to shew / arow; bright; flowers / bowers; Tree / victory; bowes / vowes; spring / King*. In each mode the song seems to be about to establish a harmony or at least one of the dissonances the Jacobeans found so attractive in their music; but all of the disharmonies are just a little too close to one another for this to succeed. In the rhymes, for example, the *to shew / arow* vowel is repeated in a muffled and unsatisfying way in *flowers / bowers* and *bowes / vowes*. What these irregularities are pointing to is the *possibility* of regularity, that harmony is incipient in the as yet incomplete ratios and patterns of allusion. (Perhaps we should note that Princess Elizabeth was not fourteen until August 1610. In June, the play between 13 lines and 14 court ladies (13 other than herself) would have been a singularly appropriate compliment. The song which follows has 14 lines.)

17 *The Jonsonian Masque*, corrected edition (Berkeley, Los Angeles and London, 1981), pp. 104-5.

18 In his essay 'Samuel Daniel's Masque *The Vision of the Twelve Goddesses*', *Essays and Studies* N. S. 24 (1971), pp. 22-35 (especially 31-4), Geoffrey Creigh has argued that there is an 'underlying Platonic theme' in Daniel's earlier masque (of 1604). In this case Plato is interpreted chiefly through Seneca's *De Beneficiis*.

19 *The Jonsonian Masque*, Chapter 5.

20 See Jonas Barish, 'Jonson and the Loathèd Stage', *A Celebration of Ben Jonson*, ed. William Blissett, Julian Patrick and, R. W. Van Fossen (Toronto, 1973), pp. 27-53. In this excellent essay Barish shows just how complicated Jonson's position is. He notes (pp. 38-9) that one ground 'for Jonson's distrust of play and masque is the inherent impermanence of both forms. Jonson belongs in a Christian-Platonic-Stoic tradition that finds value embodied in what is immutable and unchanging, and tends to dismiss as unreal whatever is past and passing and to come. What endures, for him, has substance; what changes reveals itself thereby as illusory. His non-dramatic poems recur repeatedly to the ideal of the unmoved personality, the soul that can sustain itself in virtue when all is flux around it.' Against this, my comment about *The Masque of Queens* will seem, as it is, an oversimplification. Yet it is clear that Daniel thought Jonson was fudging some of these issues, and his notions of the impermanence of the masque are, as we have seen, far more radical than Jonson's.

DAVID LINDLEY

Music, masque, and meaning in *The Tempest*

◆⊜◦⊜◆

The Tempest employs more music than any other Shakespeare play. It is also the play that most insistently echoes the manner of the masque. Both these aspects of the work have been much commented upon, but in the general revaluation of *The Tempest* which has seen the older view of it as a celebration of reconciliation replaced by a critical consensus stressing its inconclusiveness, ambiguity, and doubt, the music has consistently been accepted as imaging and enacting ideals of harmony and concord, whether or not those ideals are finally attained.[1]

This attitude to the play's music rests upon the view that Shakespeare was employing the standard Renaissance theory that earthly music reflected the celestial harmony of the spheres, and by that analogy was empowered to affect and influence humankind. There can indeed be no mistaking the fact that the power of Ariel's music to allay the fury of the elements and to calm Ferdinand's passions in Act I or to heal the perturbed minds of the noble lords in Act V are fully comprehensible only in a context where an audience might readily supply this symbolic significance to the music they hear. Nor can one doubt that the failure of Antonio and Sebastian to hear and respond to the music that lulls the other lords to sleep in Act II, Scene i is emblematic of the moral disharmony of their natures.

But music in the theatre need not summon up this kind of symbolic significance, for, as Duke Vincentio recognises, 'music oft hath such a charm / To make bad good and good provoke to harm'.[2] We have to recognise that music may delude or spur illicit passions as well as cure, heal, and restore. We do not applaud Orsino's indulgence of appetite with music's moody food, for example.

In the experience of a theatre audience music is much too varied in its stimulus and dramatic significance to be tidily packaged in a neo-Platonic wrapper. But in the world of the court masque the power of music and its emblematic significance is much more firmly controlled and directed. Part of the argument of this essay is precisely that *The Tempest* exploits and explores the tensions between these different dramatic possibilities.

Some of these tensions are apparent in the play's final song, 'Where the bee sucks'. Critics have been moved to eloquence by it. 'Ariel's song is pure lyric and pure joy', writes Mary Chan, while Seng claims: 'For the brave new world of redeemed man which is to succeed on the old one of crime and punishment there could hardly be a better hymn of praise than Ariel's song of summer and freedom.'[3] But these and many other determined efforts to bestow symbolic significance on this song fail to attend to its actual effect in its dramatic context.

Prospero has called for a 'solemn air' to restore the unsettled minds of the nobles. As the charm begins to work he resumes the mantle of his lost dukedom. This is the climatic moment of the story that *The Tempest* narrates. Prospero has successfully courted his 'most auspicious star', has regained the lost dukedom, ensured political harmony by betrothing his daughter to the son of his former opponent, and yet to accompany the gesture that signals this triumphant conclusion we are offered no ceremonious fanfare but a song about lying in cowslips.

The disparity between the song and the dramatic action it accompanies forces the audience into reflection. At first the close juxtaposition of the song with the curative heavenly music suggests that they both belong to the same symbolic realm, but as the words of the song register, the difference between them is sharply established. One is the impersonal sonority of the heavens, the other entirely personal and spontaneous song. This is the first time that Ariel has sung his own words, and their self-indulgence links it with other 'unscripted' songs in the play, Stephano's 'The master, the swabber, the bosun and I' and, more obviously, Caliban's song of freedom, 'No more dams I'll make for fish'.

For all the differences between these singers, the fundamental similarity of the songs cannot be ignored. They alert us to a different musical possibility from that allowed by a neo-Platonic theory. Music here is an outburst of individual feeling, a gesture whose expression is entirely circumscribed by the individuality of the singer. Such song, as Mark Booth has pointed out, invites us as audience to submerge ourselves in an indentification with the singing voice, hence the appeal of the simple, quasi-pastoral lyric that Ariel sings. But at the same time, the failure of the song to support the action for which it is the incidental music confirms the truth of Booth's observation: 'A song, set in a play, but set out of the play too by its music, facilitates our indulgence in feelings that may be undercut before and after the music plays'.[4] Here it is not so much the feeling itself that is undercut, as the disparity between Prospero's abandonment of magic and return to the real world and Ariel's fugitive fantasy that is highlighted. When one adds to this the fact that Ariel, the singer whose feelings we have briefly been persuaded by their musical utterance to take as our own, is an insubstantial figure (quite unlike the obstinately corporeal Stephano and Caliban) then the unsettling elusiveness of this song is plain.

Uncertainty of response is a characteristic effect of most of the musical events in the play. The first song is 'Come unto these yellow sands'. Ferdinand concludes that its music 'waits upon / Some god o' th' island', and reinforces his attribution of celestial origin by his account of its power:

> This music crept by me on the waters
> Allaying both their fury and my passion
> With its sweet air: thence I have follow'd it
> Or it hath drawn me rather.   (I.ii.394–7)

No neo-Platonist could wish for better demonstration of the potential of music, no Orpheus could work more marvellously than the singing Ariel. We are willing as an audience to consent to the power Prospero exercises through music precisely because we are able to supply for it the necessary conventional symbolic significance.

Yet there is an unease about the song. Though it sounds fine at first, the burden of the song, sung by 'watch-dogs' and 'Chanticleer', jars with the lyric's romantic opening. A sense of discomfort is fully justified when, at the end of the play, the sprites who sang 'bow-bow' appear in doggy habit to chase Stephano and Trinculo from Prospero's cave. The refrain of the song hints at the capricious, even malevolent side of Prospero's magic and its instruments, demonstrated clearly when he orders his spirits to 'hunt soundly' the conspirators. The 'god o' th' island' can threaten as well as invite, as Ferdinand himself is soon to realise.

The celebrated 'Full fathom five' follows almost at once. Much can be said about this exquisite and potent lyric, its proleptic significance in imaging the 'sea-change' the characters experience, its immediate effectiveness in preparing Ferdinand for his meeting with Miranda, or the way its eerie transformations bespeak the power of the art which contrives it. But at the same time an audience must realise that at the simplest level the words of the song are untrue. Already assured that 'there's no harm done', we are uncomfortably aware that Ferdinand's statement, 'this ditty doth remember my drowned father' reflects an understanding of events entirely contrived by Prospero.

We are caught, therefore, in a double response to this song. Persuaded by Ferdinand's attitude, we accept the emblematic significance that music always possesses as a potential in Renaissance drama; but at the same time our superior awareness of the true narrative state of things makes us uneasily conscious of the compromise with truth that Prospero's designs necessitate.

In two other episodes later in the play there is a similar compromising of music's symbolic significance as it is subordinated to Prospero's designs.

Ariel's music charms Alonso, Gonzalo, and others to sleep in Act II, Scene i apparently only so that Antonio's and Sebastian's conspiracy

David Lindley

might have space to declare itself. Prospero's magic arts thus create the conditions for the instigation of vice as well as for the harmonising of discordant passions. More significant is the episode in Act III, Scene ii, where the tune of the catch 'Flout 'em and scout 'em' is taken up by Ariel's pipe, much to the amazement of Stephano and Trinculo. They, like Ferdinand, follow the celestial music, only to be led into a bog.

However one might contain these episodes within a standard view of music's symbolic significance, by pointing out that where the virtuous Ferdinand is rewarded the base conspirators are duly punished, this should not obscure the fact that by responding to music Alonso and his followers are rendered vulnerable (though by music also they are preserved) and Stephano and Trinculo are reeking of horse-piss. For the audience, and indeed for the characters on stage, the music that lulls the nobles to sleep and the transformed music of the vulgar catch are the same as the music of Ferdinand's song. What distinguishes one from the other is not the nature of the musical harmony, nor the effects they have, but the consequence Prospero derives from his manipulative power.

As will become clear later this focussing on music as a means of power is of great significance for the play as a whole, and for its use of the masque genre in particular. For the moment we might turn from Ferdinand's wonder at the celestial music to Caliban's celebrated response to the island's sound. He tells Stephano and Trinculo:

> Be not afeard; the isle is full of noises,
> Sounds and sweet airs, that give delight, and hurt not.
> Sometimes a thousand twangling instruments
> Will hum about mine ears; and sometimes voices,
> That, if I then had wak'd after long sleep,
> Will make me sleep again; and then, in dreaming,
> The clouds methought would open, and show riches
> Ready to drop upon me; that, when I wak'd,
> I cried to dream again.
> (III.ii. 133–41)

The fact that his response is so similar to Ferdinand's complicates the simple moral scale where sensitivity to music is a mark of virtue. It suggests a moral neutrality in music's effects. For if, in the myth most often used to support the neo-Platonic view of music, Orpheus made rocks, stones, and trees move, it says much for music's power, but indicates also the involuntariness of response to it, and therefore the potential danger of its effects in the hands of an unscrupulous manipulator. But the most important aspect of this speech is Caliban's account of the way music persuades him to sleep and to dream of innumerable riches, only to wake and, waking, to cry to dream again. For it is this pattern of response that underlies the two biggest set-pieces of the work, the two masques which immediately follow this speech.

In the first a banquet is laid before Alonso and his company. As

Prospero watches, his spirits enter to 'solemn and strange music'. Unlike Stephano and Trinculo the nobles are not frightened, but respond to the sweetness of the sound. They, like the dreaming Caliban, are offered riches in the form of food that they desperately need. But just as Caliban can never capture his dream-treasure, so they are denied their banquet as it is taken away 'by a quaint device' and Ariel rebukes the 'three men of sin'.[5]

No sooner is this scene over than Prospero prepares for the next Masque. He addresses Ariel:

> Thou and thy meaner fellows your last service
> Did worthily perform; and I must use you
> In such another trick. Go bring the rabble,
> O'er whom I give thee power, here to this place:
> Incite them to quick motion; for I must
> Bestow upon the eyes of this young couple
> Some vanity of mine Art: it is my promise,
> And they expect it from me.   (IV.i.35–42)

The connection between this and the previous device is unambiguously made; performed by the same spirits, it is 'such another trick'. The oddity that Prospero introduces what should be one of the play's central emblematic statements with such apparent contempt may be left on one side for future consideration.

The masque proceeds. Iris, Ceres, and Juno gravely meet and promise richness and fertility to the betrothed couple. Iris then summons the 'Naiads of the windring brooks' and 'sunburn'd sicklemen' to dance before the couple. Since there are no courtiers on Prospero's island, it is the spirits who must take the place of masquers and perform the dance which, in Jonson's phrase, may 'make the beholders wise'.[6] The conjunction of watery female semi-deities and fiery male reapers draws upon the conventional symbolism that Jonson, for example, uses in *Hymenaei*:

> Like are the *fire*, and *water*, set;
> That, ev'n as *moisture*, mixt with *heat*,
> Helps everie naturall birth, to life;
> So, for their Race, joyne *man* and *wife*.[7]

The dance, therefore, suits well with the promise of fertility that the three goddesses make in their song to the couple.

Anthony Stafford's gloss on this symbol reveals a further appropriateness to the concerns of the masque. He writes:

To the same ende did the Romanes of old, carrie before the married couple, fier, and water (the former representing the man; the later, the woman,) what else signifying, then that the woman should expect till heate bee infused into her by her husband? it being as much against the nature of an honest spouse, as of the coldest water, to boile of her selfe; and on the contrarie side, that the bridegroom should distill warmth into his own water and heate it, but not over-heate it.[8]

Prospero at the beginning of the act had warned the couple against anticipation of the wedding night, and then returned to the theme as he sternly rebukes Ferdinand:

>   do not give dalliance
> Too much the rein: the strongest oaths are straw
> To th'fire in th' blood: be more abstemious,
> Or else, good night your vow!

Ferdinand replies:

>   I warrant you, sir;
> The white cold virgin snow upon my heart
> Abates the ardour of my liver.   (IV.i. 51-6)

This ideal control, imaged in snow and fire, is sustained throughout the masque (from which Cupid is excluded) and is symbolised in the graceful dance of the temperate nymphs and sunburned sicklemen.

Through this masque Prospero enforces upon Ferdinand and Miranda the difference between a chaste conjunction issuing in happy fertility and the beastly lust that would have peopled the isle with Calibans, or brought forth Stephano's 'brave brood'. The urgency of his warnings to the couple before the masque begins suggests that Prospero is by no means certain that, without the persuasive effect of his 'harmonious vision', he can trust them to understand the difference.

The entertainment, then, works according to the ideal prescription for the masque, leading the spectators to fuller understanding through their contemplation of an image which impresses itself upon them by the power music, dance, and word have to imitate the deeper harmonies of the universe. But though these spectators are of a morally unblemished nature, this show, like the lords' banquet, is snatched away as with 'a strange, hollow and confused noise' the spirits 'heavily vanish'. On their departure Prospero launches into the play's most famous speech, fusing the terminology of masque and reality to remind his audience that the vision, however harmonious, must fade, and they, like Caliban, may cry to dream again.

The pattern of these two scenes is further emphasised by the last trick of Prospero's devising, as Ariel loads a line with glistering apparel to distract Caliban and his fellow conspirators. This illusory richness (which has no real narrative necessity, since Prospero could simply have set his dogs on them when they arrived) is functionally the same as the two shows that precede it. This offering of the island also proves a false treasure.

The frustration common to all these scenes might indeed be held to form the 'deep structure' of the play (to borrow a linguistic term). It is realised in many of the surface incidents of the play. Ferdinand is offered Miranda, but then reduced to servitude; Caliban mistakes the promise first of Prospero and then of Stephano to his discomfiture; the villainous Antonio and Sebastian have Alonso presented to them as a victim, only for him to wake up before they can seize the prize. Most notably, Prospero himself has sought the goal of wisdom only to lose his dukedom in the process, and then, on regaining the dukedom must resign the art he has devoted his life to acquiring.

It is the omnipresence of this pattern that helps to account for the uncertainty of the play's effect upon an audience, since it belongs to tragedy rather than to romance. Unease is clarified in the emphasis the pattern receives in the three masque-like episodes, for masques are by their very nature affirmative offerings, made to a married couple, a patron or a monarch, and their standard pattern moves from inhibition to celebration. In standing on its head the masque genre that it employs *The Tempest* examines the problematic nature of the form, and articulates many of the difficulties and dilemmas that attended it throughout its life.[9]

The Jacobean court masque was continually under attack, most frequently on the grounds of its excessive expense and vainglorious display. The standard defence was an appeal to the notion of princely magnificence: conspicuous consumption is a sign of the richness and importance of a court that would be demeaned by anything less than elaborate and costly show. In *The Tempest* there is the paradox that all its goodly visions issue not from the self-projection of a rich and stable court, but from the power of a magician who inhabits a 'full poor cell' on a desert island. The actors are not the lords and ladies of James's court, whose richness and magnificence might properly become them, but spirits. The play seems to insist that the true riches of the island are the quick freshes and the fruits that Caliban showed to Prospero, rather than the sumptuous banquet that the lords reach for in vain. One might, indeed, see the relationship between the first two set-pieces as antimasque and masque making precisely that point by their juxtaposition. But Prospero's masques are, from this point of view, vanities indeed, having no basis in economic and political reality. Their defence must be sought elsewhere.

Jonson saw the heart of the masque, and its most serious validation, in its capacity to 'lay hold on more remov'd mysteries'.[10] But making this claim raises further problems. In the first place the arcane hieroglyphs of the masque, since they are comprehensible only to the learned, could make little impression upon the actual audience of Jacobean courtiers, preoccupied with the elegant trappings of ostentation. Secondly, the ideal relationship of performer and role, where the noble personage became (in both senses of the word) the part that he played, was always vulnerable to the uncomfortable knowledge that the glorious surface only partly concealed a less than ideal reality.

As more and more people became disillusioned with the excesses and corruptions of James's court, the gap between the masque ideal and the reality it was supposed to reflect became ever harder to paper over, and the educational potential of the masque less and less easy to credit. Writers both for the court and for the public theatre were moved to explore that gap. Tragedians used the discontinuity between image and reality to bitter satirical ends; Daniel expressed increasing disquiet at the vanity of masques; Jonson attempted to take on critics directly in works like *Love Restored*, and Campion in *The Lords' Masque* anxiously insisted upon the necessity of the masquers remembering the significance of the roles they played as they returned to their normal world.[11]

The Tempest grows out of this general disquiet, and attempts itself to grapple with the problems it raises. While the characters in the play are not themselves participants in the masque, yet the final scene of the play does approach indirectly the question of the relationship between a masquer and the role he enacts. For Prospero arranges as the conclusion of his work of reconciliation a masque-like emblem as he discloses Ferdinand and Miranda playing chess. He promises to requite Alonso's restoration of his dukedom with 'as good a thing'; he will, in terms that echo masquing vocabulary, 'bring forth a wonder to content ye'. The emblematic use of the loving couple is very like Campion's later use of the figures of Princess Elizabeth and Frederick Elector Palatine as the concluding symbol of his *Lords' Masque*, but whereas in Campion's work the masquers and audience turn to do homage to the couple sitting in state, Shakespeare's lovers are preoccupied with each other, and their ideal status is immediately undermined by Miranda's challenge, 'Sweet lord, you play me false'. Whatever the precise significance of the exchange which follows, it is obvious that Ferdinand and Miranda resist the possibility of being subsumed into an iconic gesture.

This resistance accords with Miranda's own modest deflection of Ferdinand's attempt to turn her into a masque-like goddess at the beginning of the play. It also fits into the way the final scene as a whole plays with the masque's climatic moment of disclosure. When Alonso first sees Prospero he cries out:

> Whether thou be'st he or no,
> Or some enchanted trifle to abuse me,
> As late I have been, I do not know.   (V.i. 111-3)

(The paradox of trifles that torment is itself a record of the play's deeply ambiguous attitude to the status and effect of theatrical illusions.) But then Miranda herself looks at the 'goodly creatures' before her as if they were a masquing company. The ingenuousness of her amazement is obvious to the audience, and ironically underlined by Prospero's "Tis new to thee'. Thus, where the court masque moves securely and triumphantly from the world of illusion to the court reality it had translated, transcended, and imaged, Shakespeare's dissolution involves a blurring of realms, and much more uncertainty about the boundaries of the too easily opposed worlds of illusion and reality. In so doing it unsettles the audience's response. Are we to be glad that Ferdinand and Miranda are human in a way that Campion's Frederick and Elizabeth are inhibited from being, and do we therefore register this conclusion as a satirical barb aimed at the insulations of the court masque? Or do we regret that Miranda's naïveté, like the optimistic idealism of Gonzalo, is bound to founder on the ambitious pragmatism of Antonio and Sebastian? The problem is not merely an intellectual one, but a dilemma of feeling and response, a dilemma that is most pressingly active in our response to music. For music's capacity to work directly upon feeling is, in the masque, sanctified by its necessary connection with the divinely harmonious universe. In *The Tempest* we respond as fully to music's lure, but the rightness of our submission is continually questioned.

But though the ending of the play, with its ambiguous relationship to a masque's dissolving, follows upon scenes which have asserted the impossibility of a masque's converting the truly wicked and indicated the frailty of such visions even for the morally unblemished, the play does not therefore retreat to the cynicism of Bacon's verdict; 'these things are but toys'.[12] For though Prospero had introduced his betrothal masque as a vanity, yet he is concerned enough about its effect to command the spectators' attention, 'Or else our spell is marr'd'. He stresses, as Jonson so often does, the importance of the spectator's conspiracy in enabling the masque to work.

It is through the presentation of the dilemmas of Prospero, the maker of masques and convenor of the company of musical sprites, that Shakespeare tests the importance and the limitations of the masque genre. For though the constant state of tension in which Prospero exists throughout the play may be explained by the narrative necessity he is under to seize this one opportunity to regain his dukedom, his emotional state can best be understood as arising from a desperate sense of the fragility of the power his art gives him, coupled with an equally urgent sense of the significance of that art.

The outbursts of anger that structure the long second scene of Act I are all aroused by the failure of others to observe a properly obedient attitude towards him. This is not mere despotism, but a precarious fear that those over whom he can or should exercise control resist or abuse the roles he fashions for them. Throughout the play Ariel, executant of Prospero's designs, is continually checked up on, commanded to faithful reproduction of his script, overlooked in performance, commended for actorly success. Prospero is as anxious as Hamlet in his producer's guise, as nervous as any caricatured author on the first night of his play.

Prospero cares so intensely not primarily because he himself stands to gain from his magic (the lack of triumph at his resumption of the ducal mantle is, however disconcerting, in accord with the lack of real ambition in Prospero's character), nor even because of his love for his daughter and hope for her future, but essentially because the efficacy of his art is itself to be the validation of a lifetime spent in acquiring it. This is the first and only time that his magic is put to the real test of confronting the complexities of human wickedness, desire, and frailty. Compared to this his past magical exercises, retailed in Act V, are mere sideshows, and his Medean speech not the triumphant assertion of theatrical power that Kernan describes[13] but a frenzied effort to boost his own confidence before he turns to undo the charm upon the nobles and finds out whether his magic has actually worked upon stubborn human nature. Prospero's anxiety raises precisely the question of the capacity of masque image to work upon an audience that the masque itself resolutely sidestepped and contained.

But if it is the sense of the fragility of his powers that troubles Prospero, the audience's response is further complicated by the fact that they are unsure, during the course of the play, exactly what purpose Prospero intends to serve. At times he seems only to exult in revenge and to be persuaded to forgiveness by Ariel very late in the play. But yet he takes care for the future of his daughter and troubles to attempt to induce repentance in the minds of the lords.

This is a highly significant complication since it establishes as a central issue in the play the responsibility of the poet in constructing his work to some purposeful end. Merely to exercise power, to perform tricks, would indeed be a vanity. Magic power exists to be harnessed, but it is the nature of the magician's designs that determines the moral value of that power. Under Prospero the island resounds to sweet noises, where for the witch Sycorax the only music was the shriek of the imprisoned Ariel. Prospero must liberate the lords from their charmed imprisonment as he had earlier released Ariel if we are not to condemn him as he condemns Sycorax.

In *The Tempest*, therefore, the masque genre is subjected to a double examination. On the one hand its moral effectiveness is determined (and circumscribed) by the nature and limitations of its beholders; but on the other hand it is also vitally dependent upon the nature and purposes of its contriver. It reflects the sensitivity of Ben Jonson both to the ignorance of his audiences and to the vanity of Inigo Jones, a contriver of masques who (in Jonson's view) saw no further than 'shows, shows, mighty shows'.[14]

The radical element in Shakespeare's work is the recognition, through the examination of Prospero's predicament, of the fundamentally rhetorical nature of the masque. It is an instrument of power, of coercion and manipulation, resistible and corruptible. It is not enough simply to lay hold on some neo-Platonic idea, and, by reproducing it claim that it will therefore 'work'.

This understanding corresponds very significantly with the new view of music and its effects that was at this time taking hold. For the older, idealist notion of music's correspondence with the music of the spheres was being replaced by a rhetorical model of its affects. Monody and declamatory song were the vehicles of this change, and it was especially in the masque with its professional virtuoso singers that the style flourished.[15] To see rhetoric and neo-Platonism as opposites is of course a far too crude distinction. Nonetheless it is the element of persuasion that rhetoric brings with it that threatens the security of the correspondence between ideal and human reality that sustained the masque and the theories of *musica speculativa*. It is our awareness that the songs Ferdinand hears are part of Prospero's rhetoric as well as the images of celestial harmony he takes them to be that opens up the play's enactment of the problems that attend the making of masque and music.

This does not, of course, deny the validity of masque or of music. Their power exists, and may be harnessed for good or for ill. The play as a whole interrogates a series of familiar Renaissance debating topics. Art versus nature, action versus contemplation, reality versus illusion are but some of the subjects the play considers, and for all of them no simple preference is established. Most significant for the question of the validity of transitory masque is the opposition between Caliban and Ariel, beast against spirit, earth and water versus air and fire, body against soul.

This last distinction is used by Jonson to characterise the masque, and to defend his part in it. The display is its body, the mystery the poet shadows is its soul, 'impressing and lasting'.[16] In a very similar analogy Renaissance musicians compared the words of a song to the soul, the musical notes to the body, for only through the words are the fluctuating and transitory impressions of sound given direction and lasting purpose.[17]

In *The Tempest* both these notions are severely tested. When the play ends it is not the spirit who remains, but the thing of darkness that Prospero must acknowledge his and transport back to Milan. In the final scene it is the instrumental music that is curative, and Ariel's last song that slips into solipsism.

Conventional justification of masque and of music is therefore questioned. The self-regarding, inconsequential beauty of 'Where the bee sucks' signals the basic fact that music, like the magic powers it enables Prospero to deploy and the masquing visions he creates with its aid, is of itself nothing and the riches it promises an illusion. Prospero's shaking of the earth is similarly a self-indulgence unless it is played to some purpose before an audience, just as Ariel's singing acquires a positive function only when scripted by Prospero and directed to human listeners.

But to recognise, as the play does, that it is the body we are stuck with,

David Lindley

the life of action that must ultimately claim us, does not mean that music and the masque must be dumped, valueless, into the sea along with the books of magic. For the power of art is perenially available. Prospero denies himself the means of access to magical powers, not the validity of their exercise. For all their inadequacies music and masque have succeeded in bringing Alonso to repentance, and have imaged the love of Ferdinand and Miranda as something more than mere political convenience. Furthermore, as an audience we cannot deny the power of theatrical illusion when it is only through the masque–play that Prospero creates that we can encounter the meditation upon the limitations of masque and music that Shakespeare offers to us.

Stephen Orgel has rightly suggested that *The Tempest* is the 'most important Renaissance commentary' on 'court masques and plays'. Mary Chan claims that it 'shows the validity of the masque's conceptual basis', while, by contrast, Ernest Gilman calls it 'a delicately subversive maneuver staged in the enemy camp and hinting at the bedazzled, insulated self-regard of such entertainments'.[18] The truth is that *The Tempest* resists such simplification of its stance, presenting instead a multi-layered and deeply ambivalent attitude.

It does so because, though it reflects many of the substantial uncertainties about the masque genre current at the time of its composition, it actively involves the spectator in feeling, not merely contemplating the problems. Thus we, like the spectators on stage, are frustrated and disappointed as harmonious visions end in discord. We recognise the compromises that follow upon Prospero's manipulative aims, yet we respect the urgent desire that led him to a life of contemplation to secure the power he exercises. At the end of the play Prospero's wistful farewell to Ariel is echoed by our own regret as we tender the applause that releases Prospero from his island, but banishes us from the theatre. But perhaps most important of all in engendering the audience's complicity in the play's paradoxical statement is the music. Not only are the characters on stage pushed hither and thither by Prospero's music, but it works its end upon our senses also, with an undeniable insinuation. The symbolic view of music is comprehensible as an attempt to validate morally the experiential truth of music's power. *The Tempest*, by unpicking without ever quite denying that analogy does not merely reflect a historical moment, the time of 'the untuning of the sky', but forces us as an audience to go beyond a simple criticism of the fragility of the world of the stage. The Platonic theories that sustain a Sidneyan belief in art's golden world are crumbling, but we are left 'wishing it might be so'.

NOTES

1 One of the most persuasive comments on the play's darknesses is W. H. Auden's poetic descant, *The Sea and The Mirror*. A characteristic early

statement of changing attitudes is Rose Zimbardo, 'Form and Disorder in
The Tempest', *Shakespeare Quarterly*, 16 (1963), pp 49–65. A traditional
view of the music is articulated by John P. Cutts, 'Music in *The Tempest*',
Music and Letters, 39 (1958), pp. 347–58. A less straightforwardly symbolic
reading informs Theresa Coletti, 'Music and *The Tempest*', in *Shakespeare's
Late Plays*, ed. Richard C. Tobias and Paul G. Zolbrod (Athens, Ohio,
1974), pp. 185–99.

2 *Measure for Measure*, IV.i. 14–15.

3 Mary Chan, *Music in the Theatre of Ben Jonson* (Oxford, 1980), p. 328;
Peter Seng, *The Vocal Songs in the Plays of Shakespeare* (Cambridge, Mass.,
1967), p. 271.

4 Mark Booth, *The Experience of Songs* (New Haven and London, 1981),
pp. 14–23; 118.

5 For a study of the manifold implications of the banquet see Jacqueline E. M.
Latham, 'The Magic Banquet in *The Tempest*', *Shakespeare Studies*, 12
(1979), pp. 215–27.

6 Herford and Simpson, 7, p. 489.

7 Herford and Simpson, 7, p. 215.

8 *Niobe* (1611) sig. C2–3.

9 Ernest B. Gilman discusses the manipulation of the masque genre in his
' "All eyes": Prospero's Inverted Masque', *Renaissance Quarterly*, 33 (1980),
pp. 214–30, though he sees the conspirators as an 'antimasque', and does not
discuss the other shows.

10 Herford and Simpson, 7, 209.

11 See Inge-Stina Ewbank, ' "These pretty devices": A Study of Masques in
Plays', in *A Book of Masques*, ed. T. J. B. Spencer and Stanley Wells
(Cambridge, 1967), pp. 405–48; Ralph Berry, 'Masques and Dumb Shows in
Webster's Plays', *The Elizabethan Theatre*, 7 (1981), pp. 124–46, and, in the
same journal, pp. 111–23, Cyrus Hoy, 'Masques and the Artifice of Tragedy';
Jeffrey Fischer, '*Love Restored*: A Defense of Masquing', *Renaissance
Drama*, 7 (1977), pp. 231–44; David Lindley, *Thomas Campion* (Leiden,
forthcoming), Chapter 4.

12 Francis Bacon, 'Of Masques and Triumphs', in *Essays*.

13 Alvin B. Kernan, *The Playwright as Magician* (New Haven and London,
1979), p. 143.

14 'An Expostulation with Inigo Jones', *The Complete Poems*, ed. George
Parfitt (Harmondsworth, 1975), p. 346.

15 See John Hollander, *The Untuning of the Sky* (Princeton, N.J., 1961) *passim;*
James Anderson Winn, *Unsuspected Eloquence* (New Haven and London,
1981), Chapter 4; and for the music, Ian Spink, *English Song, Dowland to
Purcell* (London, 1974).

16 Herford and Simpson, 7, 209.

17 See, for example, Monteverdi's observation that musical pieces without
words were 'bodies without soul', in Oliver Strunk, *Source Readings in
Music History* (New York, 1950), p. 406.

18 Orgel, *The Illusion of Power* (Berkeley, Los Angeles and London, 1975),
p. 45; Chan, *Music in Ben Jonson*, p. 330; Gilman, ' "All eyes" ', p. 220.

SARA PEARL

Sounding to present occasions: Jonson's masques of 1620-5

CRITICISM OF JONSON'S MASQUES has made great strides in the last few decades. Thanks to the studies of John. C. Meagher, Stephen Orgel, and, most recently, Graham Parry,[1] it is no longer possible to view this part of the Jonson canon as an embarrassing appendage, in which the author, for the right reward, was willing to prostitute his muse to the provision of emptily sycophantic royalist ephemera. We must now recognise that the masque in Jonson's hands had a serious purpose and is artistically successful and complex. Nevertheless, current comment remains deficient in at least two ways. One is a tendency, despite the existence of such striking parallels as those between *Epicoene* and *Hymenaei*, to treat the masques in isolation from the rest of the dramatic canon.[2] The other is a failure to probe beyond the general meaning of the allegory to its particular meaning, by way of an awareness of the specific issues of royal policy to which each masque is a response, and on which it is a commentary. The aim of this essay is to demonstrate the value of these methods of analysis.

My subject is the series of Twelfth Night masques from 1620-5, written during the ten-year period when masque writing represented Jonson's only dramatic endeavour, and the play which followed them, *The Staple of News* (1626). The masques are *News from the New World Discovered in the Moon*, 1620; *The Masque of Augurs*, 1622; *Time Vindicated to Himself and to His Honours*, 1623; *Neptune's Triumph for the Return of Albion*, 1624; and *The Fortunate Isles, and Their Union*, 1625. By this date the court was well used to regarding the Twelfth Night masque as an occasion of great political significance, both in terms of the foreign ambassadors who attended (they frequently squabbled over invitations), and in terms of the masque's content, which would be carefully scanned for clues to royal intentions. The masques of 1620-5, which have not been singled out as a group before (except to receive the summary verdict that they are at once over-elaborate and facile compared to Jonson's masques of the previous decade[3]), provide a sustained debate on a set of issues of intense interest to both James and Jonson. They propose the view that comment on matters of state was beyond the capacities of ordinary people, that such matters involved a concept of higher truth available only to James. In particular, the masques are centred on James's views on Britain's position in relation to Europe, a key political question during these years. As the interpreter of royal policy, Jonson continues to cast himself as the same 'high, and aloofe' poet one encounters in the plays and non-dramatic verse, above the mass of mankind, and in this way very like the king. This analogy is also a constant theme of these five masques. All of them remind the audience that they must be educated into an understanding of Jonson's art, just as they must submit themselves to the mysteries attendant on James's kingship.

Jonson returned to the stage in 1626 with *The Staple of News*. The play contains, as Herford and Simpson note, many verbal borrowings from the masques of 1620–5, but this was not a matter of the haphazard retrieval of lines and passages which happened to be running in Jonson's head. As I shall indicate, the repetitions are there because in many ways *The Staple of News* is a gathering together and re-inspection of the ideas which the masques examine.

In 1620, the date of *News from the New World*, Britain's European policy seemed of supreme importance. There was great concern over the war in Europe, particularly in relation to the hoped-for restoration of the Palatinate to Frederick, James's son-in-law, and more generally because of the increasing power of the Catholic forces. Public anxiety was such that it created the conditions for a new industry: the regular printing and dissemination of European news. This was something entirely without precedent. For the first time ordinary people were able to discuss, assess and interpret national and international political events for themselves. 1620 was the year in which the first English newspapers began to appear, in the form of translations of Dutch news-sheets. Their pro-Protestant bias was not always disguised. They occasionally referred to the Imperialist army as 'the enemy', and minimized Catholic victories; some even bore Frederick's arms.[4] One compiler, Thomas Gainsford, had himself written a radical pamphlet, immediately impounded, in which the Spanish ambassador was portrayed as a fifth-columnist, eroding from within the processes of English government.[5]

James's attitude was very different. Declaring that the Palatinate question was a private quarrel between Frederick and the Emperor, he rejected the popular view that Protestantism in Europe was being dangerously threatened, and that the Protestant cause should be taken up as part of an ideological crusade against Catholicism. He carefully avoided firmly defined policies, disliking the polarization of allegiances they implied, and hoped instead for consensus in political questions. At the same time his response to the notion of public discussion was emphatically hostile. When irritation at what was taken to be his fence-sitting grew, as it did in 1620 when after the annual sermon at Paul's Cross he made a speech, not about the Palatinate crisis as people had hoped, but about the rebuilding of St Paul's,[6] James countered by asserting that questions of foreign policy were 'mysteries of state' which attracted 'too much bold censure'; they were 'no Theames or subjects fit for vulgar persons', being 'far beyond their reach or capacitie'.[7] He backed up this line with a spate of proclamations, forbidding anyone to debate the issue[8], and by 1621 the court had become so nervous about indulging in discussion that the royal progress for that year was conducted in 'profound silence'.[9] In 1622, when news of the final negotiations to marry Charles, the Prince of Wales, to the Spanish infanta began to circulate and produce mounting alarm, James decided to enforce the proclamation that the gentry should spend Christmas away from London at their country estates. The official reason was to preserve tradition, the 'real and secret' reason, as the Venetian ambassador noted, to prevent them meeting to criticise the match.[10] It was against this background of popular eagerness to obtain and debate political news and unrelenting royal censorship that Jonson's masques of 1620–5 were written.

What was Jonson's attitude to the political situation? It is clear that political matters interested him since his library contained books that represented both extremes of Protestant and Catholic opinion. He owned a copy of the banned *Vox Populi* by Thomas Scot and also of Scipio Mirandula's *Congratulations on the projected marriage between Charles I of England and Maria, Infanta of Spain*.[11] But in all his poems (the most private area of his work) written during the period of disquiet regarding James's continental policy, he is careful not to appear aligned to any extreme view. In a poem of about 1620, when English volunteers were being recruited to aid Frederick, he hotly recommends fighting to 'revive / Mans buried honour'.[12] But the poem concentrates not on the honour of the cause, but, *à la* Rupert Brooke, on the honour of purifying oneself by leaving behind an effeminately fashionable London life. In 1623 Jonson carefully disclaims all interest in foreign policy:

> What is't to me whether the French Designe
> Be, or be not, to get the *Val-telline?*
> Or the States Ships sent forth belike to meet
> Some hopes of Spaine in their West-Indian Fleet?
> Whether the Dispensation yet be sent,
> Or that the Match from *Spaine* was ever meant?[13]

He would fight 'without inquirie' to regain the Palatinate, not for a political or religious cause, but 'for honour', and put thus he is able to claim without inconsistency that, as James emphatically wished, in all things his 'Kings desire' should be paramount.

Jonson takes up the theme of censorship in 'An Execration upon

Vulcan', written at the same date. He treats this sensitive issue in a comic way by imagining the fire that burned his books as a monstrously unjust censor. Vulcan irrationally attacks his work although it is free from 'treason', 'heresie', 'Imposture', 'witchcraft, charmes or blasphemie' (15–16). Jonson details all the bad writing (the productions of others) that Vulcan should have concentrated on: the romances, scurrilous political writings, newspapers, and fanatical religious prophecies. At the end of the poem he holds himself up as a right-minded censor, able to enforce the proper powers of criticism and distinguish between the good and bad in politics and art.

Identifying and linking the false in politics and art is the moral impetus behind *News from the New World*. Jonson presents three characters, a printer, a chronicler, and a factor, whose methods of manufacturing news to satisfy the public's appetite are a satiric jibe at the news industry. The printer, knowing that men will 'beleeve nothing but what's in Print' (63), does not concern himself with the truth. He will 'give anything for a good Copie now, be't true or false, so't be newes' (18–19), and republishes his news as soon as the public forgets it. The factor provides for different factions by composing 'Puritan newes', 'Protestant newes', and 'Pontificiall newes' (42–3). Like many of the avid private news-letter writers and readers of the day he believes that news should not be printed but remain as unpublished letters since as such they retain the prurient appeal of private gossip. The chronicler masquerades as a historian who is 'for matter of State' (21). He presents trivial gossip about the court as though it were the stuff of history: 'I have noted the number, and capacity of the degrees here; and told twice over how many candles are i'th'roome lighted ... because I love to give light to posteritie in the truth of things' (27–31). All three newsmongers, then, do not record the truth but create fantasies. Jonson's epigraph to the masque 'Nascitur e tenebris: & se sibi vindicat orbis', 'a world is born out of darkness and sets itself free', itself suggests this process of false creativity, a monstrous birth. In *The Staple of News*, which reproduces this masque's dramatisation of different attitudes to news, this analogy is repeated. The news office is described as a new born child that 'ha's the shape– / And is come forth' (I.v.73), helped into the world by Cymbal's midwifery.

The heralds in *News from the New World* also offer news that is 'Newe as the night they [the news] are borne in; / Or the phants'ie that begot 'hem' (3–4). They have, they say, been sent by Jonson to proclaim the news that he has discovered in the moon. The newsmongers imagine that Jonson has actually been there, and suggest scientific ways in which it might have been done. The heralds dismiss their literal-mindedness and state that this news comes not by 'Philosophers phantasie. / Mathematicians Perspicall. / Or brother of the Rosie Crosses intelligence, no forc'd way, but by the neat and cleane power of Poetrie, / The Mistris of all discovery' (100–4). Jonson is a 'servant' of poetry 'in search of truth': in this sense he has 'been there' (106–7). Thus the news from the moon is presented as possessing an artistic truth which elevates it from the false creations of the newsmongers.

The truth that the heralds report as Jonson's discovery turns out to be an imaginatively satiric version of London. The moon is described as physically just the same as the earth: it is 'found to be an Earth inhabited!' (128), 'but differing from ours' (136). Unlike contemporary London, the moon is free from the religious and political dissension that James so much disliked. 'All the discourse there is harmonie' (196); there are 'no controversies' (200). Lawyers are dumb, and Puritans are 'walkers onely' (206), they do not sermonize or prophesy. But in some ways the moon is like London. Great ladies arrange secret meetings, though in the clouds rather than Hyde Park (249), and go on fashionable trips, though to the 'isles of delight' rather than Tunbridge Wells (268). Another ironic resemblance alludes to a subject of royal displeasure which James must have been making very apparent at the precise date of the masque. On the Isle of Epicenes women dress like men with 'not heads and broad hats, short doublets, and long points'; they 'laugh and lie down in the Moone-shine, and stab with their ponyards' (278–81). It can hardly be a coincidence that on 24 January 1620 James ordered the clergy of London to preach against the 'insolencie of our women, and theyre wearing of brode brim'd hats, pointed doublets, theyre haire cut short or shorne, and some of them stilettoes or poinards'.[14]

Jonson's true discoveries in the moon finally turn out not to be the masque's real news at all. The heralds have 'adventured to tell your Majestie no news; for hitherto we have mov'd rather to your delight, than your belief' (299–301). Naturally, since their news so flatteringly reflects James's opinions on 'controversies' and female dress, it is 'no newes' to him. It is also 'no newes' in another sense, since it is a less important announcement than the final revelation of the masque: the loyal support of James's own courtiers. The antimasque of Volatees, a troupe of feather-covered moon-men, are banished by the courtiers, led by Prince Charles as Truth. Unlike the newsmongers and the inhabitants of moon-London, the courtiers are 'a more noble discoverie worthie of your eare, as the object will be your eye' (302–3). They are a 'race' of James's own, 'form'd, animated, lightened, and heightened by you' (303–4). In an inversion of the normal process of gazing up at the moon from the earth, they have been admiring James from 'above the Moone far in speculation of your vertues, have remain'd there intranc'd certaine houres, with wonder of the pietie, wisdome, Majesty reflected by you, on them' (304–7).

In this way Jonson's true art has revealed the Truth—in the shape of Prince Charles—both, Jonson implies, ultimately created by James. In a gathering up of images at the end of the masque Jonson urges the court to 'Read' James 'as you would doe the booke / Of all perfection' (340-1). James now represents the true version of reality, providing the correct text in opposition to the mistaken and seditious versions that political gossip and newspapers propagate.

Jonson did not write the next Twelfth Night masque, performed in 1621. We do not know the author of this piece, nor do we have the text, but Chamberlain reported[15] that it contained a Puritan who was brought on to be 'flouted and abused'. Chamberlain thought that the directness of its stand against radical Protestantism was both 'unseemly and unseasonable'. As he points out, its tactlessness lay in the fact that Catholic France was persecuting the Huguenots, to whom many Britons, as Protestants, felt sympathetic. If the French ambassador was at the masque, he would no doubt have assumed that this gave the seal of James's approval to his government's policy.

The political implications of Jonson's 1622 masque, *The Masque of Augurs*, are less overt. It concentrates on creating an image of future peace by imaginatively removing Britain from the problems of the Continental wars. Before this final vision, Jonson uses images of false and debased creativity in the antimasque that will contrast with the true arts of government and poetry practised by James and himself. He also suggests how the audience should view the masque and connect it with their own lives. Understanding art is thus linked with understanding the proper relationship between courtier and king. A bargeman, a brewer's clerk, an ale-wife, and a bear-ward from St Katherine's (a lower-class, dockland area of London) invade the court buttery hatch. They sing a scatological drinking song to accompany their dancing bears. However much some members of the court may have enjoyed such rowdy entertainments, Jonson makes it clear (while providing them) that they are inappropriate for the court. The ale-wife persuades the Groom of the Revels to allow the dancing bears to appear by assuring him absurdly that they are 'Beares both of qualitie and fashion' (132). At the same time, Jonson suggests that James, who was anyway fond of bear-baiting, is generous enough to accept any entertainment if it is offered in the right spirit. Notch, the brewer's clerk, rebukes the Groom of the Revels, who has tried to dismiss him, by pointing out that the court is a place of love, not exclusion: 'our comming was to shew our loves, sir, and to make a little merry with his Majestie to night' (62-3). This fantasy of a relationship of love and generosity between the king and his meanest subjects prepares us for the prophecy of the main masque, where it is foretold that James will 'live free / From hatred, faction, or the feare / To blast the Olive thou dost weare' (386-8).

Jonson provides a mirror image of court life in this masque: it is set in the court buttery hatch in order to implicate the court audience more directly in the process of interpretation, as they see themselves in a familiar domestic setting. It is the court official's behaviour in the masque, rather than the presenters of the bears, that is put under the closest scrutiny, and Jonson satirises his petty officialdom and corruption. The bear-ward suggests that the Groom has been taking the court supplies for his own use, and the Groom replies 'I may doe it by my place' (41). In fact, when this masque was performed in 1622, Cranfield had recently finished reorganising the court finances in order to reduce corruption among officials. Persistent efforts ended with a saving of £1800 a year on the household, just by, as Cranfield put it, not abridging anyone's diet, but 'only their stealings and knaveries'.[16] The knavery of Jonson's lowly court officer was no doubt a reminder of the recent purge.

The second antimasque put on by the St Katherine's presenters is as vulgar as the bears, but in a different way; it juxtaposes a different kind of debased art. Vangoose, 'a rare Artist', characterises his masque as entirely different from that of Jonson and Jones, who lack originality: 'dey have no ting, no ting van deir owne, but vat dey take vrom de eard or de zea, or de heaven, or de hell, or de rest van de veir Elementen' (101-3). Vangoose is proud of his intellectual isolation and powers of creativity. His masque is a 'dainty new ting, dat never vas nor never sall be, in de *rebus natura*, nor *de forma*, nor de hoffen, nor de voote, but [is] a *mera devisa* of de brain' (106-8). He rejects nature and historical example, and like Jonson's Littlewit or Swift's spider, he relies entirely on his own originality. He offers to conjure up the whole of the Turkish court by his trick reflecting glasses, and when this is turned down decides to show the world's pilgrims that 'make de fine Labyrints, and shew all de brave error in de vorld' (253-4). He has composed this masque because Jonson and Jones do not have a masque ready, they are 'barren' and 'lost' (100). By maintaining the fiction that he did not write either the antimasque of bears or Vangoose's antimasque, Jonson marks these out as debased productions against which his own art may be judged. James, too, would have found Vangoose a particularly suitable target for attack, as Vangoose is described as 'a *Brittaine* borne' who affects a Dutch accent. In 1622 such Dutchified Britons would have held little appeal for James, who was currently stressing his hostility to the idea of aiding the Netherlands against the Spanish after the expiry of the Truce of Antwerp the year before.

Vangoose expresses the kind of wilful eccentricity that Jonson most disliked when he claims that antimasques should be irrelevant to the masques they precede. It is 'all de better, vor an Antick-maske, de more absurd it be, and vrom de purpose ... If it goe vrom de *Nature* of de ting, it is de more Art' (265-7). However, as Jonson points out, the 'perplex'd Dance' of 'straying and deform'd Pilgrims, taking severall pathes' (270) *is* relevant because it provides an image of error and confusion abroad which James, in Britain, will reject. Apollo indicates that 'whilst the world about him is at ods', James sits

> Crowned Lord here of himselfe, and smiles.—
> To see the erring mazes of mankinde;
> Who seeke for that, doth punish them to finde.   (315-18)

This scene clearly refers to James's foreign policy. 'Neighbours' gaze enviously at James's 'fortune', 'stand amaz'd' at his 'wisdome', and 'wish to be / O'recome, or governed' by him (405-7). Europe is thus envious of James's much vaunted peace policy, or in other words, of his non-intervention in their Continental quarrels.

At the end of the masque, the augurs prophesy continuing peace and prosperity for Britain. Charles, as James's son, will continue his policies. Evidently it was a comforting belief in a time of such political uncertainty that Britain's future could be predicted so confidently, and thus controlled and made safe. Jonson uses the methods of the augurs, with their prophetic trances and their reading of the future through the flights of birds, to give the authority of classical precedent to this rosy futuristic vision. Jonson's art, unlike Vangoose's, makes proper use of historical and literary antecedents to reveal art's true mysteries.

The architecture of the masque also stresses the links between James's present and future court and the classical past. Unusually, Jonson complimented Jones on 'the scene', describing it as 'full of noble observation of Antiquitie, and high Presentment'.[17] *The Masque of Augurs* was the first masque to be put on in Jones's new and as yet uncompleted Banqueting House. In this grand Palladian setting, the masque opened by revealing a backdrop that represented another of Jones's building successes: the court buttery at St James's.[18] We do not know what this room looked like, but in view of Jones's other architectural designs we can assume that it was classical in style. For the main masque this backdrop was withdrawn to reveal a complex perspective scene leading to the college of augurs, a temple based on the Pantheon.[19] Thus the masque's backdrops were linked to the masque's actual setting, and the combination of these real and depicted examples of classical but new architecture gave visual embodiment to the idea that James's rule recreated the splendours of the classical past in the present.

In *Time Vindicated to Himself and to His Honours* of 1623 Jonson returns to the theme of popular comment on state affairs explored in *News from the World*. Like *The Masque of Augurs*, however, this masque had as its back-scene a representation of a building by Jones; in this case, the facade of the Whitehall Banqueting House.[20] This impressive classical building vindicates the fame of the time by providing a visual contrast to the grotesque figures of 'the curious' dressed to represent 'Eares', 'Eies', and 'Nose' who cavort in front of it. The curious fail to recognise the splendours of their setting and of James's rule and are 'ill-natur'd, and like flies, / Seeke *Times* corrupted parts to blow upon' (266-7). They campaign for the removal of censorship so that 'men might doe, and talke all that they list' (44). Contrary to James's proclamation, they 'might have talk'd o'the King—Or State.—Or all the World. / Censur'd the Counsell, ere they censure us. / We doe it in *Pauls*.—Yes, and in all the tavernes' (207-12). They long for the disruption of society, delighting in 'the impostures, / The prodigies, disease, and distempers, / The Knaveries of the *Time*' (50-1).

As the St Katherine's presenters in *The Masque of Augurs* are led by Vangoose, the champion of the curious is Chronomastix, or time's scourge. He is in part a caricature of George Wither, who was known for his sweeping and radical satires. Chronomastix, like the curious, is one who pretends to hate social maladies but actually delights in them. He will only 'look on *Time* and love the same' when the curious 'censure whom we list, and how we list' (83-4) and chaos reigns. The artistic reasons for the attack on Wither are not far to seek. In his *Motto* of 1621 Wither criticises poets who, like Jonson, have patrons and write for money: 'I have no muses that will serve the turne', Wither wrote, 'At every triumph and rejoyce or mourne'. He stressed his independence by dedicating his work 'To anybody', and declared that 'Gods two *Testaments*' and 'the world' were the only books he cared for,[21] a view which Jonson, who regularly advertised his attachment to classical literature, would have found particularly contemptible. Most important, he is, in Jonson's masque, an arrogant individualist whose sole aim is to 'get my selfe a name' (95). Although Wither claimed that he despised worldly success, Jonson makes Chronomastix announce that 'To serve *Fame* / is all my end' (94-5). Chronomastix proceeds to conjure up an antimasque of his 'faction and friends', a selection of Londoners who, like the curious, 'know all things the wrong way' and admire his satire of the times. But such popular success is shown to be inimical to Fame, who rejects Chronomastix: '*Fame* doth sound no trumpet / To such vaine, empty fooles: 'Tis Infamy / Thou serv'st' (98-9).

Chronomastix, the curious, and the Londoners who support them all practise the kind of satire that Jonson saw as socially subversive. Jonson distinguished between constructive satire which attempted to cure the ills of society and destructive, which aimed to destroy society itself. As he asserts in *Discoveries*:

> nothing is of more credit, or request now, than a petulant paper, or scoffing verses ... Rayling, and tinckling *Rimers*, whose Writings the vulgar more greedily reade; as being taken with the scurrility, and petulancie of such wits. Hee shall not have a Reader now, unlesse hee jeere and lye ... to heare the worthiest workes misinterpreted; the clearest actions obscured; the innocent'st life traduc'd; And in such a licence of lying, a field so fruitfull of slanders, how

can there be matter wanting to his laughter? Hence comes the *Epidemicall* Infection. (273–93)

Here, as often, Jonson connects his own writing, 'the worthiest workes', with James's policies, 'the clearest actions', as equal targets for slander. But Jonson worried that the distinction between his own satire and that of a more radical temper was not all that clear. He claimed in *Discoveries* that his satires had often been misunderstood. Enemies had quoted them out of context and given them a political meaning that was not intended. 'The Age is growne so tender of her fame', he complains, 'as she cals all writings *Aspersions*' (2300–1). Indeed, after *Time Vindicated* was performed, Chamberlain reported that Jonson was 'like to heere yt on both sides of the head' for introducing the character of Chronomastix, since criticising society had become 'so tender an argument that yt must not be touched either in jest or in earnest'.[22] Jonson's careful distinction in the masque between writing political satire and writing an attack on political satire was evidently not sufficiently clear. No doubt James liked to see himself as the good king of Jonson's *Discoveries*, a 'mercifull *Prince*', 'safe in love, not in feare', who 'needs no Emissaries, Spies, Intelligencers, to intrap true Subjects', and 'feares no Libels, no Treasons. His people speake, what they thinke; and talke openly, what they doe in secret' (1191–5). The mere presence of the curious in *Time Vindicated*, however, with their libels and treasons, seems to have been enough to call this ideal image too disconcertingly into question.

The masque ends with a specific reference to the current cause of rumour and faction, the European war. Having shown the courtiers being freed by Love from Hecate's obscuring spells, after which they stand revealed as 'certaine glories of the *Time*' (281) united by their loving duty to James, Jonson urges that they sublimate any desire for war into a desire to go hunting, hunting being war's peacetime equivalent, 'the noblest exercise' (516), and, of course, James's favourite pastime. The idea is then given an ingenious metaphorical extension. The courtiers should not 'hunt Mankind to death', but take as their example James, who

> hates all chace of malice, and of bloud:
> And studies only wayes of good,
> To keepe soft Peace in breath. (529–31)

The idea of hunting men thus embodies both the foreign war and the political strife ('malice') which it was causing at home.

In *Time Vindicated* Jonson pilloried Wither above all for the way that he courted a cheap brand of popularity by whipping up feelings of ingratitude against James. Jonson's next masque, *Neptune's Triumph for the Return of Albion* of 1624, takes up the same theme of popular and vulgar political views, but treats it very differently. *Neptune's Triumph* concerns Charles's return from Spain without the Infanta in the previous

October, after which official policy had been readjusted and brought into line with the public rejoicing with which the failure of the match had been greeted. Accordingly, Jonson finds himself confronting the paradox (for him) that something so *popular* can also be right. The masque centres on a debate between a poet and a cook (the two different aspects of Jonson as masque-maker, at once moralist and entertainer) concerning the problems of pleasing 'the palates of the ghests' (48-9) and satisfying '*Expectation*'. The Poet regards expectation as a 'pressing enemie' (56) since the audience will want 'more than they understand' (61). The Cook argues that the 'severall tasts' (50) of the spectators must be catered to by the artist.

The Poet's masque seeks to suggest the irrelevance of the political popularity of the event it celebrates. The Poet creates an allegory of the return from Spain in which Neptune (James) has despatched a floating island to bring back his son Albion (Charles) from the '*Hesperian* shores' (143). Jonson skilfully assimilates the fact that he is writing some time after the event by making the Poet explain that now the popular celebrations have died down, the voyage can be explained without the distortions of sensational reporting; before 'It was not time / To mix this Musick with the vulgars chime. / Stay, till th'abortive, and extemporall dinne / Of balladry, were understood a sinne' (161-4). Political events are best understood when they are distanced both by time and by being allegorised; the mythic content gives them a heroic meaning beyond a mere discussion of contemporary politics. When the floating island is revealed and the Poet's account is dramatised in the masque proper, the chorus underlines this point. The audience are reminded that it is 'no common Cause' (349) which is being celebrated, and that the heavens have given their 'consent' to the 'publike votes' (351-3) for Charles's return.

The Cook's masque is a vulgar and outlandish anticipation of the Poet's. He 'would have had your Ile brought floating in, now, / In a brave broth, and of a sprightly greene' (185-6), 'with an *Arion*, mounted on the backe / Of a growne Conger' (189-90). Such productions are, of course, entirely suitable for the antimasque. The Poet, unlike Jonson, dismisses antimasques as not being 'A worthy part of presentation / Being things so *heterogene* to all devise, / Mere *By-workes*, and at best *Outlandish* nothings' (220-4). The Cook shows that this is not so. He will satisfy the audience's appetite with 'a *metaphoricall* dish' (223) of 'persons, to present the meates' (241). The people who go into his cooking pot are those who 'relish nothing, but *di stato*' (245), or matters of state, but 'know all things the wrong way' (247). They include the newspaper writers and readers: those who have discussed the Spanish match and gossiped about such matters as the elephant and camels (which for good measure also go into the pot) which were paraded in the London streets as a gift from Spain.[23] In this way the Cook, although claiming to satisfy popular tastes, provides a covert attack on them; as he indeed says, his wit 'may jumpe with' the Poet's (234).

Significantly *Neptune's Triumph* was never performed. The reason according to Chamberlain was the unresolved quarrel between the French and Spanish ambassadors over who was to be invited, although the official excuse was that the king was unwell.[24] The masque must have pleased Buckingham and Charles, the chief masquers, who had returned from Spain unwilling to continue negotiations for the marriage. James, however, had not yet given up hope for the match and might have feared that the overtly anti-Spanish tone of the masque would offend the Spanish ambassador. It is certainly the case that the masque would not please 'the severall tasts' of 'every Nation' as the Cook had recommended. Perhaps Jonson's barbed defence of popular opinion conflicted too much with the king's own wishes for the masque to be performed.

The Fortunate Isles, and Their Union was Jonson's last masque of the 1620s and was written a year after *Neptune's Triumph*, in 1625. Although it uses some of the same material, including the floating island, it is far less anti-Spanish. The Venetian ambassador recorded that since the Spanish ambassador and his retinue were present 'it is believed that many jests against the Spaniards were omitted on their account'.[25] James was keen to keep on even terms with Spain despite the failure of the match and the growing probability that Charles would marry a French princess: an event anticipated in this masque as the union between the rose and the lily. The main idea behind *The Fortunate Isles*, however, is not Britain's allegiance to any foreign power, but her own nationalistic pride and separateness.

The masque opens with a satire on the Rosicrucians. Merefool (like Fitzdottrel in *The Devil is an Ass*, Vangoose in *The Masque of Augurs*, and the newsmongers in *News from the New World*) is a seeker after magic and mystery. He is one of the 'Bretheren of the *Rosie-Crosse*', who has been praying for a mystical experience. Johphiel, an 'aery spirit', visits him and promises that he will be 'The Constable of the Castle *Rosy-Crosse*', 'Keeper of the Keyes / Of the whole Kaball', 'Principall Secretarie to the Starres' (133-6), 'Reade at one view all books' and 'speak all the languages / Of severall creatures' (143-4). Johphiel offers to conjure up any historical or mythical character, but unfortunately those that Mere-fool requests—they include Zoroaster and Hermes Trismegistus, mystics whom the Rosicrucians especially admired—are engaged on other business and cannot appear. Johphiel suggests instead two English writers, Skelton and Scogan. They appear and bring in a masque of figures from traditional English ballads. When Scogan first enters he announces that he and Skelton have been called with 'a morall intent' (315), and this intent turns out to be disabusing Merefool of his mystical fantasies. When the masquers disappear Johphiel tells Merefool that he has been watching not 'the company o'the *Rosie-crosse*' but 'the company of *Players!*'

(431-2). He begs the king's pardon and suggests that Merefool should be banished for his foolishness and credulity.

The political point of exposing Rosicrucianism was particularly pertinent in the mid 1620s. An attack on this mystical cult was a compliment to France, since a propaganda war against it was currently being waged there. Moreover, the ideas of the Rosicrucians were not attractive to James. He disliked their idealistic, apocalyptic, and mystical methods of thought and their links with radical Protestantism. Scholars influenced by the cult found no royal support. James refused to receive John Dee, and Robert Fludd encountered difficulties in publishing his work in England. Rosicrucianism was a Pan-European movement which might dangerously divert members' allegiance away from their monarch to a wider Protestant and mystical brotherhood. James's peace policy of non-intervention on behalf of the anti-Catholic cause in Europe was flatly opposed to this brand of internationalism, and the specifically English figures that are conjured up in the masque underline the king's attitude.[26]

The ending of the masque also emphasizes the nationalistic theme. Jonson repeats the device of the floating island that he had used for *Neptune's Triumph* in the previous year. There the island symbolised Charles's return from Spain; it represents his invulnerability and safe removal from Europe home to Britain. In *The Fortunate Isles* the emphasis is different. The floating island 'Macaria', or the blessed, is spoken of as Britain's geographical neighbour. This association of Britain with the fortunate isles had many precedents in classical mythology and literature. The isles were supposed to be on the western extreme of the world and were where the souls of the blessed were sent after death. Virgil refers to Britain as 'wholly sundered from all the world', and Horace places Britain at the edge of the earth. Later writers repeat this idea, among them Erasmus, Selden, and Drayton, and Camden notes in his *Britannia* (1610) that 'the plentiful abundance, these goodly pleasures of *Britain*, have perswaded some, that those fortunate Ilands, wherein all things, as Poets write, doe flourish in a perpetuall spring tide, were sometime here with us'.[27] In Jonson's masque the fortunate islands 'adhere to your B R I T A N - N I A ' (448) and 'the aire, the soile, the seat combine / To speak it blessed!' (488-9). As in Camden's account, it is perpetually spring, and a profusion of specifically British spring flowers grow. The emphasis is a cheerfully nationalistic one: Britain as part of the fortunate isles is proudly isolated from the rest of the world. Jonson also makes the association especially appropriate to James. The fortunate isles were supposed by Plutarch and Lucian to be the retiring place for heroes, where Saturn slept: a place where there was, as Jonson says, 'no sicknes, nor old age' (508). It was an attractively fanciful idea to put before James, who was an old and ill man when the masque was performed, and was to die a few months later.

In Jonson's masques of 1620-5 there is a constant process of distinguishing between false mysteries and true ones; a constant impetus to discriminate and judge. Rejecting the popular requires a sophisticated response, and Jonson reiterates the concept that those who wish to interpret either politics or art must be 'understanders'. Crucial to this is the notion that one will only understand up to the level of one's abilities. To expect the work to provide more is arrogance. In *News from the New World* the herald asks the factor of news 'in what case were you and your expectation' (115) if the moon proves to be different from his idea of it. In *Time Vindicated* Fame criticises the curious for discussing 'more than you understand' (13), and in *Neptune's Triumph* the Poet asks the Cook 'But what if they [the audience] expect more than they understand?' (61). The onus of correct interpretation is thus thrust onto the audience; it is their skill and tact in understanding the masque that is crucial to its political and artistic point.

This idea is fundamental to *The Staple of News*. A group of gossips, Mirth, Tattle, Expectation, and Censure, act as an on-stage audience to the play and comment on the action throughout. In the Induction the Prologue warns them to 'expect no more than you understand' (30-1), but the gossips discuss their opinion of the play before it even begins. Later, they begin to extract a political message. Censure connects '*Aurelia Clara Pecunia*' the '*Infanta* of the *Mines*' with the Spanish Infanta, 'Plaine in the stiling her *Infanta*, and giving her three names' (2 Int. 25-6). Mirth speaks for Jonson when she replies 'Take heed, it lie not in the vice of your interpretation: what have *Aurelia, Clara, Pecunia* to do with any person? do they any more, but express the property of *Money*, which is the daughter of the earth, and drawne out of the Mines? Is there nothing to be call'd *Infanta*, but what is subject to exception?' (2 Int. 27-32). Jonson is clearly teasing the audience by describing Pecunia as he does. Like the gossips we cannot help connecting her with the Spanish princess, but as Mirth points out, there is in fact no real connection: it is simply 'the vice of your interpretation'.

Such pointers to the dangers of hunting for political allusions were evidently ignored by the play's first audiences, for Jonson felt obliged to add to the printed text an admonitory note addressed 'To the Readers'. Significantly, this is placed before the third act, where the news office reveals its news of foreign affairs. The news is extravagantly absurd, reporting impossible changes of allegiance and status, and fantastic military tactics by the King of Spain, the Emperor, and Spinola. The aim is to parody the horror stories of encroaching Catholic hegemony over Europe. In the address to the readers Jonson sternly observed that 'the *Allegory*, and purpose of the *Author* hath hitherto beene wholly mistaken, and so sinister an interpretation beene made, as if the soules of most of the *Spectators* hath liv'd in the eyes and eares of these ridiculous Gossips that tattle betweene the *Acts*' (2-7). The audience must 'consider the *Newes* here vented, to be none of his *Newes*, nor any reasonable mans, but *Newes* made like the times *Newes* (a weekly cheat to draw money)' (8–10). By making his news 'like the times *Newes*' (i.e. sensationally distorted), but not like 'any reasonable mans', Jonson is guying the tastes and expectations of the audience. His '*Allegory*, and purpose' is not to report and analyse the current political situation but to show how wrongly an audience can interpret political comment. Jonson is declaring his dislike of fictionalised versions of current events such as Scot's and Gainsford's anti-Spanish pamphlets, or Middleton's *A Game at Chess*, to which there is a mocking reference in the play (at III.ii.198–211). Jonson offers his work not, like these productions, as political satire, but as a critique of political satire.

Jonson defeats not only political expectations in *The Staple of News* but artistic ones. As in the masques, truth in politics is linked to true art. The gossips complain that the play lacks a proper fool and a proper devil; they judge by the standards of an old-fashioned, rather than a modern, morality play. They are horrified by the way that Jonson has allowed the news office to 'fall most abruptly' (4 Int.75) halfway through, and demand that it be reinstated with an apology from the author. Most of all they are furious that Jonson has tricked them into believing that Pennyboy Canter, the moral spokesman of the play, was a real beggar: 'Absurdity on him, for a huge overgrowne *Playmaker*! why should he make him live againe, when they, and we all thought him dead? If he had left him to his ragges, there had beene an end of him' (4 Int. 8–11). Here Jonson exerts his own artistic powers and licence; it is a way of indicating that his imagination overrides the false fictions which the audience, the gossips, and the newsmongers share.

As in *News from the New World*, where the factor looks forward to establishing 'a Staple for newes' (45), Jonson sets his own creative, artistic truth against the false manufacture of gossip. In the Prologue for the Court he wrote that '*Wherein, although, our* Title, *Sir, be* Newes, / *Wee yet adventure, here, to tell you none*' (9–10). An ironic contrast is pointed out between Pennyboy Canter's moral comments and news: 'No more o' your sentences, *Canter*, they are stale, / We come for *Newes*, remember where you are' (III.ii.14–15). By the end of the play his 'sentences' have turned out not to be tired platitudes but truer and newer and therefore less 'stale' than the play's news. Thus Pennyboy Canter's moral and social lessons emerge as the real news of the play supplanting the political fictions of the newsmongers.

The jeerers in *The Staple of News* are a re-working of the curious of *Time Vindicated*, who negatively and destructively criticise all around them. They claim to 'jeere all kind of persons / We meete withall, of any rancke or quality' (IV.i.7–8). Cymbal, their 'tinckling *Captaine*' and chief of the news office, encourages them to 'deride / The wretched: or with *buffon* licence, jeast / At whatso'er is serious, if not sacred' (V.vi.9-11). But at the end of the play Pennyboy Canter demonstrates that such detractors are easily defeated. Their 'amazement, and distraction' in the face of truth marks them as a 'guilty race of men, that dare to stand / No breath of truth: but conscious to themselves / Of their no-wit, or honesty, ranne routed' (V.vi.3-5). However, while Pennyboy Canter condemns the jeerers as the 'scumme, and excrements' of men, he is careful to add that they are simply wicked individuals, unworthy of their noble professions—that of courtier, herald, doctor, and poet: he does not 'hate / Their callings', but 'their manners, and their vices' (IV.iv.138-9) as individual men.

Jonson's aim in singling out individual detractors of the time is to stress that it is the individual's responsibility to behave well. As he wrote in *Discoveries*, 'But they are ever good men, that must make good the times: if the men be naught, the times will be such' (247-8). To bring about a perfectly adjusted society an individual must learn how to behave perfectly. This dictum was obviously of fundamental importance in a society where a few individuals, the king and a small circle of courtiers, held so much power. At the same time Jonson suggests that a sudden transformation into goodness is impossible: 'Men have beene great, but never good by chance / Or on the sudden'.[28] Rather, the transformation requires a slow process of self-knowledge and self-improvement. In most of his earlier work prior to *The Staple of News* Jonson appears to be mistrustful of the moral education of individuals. Characters in the masques are banished not cured, and in the plays characters are usually stripped of their illusions but not re-educated. In *The Staple of News*, however, the process is rather different. To counter the destructiveness of the newsmongers and jeerers Jonson has the central characters undergo a reformation. Suitably, the action takes place during the celebrations of Shrove Tuesday, and so looks forward to the period of soul-searching and renunciation that Lent will bring. Pennyboy Junior learns his lesson in time to redeem himself by his actions before the play ends. He puts on his father's cast-off beggar's cloak and after a period of penitence 'awakes' from his 'lethargy' to trick Picklock into returning the trust of the Pennyboy estate. Pennyboy Canter, impressed by his actions—deeds not mere promises—tells him to 'put off your ragges, and be your selfe againe', but stresses that this 'Act of pietie, and good affection' has only 'partly reconcil'd' him to his son (V.iii.22-4). The need for good behaviour, in other words, does not stop there. Pennyboy Canter also rehabilitates his brother, Pennyboy Senior, by putting the jeerers, who have been baiting him, to flight and restoring his wits. In return for 'the light you have given mee' (V.vi.41), Pennyboy Senior willingly restores Pecunia to her proper status. Pennyboy Canter's method, like Jonson's, is to educate those around him. He prays that 'all succeed well, and my *simples* take'

(V.iii.49), curing by persuasion, a milder medicine than Jonson's usual purge.

One other influence of the masques of 1620-5 needs to be noted. The dangers of popular political comment and satiric attacks on royal policy that Jonson exposed led him to treat satire differently as a medium. He begins to abandon writing satiric commentaries on society in favour of writing about the dangers of satire and comment themselves. When he returned to the public stage the change is marked, and not one for the better. Compared with Lovewit's house in *The Alchemist*, the fair in *Bartholomew Fair*, or even the projectors in *The Devil is an Ass*, the news office in *The Staple of News* lacks the solidity and autonomous energy that Jonson's best satiric creations have (as T.S. Eliot noted, Jonson's satire succeeds not so much by hitting its target as creating it),[29] and it is too compliantly a vehicle for the author's didactic aim. Jonson's main interest has shifted away from a delight in exposing social abuses to a determination to declare the individual's responsibility to perfect contemporary society. The masques themselves, however, stand out as among the most imaginative and intellectually challenging of Jonson's masque-writing career. Through their complex engagement with current political issues they fulfil his intention, announced in *Hymenaei* many years before, of making the 'voyce' of the masque 'sound to present occasions'.[30]

NOTES

1 Meagher, *Method and Meaning in Jonson's Masques* (Notre Dame, Ind., 1966); Orgel, *The Jonsonian Masque* (Cambridge, Mass., 1967); Parry, *The Golden Age Restor'd: The Culture of the Stuart Court* (Manchester, 1981).

2 See Ian Donaldson, *The World Upside-Down* (Oxford, 1970), pp. 37-45; R.V. Holdsworth, ed., *Epicoene*, New Mermaids (London, 1979), p. xxxi. For a critical study that includes a general discussion of the relationship between masques and plays, see Mary Chan, *Music in the Theatre of Ben Jonson* (Oxford, 1980). Unless otherwise indicated, all references and quotations from Jonson's works are taken from Herford and Simpson.

3 See Chan, pp. 284, 295-6; Jonas A. Barish, *Ben Jonson and the Language of Prose Comedy* (Cambridge, Mass., 1960), Chapter VI.

4 See Joseph Frank, *The Beginnings of the English Newspaper, 1620-1660* (Cambridge, Mass., 1961); S.L. Adams, 'Captain Thomas Gainsford, and the "Vox Spiritus" and the *Vox Populi*', *Bulletin of the Institute of Historical Research*, 49 (1976), p. 144.

5 'Vox Spiritus' (S.L. Adams, 'Captain Thomas Gainsford').

6 See *The Letters of John Chamberlain*, ed. N.E. McClure, 2 vols (Philadelphia, 1939), 2, pp. 297; 299-300.

7 See 'A Proclamation against Excesse of Lavish and Licentious Speech of Matters of State', December 1620, in J.F. Larkin and P.L. Hughes, eds., *Stuart Royal Proclamations* (Oxford, 1973-), 1, 495.

8 Larkin and Hughes, 1, pp. 495-6; 519-21; 531. See also *His Majesties Declaration, Touching his Proceedings in the late Assemblie and Convention of Parliament* (1621).

9 Noted by the Venetian ambassador, *CSP Venetian*, *1621–3*, 17, p. 117.
10 *CSP Venetian*, 17, pp. 530, 538.
11 See David McPherson, 'Ben Jonson's Library and Marginalia: An Annotated Catalogue', *Studies in Philology*, 71, *Texts and Studies* (1974), pp. 71; 88.
12 'An Epistle to a Friend, to perswade him to the warres', *Underwood*, 15, l.6–7.
13 'An Epistle answering to one that asked to be Sealed of the Tribe of Ben', *Underwood*, 47, 31–6.
14 See Chamberlain, *Letters*, 2, pp. 286–7.
15 *Letters*, 2, p. 333.
16 See Menna Prestwich, *Cranfield: Politics and Profits under the Early Stuarts* (Oxford, 1965), pp. 206–9; Antonia Fraser, *King James* (London, 1974), p. 171.
17 Herford and Simpson, 7, p. 625.
18 See John Summerson, *Inigo Jones* (Harmondsworth, 1966), pp. 40–1.
19 See Orgel and Strong, 1, p. 342.
20 Orgel and Strong, 1, p. 354.
21 *Wither's Motto* (London, 1621), sigs. B1v, D1.
22 Chamberlain, *Letters*, 2, pp. 472–3.
23 Chamberlain, *Letters*, 2, p. 507.
24 *Letters*, 2, pp. 538–9.
25 *CSP Venetian*, 18, p. 564.
26 See Frances Yates, *The Rosicrucian Enlightenment* (London, 1972) for an account of the movement and its reception.
27 See J. W. Bennett, 'Britain among the Fortunate Isles', *Studies in Philology*, 53 (1956), pp. 114–40. An interesting anticipation of Jonson's use of this setting is *Every Man out of his Humour* (1599), which is set in 'The Fortunate Island'.
28 'An Epistle to Sir Edward Sacvile, now Earle of Dorset', *Underwood*, 13, ll.124–5.
29 'Ben Jonson', in *Elizabethan Dramatists* (London, 1963), p. 80.
30 *Hymenaei*, l. 17.

JENNIFER CHIBNALL

'To that secure fix'd state': The function of the Caroline masque form

❧❦❧

UNTIL RECENTLY the Court masque has predominantly been considered as a species of poetry, both because its poetry is the most accessible surviving element and because poetry has been more highly regarded than stage spectacle, dancing, or music. Under this scheme of things Jonson's masques have been firmly established as the peak of achievement in the genre (though with an occasional attempt to oust him in favour of Milton and *Comus* as more purely poetic). The Caroline masques, the least amenable to being read as literature, have inevitably been classified as a decline and fall from this high point.[1]

D. J. Gordon's important essays began to assert a serious intention for Jones's scenes, a view now confirmed by Orgel and Strong's edition of his designs.[2] The Caroline masque, once condemned as 'mere' spectacle, now begins to receive serious critical attention. Stephen Orgel has, for example, moved from the purely literary emphasis of *The Jonsonian Masque* to working, in *Inigo Jones*, in 'complete collaboration at every stage' with the art historian Roy Strong.[3]

Orgel and Strong establish that 'Jones's aesthetics', like Jonson's, 'derive from good Platonic doctrine and have clear moral ends'.[4] Jones's intention is to show the court 'its true self', in the neo-Platonic sense of a true vision of the inner reality, the 'ideal' as opposed to mere appearance. But their approach is not without its limitations. They define 'the art of Inigo Jones' as 'the power to create a hero by controlling the way we look at a man'. This is to subordinate art to political message, and thus to confuse political with artistic power—precisely the confusion of which they accuse the masque makers. Their focus on intention and content leaves the problem of the form of the masque and the variety of its elements unresolved.[5] For them Jones's masques are redeemed by their serious intention and political message, but the 'poetics of spectacle' are not really examined, unless we are to understand poetics as being concerned only with content. The task of the critic, however, must be to analyse the work as a whole, form and content. While it is partly correct to read the Caroline masques *as* 'political statements', it would be more accurate to say that the masques *make* political statements. They are works of art and not works of political theory (even though they belong to an age that made the dividing line between the two less absolute than we would now).

It is indeed a 'measure of how far we have come from the world of the Renaissance Court' that we have difficulty in accepting the political stance of the masque, and Orgel and Strong are right to recover it for us, but they are wrong to state that the Caroline masques lack the 'sense of human uncertainties' and the 'awareness of the realities of passion or politics' which they find in Jonson's Jacobean masques.[6] For if we examine the form, as opposed to the explicit content, of the Caroline masque, we find both in Jones's scenes and in the poetry of writers like Carew continual attempts to deal with uncertainties and social realities.

The masque, in combining a variety of arts, is particularly difficult to handle in terms of form. Those critics whose main concern has been with 'judging rightly the absolute worth of one masque over another' have found the prospect of masque criticism 'gloomy', and the prospect for the Caroline masque the gloomiest of all.[7]

As long ago as 1927 Enid Welsford suggested a more productive approach. She pointed out that the study of the masque raises a number of questions about the nature and function of art. Since her illuminating study, critics have seemed to concentrate rather upon the production of solutions than upon the consideration of the questions, lacking her confidence to work 'in the interrogative rather than the indicative mood'.[8] I believe that this is unfortunate, for the process of investigation generally yields more knowledge than the too hasty construction of solutions. The masque, by not fitting our usual modern categories of art, by not being a separate, 'original' and 'sincere' artistic statement, but one written to the order of a patron who required particular things to be said, inevitably disrupts our usual critical procedures and forces us to examine our premises. I would argue, following Welsford, that the chief interest and significance of the study of the masque lies precisely in the problems it raises, which are productive and not inhibiting.

In an article in *New Left Review* Raymond Williams suggests that when we look at 'a particular work, or group of works', 'we should not look for the components of a product, but for the conditions of a practice'.[9] He suggests that we ask essentially different questions from those of traditional criticism, beginning simply with 'the recognition of the relation of a collective mode and an individual project'. He suggests that the resemblances between the individual project, the work, and the collective mode 'may exist as resemblances within and across genres. They may be the practice of a group in a period, rather than the practice of a phase in a genre.' If we are looking for the conditions of a practice 'we have no built-in procedure, of the kind which is indicated by the fixed character of an object'. Since in dealing with the masque we have no fixed object we must escape the critical procedures based upon that concept. This approach sets aside the question whether the masque is or is not 'art', and the problems of its combination of forms, by setting aside the presupposition that they must be unified. It places the study of the masque firmly in a history, but not simply as 'a product of its occasion' or in any confined sense 'a historical document'.

If the study of art is seen as part of cultural history, as the examination of an historical practice, then we can begin to see forms such as the masque in terms not of an art that is opposed to the transience of history, and so restricted by it, but one that is part of history and whose evidence is as valid as any other historical fact. We must not dissolve the forms of art into other contents, as Orgel and Strong do when they reduce the Caroline masque to a vehicle for a political ideology. Form and content cannot be divided; neither politics nor history will contain the 'hidden' meaning.

There are precedents in masque criticism for such an approach. When Enid Welsford describes the masque as a 'rudimentary' form of art—that is, an 'aesthetic revel', an 'enhancement of ordinary social activities' that has been turned into art but that remains 'nearer to life' than the work of the modern artist—her concern in studying the masque is with the 'question not of classification but of interpretation'.[10] E.K. Chambers, asserting that the masque is 'an episode in an indoor revel of dancing, its goal is the masked ball and not the opera', is also concerned with describing the conditions of a theatrical practice, not with evaluating a literary object.[11]

The court masque began as a game for courtiers, a dance by persons in disguise. In the seventeenth century a complex art form developed to give a context for this revel. In part this development merely went along with the general post-Renaissance evolution of genres in discovering new spaces for artistic exploration by the classification and organisation of artistic expression. To understand the particular practice of the Caroline form we must examine the particular artistic problem the masque sought to resolve.

The function of the masked dance, the sixteenth-century 'disguising', was to celebrate the good functioning of the community.[12] 'Strangers' appear, offer a dance and sometimes gifts and a speech, remove their masks and reveal themselves as familiar friends. In a society by and large assured of its function this was sufficient. By James's reign, indeed by the end of Elizabeth's, the rapid development of a mercantile and capitalist economy was radically undermining the traditional, rurally based feudal structure, which for some time had been more of a lingering trace than a dynamic economic reality. The aristocracy and landed gentry had increasingly to turn to new methods of economic survival.[13] The court, uncertain of its function, withdraws into itself. Where the most important entertainments of Elizabeth's court were the progress shows which depended upon sustaining the myth of a unified, basically, feudal society,[14] the central entertainment of the Stuart court is the indoor masque, presented in the carefully delimited space of the Banqueting House. In Charles's reign this withdrawal is marked politically by the eleven years of personal rule. As the positions of monarch and court became less assured it was necessary for the court shows to establish control over those elements that threatened their security. In the antimasque these threatening elements are embodied in such a way that they can be defeated, or, more precisely, obliterated by the masque vision. Where Jonson sought to reconcile the elements, to reorder the disorder and vitality of the antimasque, the Caroline masque attempts only to contain it. Spectacle more readily both encompasses the flux of creative revel and transcends it. To attempt a resolution is to risk failure. Milton, indeed, shows his masquers in *Comus* failing to deal with the reality of this threatening chaos.

It is less significant that the Stuart masque retains aspects of a game, for so do many theatrical shows, than that it poses the question as to how a space can be created and defined for its masked dance. In asking that, the masque became art. Thus the sense that the masque seeks to maintain of being part of social life is rather a mapping of its area of concern than any final definition of the genre itself. The establishment of the perspective stage and its transformation scenes as the mode of resolving the contradictions between the actual state of the seventeenth-century court and its 'idea' of itself (in the neo-Platonic sense) is the formal acknowledgement, in artistic terms, of an alienation that can only be resolved by art. Yet an art whose function is to celebrate society cannot acknowledge such an alienation in any explicit terms, nor present itself as capable of constructing resolutions. It is in this radical contradiction that the Stuart masque exists, a contradiction that becomes increasingly apparent in Jonson's later masques.

Jonson's early concern with artistic control and unity of expression in his masques, perhaps most notably in *Hymenaei* (1606), corresponded with King James's demand that the masque express his concern with political unity and control. Later Jonson becomes increasingly antagonistic to what he sees as an alienated society dominated by money. This is reflected in both theme and form of later works as he seeks an alternative to an art of analysis and control in the tradition of revel. In *Love Restored* (1612), *Christmas his Masque* (1616), *The Vision of Delight* (1617), and *Pleasure Reconciled to Virtue* (1618) we can trace an increasing emphasis on the traditional festive revel. The antimasques present an energy which the masque draws upon to create a new harmony and order. In *A Tale of a Tub* (1633), written for Charles's court long after Jonson had ceased to write masques but essentially concerned with revelling and masquing, Jonson turns to rural festivities of the previous century as a vision of natural celebration in opposition to the limitations of an artificial court.[15]

In the 1630s the aristocracy could no longer call upon a concept of universal harmony such as that depicted in the shows presented to Queen Elizabeth on her progress visits to the country estates of her courtiers. The concern of Charles's court was to establish for themselves a separate and secure space apart from the society in which their role was increasingly threatened and diminished. The court was thus, unavoidably, 'estranging itself from the values of the previous epoch', and, as Glynne Wickham suggests, the proscenium arch met their changed needs.[16] Their only way to embrace 'the country' was in the restricted and repetitious pastorals played by the Queen and her ladies, and in the perspective scenes of Inigo Jones's stage.

In tracing this brief history of the masque form I have necessarily worked within particular assumptions of seventeenth-century political and social history. Though cultural history is not subservient to other histories, it is not separable from them. Unfortunately for the literary historian the history of this period is subject to greater debate than that of almost any other. The debate centres upon whether the civil wars can be attributed to the rising power of the gentry and city merchants, and so constitute, as Christopher Hill maintains, a bourgeois revolution, or whether, as Lawrence Stone argues, 'relatively little structural change took place in English society between the fourteenth and the nineteenth centuries: what altered was the role of the various social classes within a fairly static framework'.[17] However, in either interpretation it is agreed that the aristocracy of the mid-century faced a period, whatever its outcome, of unusually rapid social change.

Lawrence Stone distinguishes two 'radically' different ideologies in the period whose 'essential contradiction' is not minimised by the fact that many people 'seem to straddle two ideals'. The old aristocratic code of hospitality and paternalism in a stable society with 'clear class distinctions' stands in opposition to the new 'capitalist/Protestant ethic' of self-improvement, thrift, hard work, and competition.[18] If we wish to account for the contradictory demands in the Caroline masque for stability and action, detachment and influence, we must be aware of the divisions within aristocratic society, the straddling of these two ideals which the masque necessarily reflected.

The Caroline court masque represents a final gesture of a feudally based aristocracy which defined itself as the ultimate order of earthly achievement. Progress, for them, was impossible, or, rather, irrelevant. The confident aspiration of the Elizabethan renaissance and Jonson's classically based educative art are alike dangerous to this enclosed world. Reason must be simply the mind's power to perceive the essence behind each inevitable and perfect appearance. It is this neo-Platonic idealism that became the official philosophy of the Caroline court, and it was embodied in the transforming scenes of Jones's masques. In the face of the new 'capitalist/Protestant' ideology Charles's court attempts to withdraw into its own space, a 'secure fix'd state' transcending the 'labouring world' whose effort is itself the mark of its imperfection.[19] The aristocrat cannot aspire to anything beyond the stable place which it is his defining virtue effortlessly to occupy. But the reality of the mid seventeenth century demanded change of the aristocrat, and the court masques had to take account of this fact.

Inigo Jones first clearly presents his transcendental and spectacular Caroline masque form in *Tempe Restored*, the Queen's masque of 1632. Its emphasis upon the process of transformation also formally asserts the difficulty of its achievement. Where Jonson saw incoherence in the lack of connecting devices in Jones's succession of images we can now, perhaps, with our familiarity with the use of montage in film and video and through modern critical approaches with concepts of art that are not necessarily classical, be less anxious about such incoherence. We are able to see the placing of one thing beside another as itself a creative act, and the relationships constructed between these images to 'speake to the Understanding' as well as 'but to the Sense'.[20]

The narrative of *Tempe Restored* begins, in a sense, where Jonson's usually ended, with the triumph of Reason. Circe's 'fugitive Favourite' has already made the decision to be 'Govern'd by Reason and not rul'd by Sense'.[21] The first scene is a 'pleasant place', the Vale of Tempe, and the first part of the masque represents the form found in Jonson's masques such as *Pleasure Reconciled to Virtue* where Will, represented by Hercules, triumphs over the disordered senses. In *Tempe Restored* Townshend and Jones present this triumph as already accomplished by their audience, through the symbolic expedient of laying the fugitive favourite 'at the feet of the Lords seates' so leaving the insecurity of the Vale of Tempe to 'flye to Vertue' in Charles's court (p. 85).

The audience's faith in the 'pleasant place' of the first scene having been thus undermined, 'the further part of the Sceane opening' reveals Circe's 'sumptuous Palace' from which she and her attendant nymphs come forth in pursuit. This is a surprising reversal of the usual process whereby the deeper reality of truth and virtue is revealed in the depth of the scene, and, following upon the fugitive lover's escape to the audience as representing 'Vertue', serves to establish the court as itself the deeper reality beyond the Vale of Tempe, leaving the vale in suspense between the court's influence and Circe's.

Harmony enters next, significantly not from the heavens, 'and under her conduct fourteene Influences of the stars, which are to come' (p. 88). Like any masque presenter she leads them up to the state, accompanied by the chorus, and presents them to the King, but explains that they themselves cannot 'hold ye long' before the 'Planeticke sway' of the stars that are to come (p. 89). The Influences 'fall into their dance. Which being past they are placed on the degrees by the Lords and Ladies where they sit to see the masque' (p. 90). This also repeats a form typical of the Jacobean masque in which the masquers moved, not under their own influence, but under that of the King. Again Jones declares his intention to review and go beyond the Jacobean form, a progression symbolised by the Influences joining the audience to see the masque, which thus proclaims the intention to go on to represent a deeper truth than theirs, or than that of the old masque forms the audience have previously experienced.

The scene now changes 'into an orientall skye, such as appears at the Sun rising'. In the foreground is 'a Haven with a Citadell' and 'afar off is seene a landscipt and a calm Sea' (p. 90). From 'the midst of the ayre' the eight Spheres appear on a 'circular' cloud which 'seem'd to have let them down as in a Chaine'. 'To the Musicke of these Spheares' the masquers descend in three separate clouds 'and above all in a Chariot' divine Beauty, Henrietta Maria herself: 'The eight Stars that first descended being by this time past the Spheares came forth, and the Clouds on which they sat with a swift motion returning up againe, and the other still descending shewed a pleasing contention betweene them as they past' (p. 91). The scene thus presents contradiction, 'contention', but in purely formal terms neutralised to yield only pleasure. There is no argument between the masquers, but the image serves to dispel the real difficulty of dissolving the space between actual and ideal, represented in the earth and the heaven of the stage scene. Here earth and heaven are united through Divine Beauty who 'will vouchsafe to stoope, / And move to Earth' (p. 92).

There remains, however, another scene, the King seated still upon the state. 'Janus was happy that could see, / Two ways at once': could see both Divine Beauty, 'Whose Image men adore', and 'Heroicke Vertue' in the King, which 'is that kind of Beautie, that attracts the mind'. By dividing real and ideal into the King in state and the Queen as masquer any real contradiction is dissolved. When this couple join together on the dancing floor the golden age is returned. The audience is thus happier than Janus, for they 'Behold, / Two that have turn'd this age to Gold' (p. 94).

Then follows an 'intermedium' in which appear, in 'a new heaven . . . differing in shape and colour from the other', Jove 'with a glory' and Cupid 'flying forth'. The lower scene is changed into a 'shady wood' from which 'at the same time Pallas, Circe and her foure Nymphs appeare' (p. 94). Circe had previously merely passed from the scene to be replaced by Harmony, in a manner that will become the convention of the antimasque presenter in the Caroline masque. Circe here returns to explain the terms of her defeat. Challenged directly by Jove and Cupid, Circe makes her destiny her choice: 'Finding thy Drift, / My Bounty, shall prevent thy Guift' (p. 95):

> This Machles Payre,
> I make, my Heire:
> All I possesse, I heere, Resigne,
> Thou hast thy will: And I have Mine. (pp. 95–6)

That is, she gives the King and Queen the control of all desires. Thus the problem of desire and aspiration, the continual threat to this stable world, is neutralised. Jove, however, counters her claim: 'She gives but what she cannot keepe' (p. 96).

Jove and Cupid return to the heavens; Circe and Pallas, desire and wisdom now harmonious together, retire into the wood with the chorus. It is unusual to leave the masque scene in a shady wood, a place of confusion and some undefined threat. As they depart the chorus addresses the Court:

> Should you, these Loanes of Love forsake
> The Gods themselves, such Sommes would take
> And pay us use. (p. 96)

That is, if the world prove unworthy of the masquers the gods will borrow them. This final scene contradicts any too easy assumption that 'old Saturn's Reigne' is 'come back againe' (p. 94).

The true relationship of the masque to history is in its form, not merely in its content. Thus the precariousness of the Caroline form and its emphasis upon the process of transformation, reflect the precariousness of the political situation. It is not, as Orgel and Strong suggest, merely presenting an idealised solution to political problems; it is endeavouring, with extreme effort and difficulty, to construct a mode in which resolution might be possible. The masque is a process which cannot be reduced to any one statement.

Orgel and Strong find Thomas Carew's *Coelum Britannicum* 'unquestionably the greatest of the Stuart masques, poetically superior to all but the best of Jonson, and in its range and variety utterly unique'.[22] In both form and content of poetry and scene this masque, to describe it more precisely, examines the process of constructing a mythology for the Caroline court. In *Coelum Britannicum* we remain with the stars of Charles's court with which *Tempe Restored* concluded, but Carew's fable is to account for them being so defined.

The first scene presents 'the ruines of some great City of the ancient Romans, or civiliz'd Brittaines'.[23] This refers to the contemporary conception of a classical ancient Britain.[24] The scene stands in deliberate contrast to the neo-classical Banqueting House. Mercury enters, goes up to the royal dais, and announces:

> From the high Senate of the gods, to You
> Bright glorious Twins of Love and Majesty ...
> Come I Cyllenius, Jove's Ambassadour. (ll. 47–55)

The stage scene remains unexplained. It is surprising to find the gods 'drawne down' so soon, particularly as Mercury goes on to eulogise the King and Queen in terms rather of a vision to be accomplished than one to be demonstrated. The changes, he tells us, are to be at Jove's court, which Jove is to reform in emulation of Charles's.

Thus far the only action is in the verse. Mercury's speech is full of images of light and fire—'emulous fires' (l. 68), 'infamous lights' (l. 88), 'dazeling beames' (l. 93). There is as yet some confusion between true and false lights, and, moreover, Mercury's description of the 'bright blaze' of Charles's 'Pallace' does not change the stage scene of decay: Poetry is not adequate; the more dynamic words are in creating a vision the less, inevitably, are they able to portray calm and safety. The need to create a visual image is demonstrated by the particular emphasis, in the concluding lines of this long speech, on the vision already given. Mercury points to the King and Queen enthroned in 'a triumphant chair' (l. 95) with their court about them, as if the masque were ended and this was the last scene. But the scene of ruin remains to state that this vision is insufficient. Carew goes on to consider how it is possible that the King and Queen can be insufficient, or, in other terms, how this vision of them can be made effective.

At this point Momus, 'Supreme Theomastix', mocker of the gods, appears. Mercury commands him to 'let this Presence teach you modesty' and not 'disturbe the great Affaire' (ll. 124, 175); but Momus replies 'Let it if it can', and proceeds to demonstrate that it cannot by continuing to 'acquaint it with my condition'. He finally forces Mercury to turn from the vision to come and deal with the old stars which are to be superceded by Charles's court by effecting a scene change to the old sphere borne up by Atlas (ll. 188-94).

As the presiding genius of the antimasque Momus's function is to purge any critical disbelief by turning it to laughter; to present, and dismiss, those aspects of social reality which could be brought against the harmonious vision the masque is to present. The first antimasquers represent 'naturall deformity', opposed to the ideal nature, in neo-Platonic terms, which the masquers will represent. Momus proposes the practical solution of banishing them to the New World colonies, but Mercury dismisses this suggestion.

> They cannot breath this pure and temperate Aire
> Where Vertue lives, but will with hasty flight,
> 'Mongst fogs and vapours, seeke unsound abodes.   (ll. 392-4)

A debate ensues over who is to succeed to the now emptied heavens. Momus still presides, and it is he who proceeds to summon 'any Person whatsoever, that conceiveth him or herselfe to be really endued with any Heroicall Vertue or transcendent Merit' (ll. 454-6). The function of the ensuing debate is to demonstrate that suitable persons can only be of Charles's court.

Plutus, Poenia, Tiche, and Hedone (wealth, poverty, fortune, and pleasure) now offer themselves. The first two are ugly and therefore readily recognisable in neo-Platonic terms as unsuitable. Momus calls Plutus's gold the 'true Pandora's box' (l. 477), and Mercury condemns him as an enemy to virtue. Mercury's rejection of Poverty begins to give us a clearer picture of the virtues of the new order the masque is to offer. Poenia had claimed 'Divine contemplation' and 'all the Vertues speculative' as the particular virtues that find 'secure retreat' only with her, while the 'whole race of Vertue' is 'her Off-spring'. But the gypsies she presents gain their secure equanimity only by a total rejection of the society it is the masque's whole business to order and celebrate. Aristocratic virtue must be heroic. Mercury rejects

>   forc'd
> Falsly exalted passive Fortitude
> Above the active: This low abject brood,
> That fix their seats in mediocrity,
> Become your servile minds; but we advance
> Such vertues onely as admit excesse,
> Brave bounteous Acts, Regall Magnificence,
> All-seeing Prudence, Magnanimity
> That knows no bound, and that Heroicke vertue
> For which Antiquity hath left no name,
> But patternes onely, such as *Hercules*
> *Achilles*, Theseus.   (ll. 655–66)

We see here Carew attempting to argue a resolution of the contradictory ideologies which Stone defined. A virtue that could know a 'bound' cannot satisfy the aspiration of the aristocrat who must define his place as above all servility. This place cannot be static yet must be stable, hence its virtue is nameless, that is, cannot be confined but only enacted after the pattern, the ideal in neo-Platonic terms, shown by the ancient heroes.

Fortune next claims sovereignty, for, since the end of the golden age,

>   since Astrea fled to heaven, I sit
> Her deputy on Earth, I hold her skales
> And weigh mens Fates out.   (ll. 688–90)

Her antimasque is of a battle; self-condemnatory in a search for order and peace. Mercury assigns her rule to the 'groping world', for before 'the piercing eye of Providence' which is 'fix'd and certaine', Fortune 'Losest thy being, and art not at all' (ll. 732–7). It is unusual to find God so nearly approached in a masque. Carew's reference to Providence is an attempt to recover the traditional analogical world. Whereas at one time the omnipresence of God could be assumed beyond the Joves and Dianas of the progress shows and masques, now it seems that the connection must be explicitly asserted.

The power of the individual will that Carew asserts here is strenuous. It is the 'lazy sluggard' that is fortune's prey (l. 747). The effort with which the new order must be attained is acknowledged, but it must also be distinguished from the effort of the rest of the world, doomed as that is to failure. This is the established function of the Stuart masque, for, as Orgel points out, the 'exemplary choice' of heroic virtue is 'the only truly heroic action in the world Jonson has created' in his masques.[25] But Carew is left here with a problem as to how, precisely, that virtue can be presented.

> Hedone, the final candidate, claims to be the Gole,
> The journeys end, to which the sweating world,
> And wearied Nature travels. (ll. 772-44)

She rejects 'petty low-built vertues' that 'wanted wings to reach my soaring pitch' (ll. 779-80). She appears, therefore, to offer something of the qualities that Mercury demanded. Both an end and an action, a 'soaring pitch' is in fact precisely the contradiction that the masque requires, a stable place of aspiration.

Her antimasque is of the five senses, again not entirely unsuitable to the apprehension of the masque vision. Mercury's answer is to redefine her as

> Paine,
> Greedy, intense Desire, and the keene edge
> Of thy fierce Appetite, oft strangles thee. (ll. 818-20)

It is the pattern of virtue that is to be stellified, not the abstract influence and goal. The masque is concerned with the court as embodying virtue.

Momus's task, as a satirist, to defend virtue, is now accomplished, and he retires to defend the outer margin of the sacred space against further 'suitors'. Mercury turns again to the King and Queen:

> These, with forc'd reasons, and strain'd arguments,
> Urge vaine pretences, whilst your Actions plead,
> And with a silent importunity
> Awake the drousy Justice of the gods
> To crowne your deeds with immortality.
> The growing Titles of your Ancestors,
> These Nations glorious Acts, joyn'd to the stocke
> Of your owne Royal vertues, and the cleare
> Reflexe they take from th'imitation
> Of your fam'd Court, make Honors storie full. (ll. 843-52)

Carew here defines the action of the vision to come. Silent action will arouse the gods where force and strain cannot. There is a complex reciprocating relationship between the virtues of the royal couple and the 'Nations glorious Acts', from which this vision of Charles's 'fam'd Court' gains vitality. The gods now are awakened

> And have to that secure fix'd state advanc'd
> Both you and them, to which the labouring world
> Wading through streames of blood, sweats to aspire.

Aspiration is thus equated with blood and sweat which can never reach the secure state it desires, while that desire is testimony to the value of the state Charles has achieved. Mercury continues to describe very precisely the vision the masque will present. Charles will find himself 'circled with moderne Heroes', his courtiers; Eternity will 'mould you to Stars, and fix you in the Spheare' (ll. 859, 864). The stage scene, however, remains that of the decayed sphere with its extinct stars, emphasising again that words are not adequate to create the vision Mercury describes to the King who remains, as yet, in the audience. Carew thus demonstrates both the need for the vision and the need for the king to enact it.

This is the only masque which is both presented to, and presents, the King. Carew thus fixes attention upon the process of transformation by which the King sitting in state is moulded into the ideal vision the masque will present, while at the same time asserting the coherence of the King in his two aspects as individual person and as embodiment of eternal kingship (the concept that makes possible the declaration 'the king is dead, long live the king'[26]).

Mercury concludes his speech by summoning the 'old Abiders' of Britain, and the scene finally changes to 'wild and woody' mountains where Picts, Scots, and Irish appear to dance the last antimasque. 'When this antimasque was past, there began to arise out of the earth the top of a hill, which by little and little grew to be a huge mountaine that covered all the Sceane' (ll. 883-5). This is the most spectacular scene change of the masque, intended to arouse wonder in the audience and give Charles time to leave his seat in the hall. It 'gave great cause of admiration, but especially how so huge a machine, and of that great height could come from under the Stage, which was but six foot high' (ll. 968-71). The audience is asked to admire the masque-maker's power to create visions. The three kingdoms of England, Scotland, and Ireland are seated 'about the middle part of this Mountaine' (ll. 887-8). They command it 'Open thy stony entrails wide / And breake old Atlas' (ll. 941-2). It was Atlas who guarded the pillars that kept earth and heaven apart. With the appearance of the masquers that separation is to be ended.

All the performers on the stage now turn, at the command of the Genius of Britain who sits above them all, to the Queen, who 'shoots from her eye / Diffusive joy' and then to 'Looke up, and see the darkened Spheare / Depriv'd of light, her eyes shine there' (ll. 916-17). Her eyes are 'more sparkling' than the old stars, for they move 'by a pure intelligence / Of more transcendent Vertue' (ll. 920-1). She is defined in neo-Platonic terms as the source of the true light of virtue. Her eyes

> first feele, then kindle love.
> From the bosomes they inspire,
> They receive a mutuall fire;
> And where their flames impure returne,
> These can quench as well as burne.   (ll. 923-7)

Even purity is given and not striven for. It is a definition of the aristocratic situation that desire and gratification must coexist without struggle. Once this is established the masquers, 'richly attired like ancient Heroes' descend and dance. Carew, however, goes on wrestling further with the contradiction of real and ideal. The Genius declares that they will succeed to the 'unpeopled skie' and 'governe Destinie' (ll. 980-1). The Kingdoms protest that they cannot do without them, and portray the fixed state of heaven as a restriction: 'Why should they that here can move / So well, be ever-fix'd above?' (ll. 988-9). The Genius maintains that

> their Fame shall flye
> From hence alone, and in the Spheare
> Kindle new Starres, whilst they rest here.   (ll. 993-5)

The resolution of the contradiction between ideal stability and real action is thus achieved by creating a separation between the real and ideal self that can yet be united in mutual influence.

The kingdoms remain unconvinced and repeat this fundamental question: 'How can the shaft stay in the quiver, / Yet hit the marke?' (ll. 996-7). How can real and ideal coexist? How can aspiration achieve satisfaction without leaving its original place? The Genius replies that, as the river Eridanus appeared both in heaven and on earth by acquiring 'grace', so can these heroes. This answer depends upon the grace the masquers can show in their dance.

After the masquers' main dance the scene changes to a 'delicious garden' with 'a Princely Villa' (ll. 1014-20). The chorus invites the ladies, as the conquerors of the British heroes, to join them in the revels. This scene, 'cleane differing from all the other', represents a natural world rigidly controlled, a neo-classical architecture of terraces and parterres. Garden scenes such as this were often used in wall paintings, so this scene represents a moment of near realism in which the Banqueting House is finally itself sufficient scene for the revels. The masque has succeeded in establishing the space for the dance.

Consequent upon this harmony comes the final vision of its essence. A great cloud descends to cover the whole scene, from which two more break forth bearing virtues, the one Religion, Truth, and Wisdom, the other Concord, Government, and Reputation. The lower part of the scene is occupied by 'the prospect of Windsor Castell, the famous seat of the most honourable Order of the Garter', Charles's own chosen manifestation of his new social order (ll. 1084-6). The six virtues and Eternity celebrate the King and Queen. The 'Decrepit Spheare' was not quenched by Jove, but 'ecclips'd' by the 'bright flames' of

This Royall Payre, for whom Fate will
Make Motion cease, and Time stand still.   (ll. 1093–4)

(Concord)   And as their owne pure Soules entwin'd
So are their Subjects hearts combin'd.   (ll. 1104–5)

(Government)   So just, so gentle is their sway,
As it seemes Empire to obey.   (ll. 1105–6)

Individual desire is satisfied as the power of the love of King and Queen rules their subjects in content. The clouds ascend leaving 'nothing but a sirene Skye' (ll. 1141–2). In this absolute harmony 'the Masquers dance their last dance, and the Curtaine was let fall'.

A few months after the performance of *Coelum Britannicum* Milton refutes the Caroline assertion of harmony. Even a brief consideration of his adaptations of the Caroline masque form both illuminates the court masque and indicates something of the effect the triumph of the Protestant ethic which Stone defined will have upon such celebratory forms. Circe's lover in *Tempe Restored* has only to exercise his will to escape her, and to place himself under the protection of the court to ensure his safety and her defeat. Milton challenges that assertion in *Comus* by showing the Lady as powerless to destroy Comus, Circe's son. Society is permeated by the dissipation of active virtue in luxury and excess. The Lady cannot flee revelry, symbolised by Comus, for there is nowhere to go. Milton does not celebrate society, as it was the court masque's primary function to do, but asserts individual virtue, requiring that society be changed to match the highest ideal of that individual's conception. Hence virginity becomes the image of that virtue which can only be sustained by complete detachment from the 'smoak and stir' and 'frail and feaverish being' of life in the world.[27]

The most significant change that Milton makes in the masque form is to involve his masquers in a direct struggle, in both words and action, with the antimasque. There are two groups of antimasquers in *Comus*, the first Comus himself and his crew, the second the shepherds whose dance precedes the final masque dance. Thus the whole of the struggle with Comus can be seen as a 'pre-masque'. Milton does not assume his masquers to be virtuous, but examines the preconditions of their virtue, as well as the real nature of its opposition. Milton agrees with the Court masque writers that virtue is inherent in certain individuals, but places his virtuous individuals in opposition not to an abstract disorder but to a corrupt society. Milton here not only destroys the masque's primary and essential assumption that the individual may live in society and both may be virtuous, he also goes on to present the political argument as to how the world might be changed so that virtue might live in it. Comus argues that the Lady is deceived if she supposes virginity has a value. Society gives value, and beauty must be exchanged like money, which is society's measure of value, and must be celebrated in revels lest nature's 'waste fertility' will strangle her. The Lady answers that

> If every just man that now pines with want
> Had but a moderate and beseeming share
> Of that which Lewdly-pamper'd Luxury
> Now heaps upon som few with vast excess,
> Natures full blessings would be well dispenc't
> In unsuperfluous eeven proportion,
> And she no whit encomber'd with her store.   (ll. 768-74)

But however virtuous the Lady is, she cannot make the world so, and neither, in this masque, can anyone else.

NOTES

1 See for example, Jonas A. Barish, *Ben Jonson and the Language of Prose Comedy* (Cambridge, Mass., 1960), p. 242; John C. Meagher, *Method and Meaning in Jonson's Masques* (Notre Dame, Ind., 1966), p. 178; G. E. Bentley, Introduction to *A Book of Masques*, ed. T. J. B. Spencer and S. W. Wells (Cambridge, 1970), pp. 10-12.

2 Gordon's essays are collected and reprinted in *The Renaissance Imagination* (London, 1975).

3 Orgel and Strong, 1, Preface.

4 Orgel and Strong, 1, p. 2.

5 See the review by Leonard Barkan, 'The Imperial Arts of Inigo Jones', *Renaissance Drama*, 7 (1976), p. 263.

6 Orgel and Strong, 1, p. 57.

7 Inga-Stina Ewbank, ' "The Eloquence of Masques": a Retrospective View of Masque Criticism', *Renaissance Drama*, 1 (1968), p. 237. She also commends Welsford as a more hopeful starting point.

8 Enid Welsford, *The Court Masque* (Cambridge, 1927: reissued, New York, 1962), p. 353.

9 Winter, 1973, p. 16

10 *The Court Masque*, p. viii.

11 *The Elizabethan Stage*, 4 vols (Oxford, 1923), 1, pp. 149-50.

12 See Wilfred Mellers, *Harmonious Meeting* (London, 1965), pp. 155-6, for an account of the Renaissance attitude to dance.

13 In trade or mining, for example. See Lawrence Stone, *The Crisis of the Aristocracy* (Oxford, 1965), p. 11.

14 See Marie Axton, *The Queen's Two Bodies: Drama and the Elizabethan Succession* (London, 1977) and Frances Yates, *Astraea: The Imperial Theme in the Sixteenth Century* (London, 1975), as well as Welsford, *The Court Masque*, for accounts of the Elizabethan shows.

15 Herford and Simpson, 8, p. 10.

16 *Early English Stages* (London, 1959-), 1, p. xxix.

17 Stone, *Crisis*, pp. 8–9. See also Lawrence Stone, ed., *Social Change and Revolution in England 1540–1640* (1965) for an introduction to the debate. Robert Ashton, *The English Civil War* (1978) has an annotated bibliography, and sections on court culture in his chapter on 'Tradition and Innovation'.
18 Stone, *Crisis*, pp. 8–9.
19 Thomas Carew, *Coelum Britannicum*, in *The Poems of Thomas Carew*, ed. Rhodes Dunlap (Oxford, 1959), p. 175.
20 Herford and Simpson, 8, p. 610.
21 *Aurelian Townshend's Poems and Masks*, ed. E. K. Chambers (Oxford, 1912), p. 85.
22 Orgel and Strong, 1, p. 66.
23 *The Poems of Thomas Carew*, p. 154, ll. 37–9.
24 See Inigo Jones, *Most Notable Antiquity of Great Britain Vulgarly called Stone-heng . . . Restored* (1655).
25 *The Jonsonian Masque*, p. 190.
26 See Marie Axton, *The Queen's Two Bodies*.
27 *The Poetical Works of John Milton*, ed. Helen Darbishire, 2 vols (Oxford, 1955), 2, p. 175.

DAVID NORBROOK

The reformation
of the masque

❧◦❧

AT THE BEGINNING of Shelley's unfinished tragedy *Charles the First*,
some London citizens are watching a procession of masquers on their way
to perform at court. The year is 1634; the masque is James Shirley's *The
Triumph of Peace*, performed by the lawyers of the Inns of Court. A
young spectator is dazzled by the sight:

> 'tis like the bright procession
> Of skiey visions in a solemn dream
> From which men wake as from a Paradise,
> And draw new strength to tread the thorns of life.

But the older citizens are less enthusiastic. It is no time for revelry, they
say, when the fidelity of the English church to its Protestant traditions
seems in question and when the Protestant cause throughout Europe is
imperilled. The youth admires the masquers' colourful costumes, but an
older man replies that their finery is unjustly maintained at the expense of
the poor: the masque is the symbol of the dominance of an unjust ruling
class. He points to a group of cripples and beggars in the procession: they
serve

> to point the moral
> Of this presentment, and bring up the rear
> Of painted pomp with misery!

The youth dislikes any attempt to introduce political considerations which
spoil his enjoyment of the procession's beauty: 'Oh, still those dissonant
thoughts!' He points out that the older man's political bitterness has made
him read the procession too simply: he has been watching, not real
beggars, but the disguised masquers who appear in the antimasque. They
serve as the foil to the main action, like discords in sweet music. The
youth wants to keep aesthetic judgements free from politics; the old man's
political views make him deny any aesthetic value to the masque.[1]

Shelley's play graphically presents problems which have been faced by
all writers on the Stuart masque. Historians sympathetic to the Puritan
cause have shown a degree of respect for William Prynne, who was in
prison when Shirley's masque was performed for his allegedly seditious

attacks on plays and court masques in *Histrio-Mastix*. Prynne's views became embodied in the 'Whig' interpretation of seventeenth-century history. In 1698 a Whig writer published an attack on stage-plays which contained a lengthy analysis of one Caroline masque, Davenant's *Britannia Triumphans*. He argued that this masque was idolatrous, glorifying a tyrannical monarch and mocking the integrity of the godly.[2] Many later writers have tended to assume that political and artistic decadence must go together: since James and Charles were reactionary absolutists their court masques must have been unworthy of serious consideration. But in the present century a number of scholars and critics have looked more closely at Stuart masques and have argued that the excellence of the scripts by poets like Jonson and Carew, and the scenic designs of Inigo Jones, make them important artistic achievements. Stephen Orgel has argued that 'Renaissance culture' valued display and conspicuous consumption as manifestations of princely honour and magnificence. Renaissance court poets did not see panegyric as mere flattery: praise could have a didactic function, holding up to the monarch an image which he or she ought to emulate.[3] The idea that Stuart masques involved servile flattery has been further undermined by the work of 'revisionist' historians who have questioned the idea that James and Charles were enemies of the traditional constitution and have presented a more favourable view of their political competence.[4] We are now in a better position to assess the intellectual coherence of Stuart masques.

But the new defenders of the masque have sometimes been in danger of replacing one stereotype by another. Orgel has written of Puritanism as if it were a monolithic force, an uncompromising enemy of 'Renaissance culture'. He explains Puritan hostility to masques as a manifestation of a new, reductive world-view which was unsympathetic to all forms of 'role-playing': he cites Cromwell's actions in closing theatres, selling off the royal picture collections, and ordering religious images to be defaced, as different expressions of the same Puritan world-view. Such a simple polarisation between Puritans and the rest, however, cannot do justice to the complex interaction of political and aesthetic issues in the early seventeenth century. From his reading of the *Memoirs* of Bulstrode Whitelocke, who helped to organise *The Triumph of Peace*, Shelley knew that Shirley's antimasque was not merely gloating over the miseries of the poor but trying to persuade the king to act against the monopolists on whom many people blamed economic distresses.[5] Whitelocke was to become a supporter of Cromwell, while Prynne, like many of the presbyterians who were most vehement in opposition to the theatre, became a staunch legitimist who found Cromwell's regime too radical. Shelley could sympathise with the demand of the Youth in his play for an art that would make experience more bearable by its 'skiey visions': the impulse to go beyond everyday experience could be potentially more radical than the crabbed literal-mindedness of a Prynne. In the last act of *Prometheus Unbound* he presented the apocalyptic transformation of society as a kind of cosmic masque. But Shelley could also sympathise with the Citizens' argument that art could become an anodyne, a way of glossing over political problems. In *The Masque of Anarchy* he turned masque conventions upside down, presenting the rulers of his day as the real 'antimasque' who bore the responsibility for the social unrest they were repressing.[6] The responses of some seventeenth-century poets to the Stuart masque were no less complex than Shelley's; though they did not necessarily want to abolish masques, they did believe that they needed reformation.

Criticism of the masques of Jonson and Jones goes back to the very beginning of James's reign. In fact, even before James had come to the throne the poet Samuel Daniel had been corresponding with his friend Fulke Greville about the need for a 'reformation' of court masques.[7] Elizabethan royal entertainments did not excite the same kind of public criticism as Stuart masques, but Daniel's belief that they needed 'reformation' can perhaps be linked with his and Greville's admiration for Sir Philip Sidney, whose attitude to court festivities had been somewhat ambivalent. Though he had written a masque for the queen and made spectacular appearances in tournaments, he was also anxious to be rather more than a courtier, to fight in defence of the Protestant cause. He and his friends wanted Elizabeth to intervene more actively in what they saw as an apocalyptic struggle on the Continent between Protestants and the forces of Catholic absolutism. The most famous Huguenot manifesto, the *Vindiciae contra tyrannos*, urged Protestant aristocrats to fight in defence of their traditional liberties instead of being reduced to passive bystanders in royal ceremonies, 'as if there were some Masque or Interlude to be represented'.[8] In his *Arcadia* Sidney presented masques and pastoral entertainments as the pastimes of an effeminate ruler who neglected his political and military responsibilities. Sidney and his circle were great admirers of Tacitus, who explained in his *Annals* how the Roman emperors had used spectacle as an instrument of political deception: 'Princes,' wrote Sidney's brother Robert, 'may please the people with some shows of their ancient liberties.'[9] Fulke Greville came to see King James as an equivalent of Sidney's irresponsible Basilius, and in the earlier years of the reign he began work on a *Life of Sidney* in which he contrasted his hero's Protestant militancy with the idleness and luxury that reigned at most courts. Daniel seems to have believed that the unprecedented scale of public adulation of the monarch in Jonson's masques was a sign of political decadence. He continued, however, to call not for the abolition of masques but for their 'reformation'; his own masques pointedly refrained from some characteristic Jacobean compliments.[10]

After only one season of Jacobean masques, some members of the Privy

Council were arguing that economies had to be made. In 1604 they pointed out to the king that Queen Elizabeth had never spent money on such a scale merely to subsidise ephemeral court entertainments. While costly masques might be justifiable on special occasions, it would be wasteful to stage them as a matter of course every year; the Council warned that James was making himself unpopular with his subjects. Moreover, the queen, who loved masquing, was offending a common prejudice against participation by women in theatricals. James's advisers were not noted for their political radicalism but they were already voicing in 1604 the major charges that Prynne was to bring against masques. They acknowledged, however, that the king's dignity would be undermined if he were seen to be reversing his plans and making excessively abrupt economies; the masque should not be cancelled at this stage but economies should be made in the future.[11]

James disregarded such warnings. He seems to have considered the masque to be an important means of increasing his subjects' reverence for the mystique of monarchical authority. He believed that the apocalyptic world-view which motivated so many radical Protestants, and had influenced courtly figures like Sidney, was a danger to social order and to European peace. While he retained the Calvinist settlement of the English church, he disliked close contacts between English and Continental Calvinists. He feared that some of his subjects were too 'republicanising', idolising the Dutch who had rebelled against their sovereign and speaking of the Spanish king in terms which seemed to imply a contempt for all monarchs. James resisted the call from some militant Protestants to join an alliance against Catholic powers, and aimed instead at a policy of peace and balance of power between the opposed religious blocs. To that end he became increasingly anxious to establish closer links with the Spanish monarchy.[12]

Ben Jonson was the right person to glorify James's pacific ideals. At the start of the reign he was a Catholic convert and after his return to the Anglican Church he remained strongly hostile to the more evangelistic and apocalyptic varieties of Protestantism. He was deeply suspicious of claims by individuals to divinely inspired vision: the individual imagination became subversive if it was not subordinated to public authority. He defended ritualism in the church not only on religious grounds but also because ceremony helped maintain social order and degree; his second masque, *Hymenaei*, was an extended apologia for ritual. The increasingly elaborate concluding scenes of Jacobean and Caroline masques, in which Jones's scenery transformed courtiers into images of transcendent truths, formed a secular counterpart to the cult of religous images. It is true that Jonson himself sometimes spoke disparagingly of masques: he had a running quarrel with his collaborator Inigo Jones, culminating in a final breach in the 1630s and a bitter satire against 'Showes! Mighty Showes!'.

But this was a personal rather than a political dispute: Jonson believed that painting and architecture were socially inferior, 'mechanical' arts and that he, as a learned poet, should have priority in the partnership. Jonson's political conservatism meant that he did not have any radical ideological disagreements with James or Charles.[13]

With his commitment to the Stuarts' pacific ideals, Jonson did not share the nostalgia of some Jacobeans for the Elizabethan cult of Protestant chivalry. Under Elizabeth tournaments had been as important as masques in the court calendar; under the Stuarts, as Arthur Wilson put it, 'Bellona put on Masking-attire'.[14] But James's elder son Prince Henry became the focus of a renewed cult of chivalry. Though Henry was probably not as radical as some of his admirers hoped, he does seem to have tried to move court entertainments in a more militant direction.[15] The Barriers heralding his installation as Prince of Wales aroused memories of the Elizabethan age. Henry came to political maturity at a time of intense political excitement. A shift in the balance of power in Europe seemed to be pushing James in the direction of a closer alliance with the Calvinist powers. Princess Elizabeth was betrothed to Frederick V of the Palatinate, the most militant Calvinist state in Europe. Some of Frederick's advisers may already have been dreaming of the possibility that he might become Holy Roman Emperor: commentators on *Revelation* looked to a climatic struggle between the Emperor and the Papacy as the prelude to the apocalypse. Henry was extremely enthusiastic about this alliance and is said to have helped to plan the wedding masques. It is perhaps significant that Jonson did not write a masque for this occasion. In the speeches he wrote for Henry's Barriers he had struck a cautious note, warning the prince not to become intoxicated with dreams of martial glory, and it is unlikely that he shared the enthusiasm felt by many Puritans for the German allies. But some new voices were now heard at court. The Inns of Court, which had not yet staged any major pageantry for the new king, now presented two elaborate masques. And an anonymous poet drafted a plan for a wedding masque which would have amounted to a systematic Protestant 'reformation' of the Jonsonian masque. This project did not get very far—quite apart from its expense, its apocalyptic enthusiasm would not have appealed to the king—but it provides a fascinating vision of an alternative direction in which masques might have developed under different political conditions.[16]

It had been a commonplace of Jacobean panegyric—reiterated by Jonson in *Love Freed from Ignorance and Folly* (1611) that Britain was a world in itself, enjoying a splendid isolation. The 1613 project was to take as its theme the reunification of Britain with Continental Protestantism. Jonson had tried to calm Protestant enthusiasm by using classical symbolism in his masques; the 1613 project involved a mixture of classical and explicitly Biblical symbolism. The setting of Jonson's *Hymenaei* had been a stage framed by two huge figures, Atlas and Hercules, holding up the cosmic sphere; between them was a globe from which issued the Humours and the Affections, which were eventually reconciled with Reason. The projected 1613 masque was to open with a complaint by a weary Atlas that he could no longer hold up the world because of the weight of sin and was therefore handing it over to Aletheia, Truth: only faith, rather than reason, could sustain the universe. Aletheia was to take the form of a huge recumbent statue, holding a globe in one hand and a Bible in the other. This was not the neo-Stoic Truth of Jonson's writings but the Truth of the Protestant apocalyptic tradition, a figure identified with the woman wandering in the wilderness of *Revelation* xii. She had appeared in various 'reformations' of medieval mystery plays by sixteenth-century Protestant writers and Spenser had introduced her as Una to Book I of *The Faerie Queene*. Conservatives in the church were not altogether happy with the idea, implicit in this apocalyptic imagery, that the true faith could be preserved by the pure and godly, the 'invisible church', independently of established institutions. William Laud had already clashed with the Calvinist George Abbot in the early years of James's reign over the question of the 'perpetual visibility' of the true church. The 1613 masque project was to reintroduce explicit apocalyptic imagery to the court. There was to be praise of James for receiving the Truth and ensuring that it was purely preached: this formed a striking contrast with the more conservative emphasis on ritual in Jonson's masques. Significantly, the focus was not to be confined to Britain: the nine muses, led by Urania, were to bring in three ladies representing the three parts of the world to do homage to James, and the different nations and rivers of the world were to perform a series of dances. The governing idea was that the union between Britain and the Palatinate would be an inspiration for the process of preaching the gospel to all parts of the world: when the process had been completed, the apocalypse would be near. The Muses were to call on the different nations to abandon their quarrels and recognise the pure Truth preached in Britain. At this point the globe was to split in two and reveal a vision of Paradise, guarded by an angel with a flaming sword. The Muses would lead the repentant nations into Paradise to the sound of heavenly music, and the gates would shut behind them.

Whoever devised the 1613 project had realised that the conventional masque contained within it the seeds of a more radical form. The final transformation scene represented the monarch and his court as images of perfection; but one more change of scene would show them to be no more than images and reveal the final, transcendent reality. The word 'apocalypse' means 'unveiling', 'unmasking', and several commentators on *Revelation* had compared the last days of the world to the last scenes of a play; the sudden transformations at the end of a masque formed an even more appropriate symbol. Milton was to compare the apocalyptic descent of Truth and Justice to the climax of a masque in *On the Morning of Christ's Nativity*. He believed that improvements in the arts of poetry and music could be seen as adumbrations of the apocalypse. In the 1613 project Urania, who was regularly invoked as the Protestant Muse, and the other Muses were to lead the nations into Paradise to the sounds of violins, lutes, and voices. Praise of King James would have been overshadowed by apocalyptic excitement. It is not surprising that this particular project was never carried out.

The apocalyptic hopes raised by Elizabeth's wedding were soon dissipated, however. Prince Henry had died shortly before the wedding, and it became clear that there would be no shift in the balance of power at court towards the anti-Spanish group. In the latter part of his reign James was increasingly preoccupied with negotiations for a Spanish match for Prince Charles. But this project coincided with a renewed crisis for Continental Protestantism. In 1619 Prince Frederick was elected King of Bohemia and it seemed that there might be a decisive shift in the European balance of power; but he and Elizabeth were soon driven out of their new kingdom by Habsburg forces. Many English Protestants wanted James to give full military aid to help Frederick to regain his territories, but before long the Palatinate had been lost too. James was reluctant to imperil the negotiations with Spain and wanted to achieve a diplomatic rather than military settlement. In 1619, at a time of severe financial difficulties, James began work on an expensive new Banqueting House in Whitehall as a suitable setting for the masques which, he hoped, would celebrate the forthcoming union between the houses of Stuart and Habsburg. This political crisis seems to have helped to revive the traditional hostility of some Puritans towards masques and plays. Attacks on the stage had in fact been relatively infrequent in the earlier part of James's reign, particularly because Sunday performances had been restricted. But towards the end of the reign William Prynne began work on *Histrio-Mastix* and Alexander Leighton published an attack on stage-plays. Both men were primarily concerned with political and religious issues; criticising plays or masques was a way of indirectly indicating a general discontent with the state of the nation under rulers who seemed unaware of the dangers which Protestantism was confronting. There was topical relevance in Prynne's repeated praise of rulers who had spent their money on wars and tournaments rather than court festivities.[17]

Defenders of royal policies tried to neutralise criticism by presenting themselves as champions of all culture and learning against ignorant Puritan fanatics. In August 1620 the Duke of Buckingham staged a rowdy comic masque in which one of the characters was a Puritan who marred the play. The following January a play at court ridiculed a Puritan with long ass's ears who complained that it was no time for masquing when all

Europe was in crisis.[18] But to condemn performances under specific circumstances was not necessarily to condemn them absolutely. As Margot
Heinemann has shown, people who shared the political outlook of Prynne
and Leighton did not necessarily share their view of the stage, and by the
1620s some London Puritans were taking an interest in the theatre.
Thomas Middleton was devising pageants for the city fathers which
combined elaborate spectacle with strongly Protestant propaganda, and
in 1624 he gained popularity amongst the Puritans for his apocalyptic satire *A Game at Chess*.[19] Had court masques voiced the political anxieties
of the anti-Spanish militants they would have aroused less criticism
from the Puritans and others. Indeed the Puritan propagandist Thomas
Scott compared his pamphlets, which were fictitious dialogues, to the
didactic fictions in court masques.[20] This was a reference calculated to
appeal to his patron Princess Elizabeth, who was now in exile in the
Netherlands and trying to encourage support for her cause in England.
Elizabeth loved masquing and there were regular festivities in her exiled
court. One of her supporters, the German poet Georg Rudolf Weckherlin,
had recently dedicated to her a lengthy description of Protestant pageantry
at Stuttgart.[21]

What disturbed Elizabeth's supporters about the masques of the 1620s
was that they seemed to be distracting the king from his responsibilities:
like Basilius in the *Arcadia*, he was putting off urgent diplomatic interven-
tions in order to pursue his courtly recreations.[22] John Fletcher, who
hardly corresponded to the stereotype of a Puritan fanatic, wrote to his
patron the Countess of Huntingdon that he would not discuss

> whether ytt be true
> we shall have warre with Spaine: (I wold wee might:)
> Nor whoe shall daunce i'th Maske: Nor whoe shall write
> those brave things done: Nor summe up the Expence;
> nor whether ytt be paid for ten yeere hence.[23]

Sir Francis Nethersole, one of Elizabeth's representatives, complained in
January 1620 that it was hard to gain access to the king because he spent
most of his time watching the rumbustious masques staged by his favourite, the Duke of Buckingham, and his young friends. One of these young
courtiers was given a large grant of land 'for masking and fooling'.[24]
Satirists disliked the company the king was keeping:

> At Royston and newmarkett he'le hunt till he be leane
> But hee hath merry boys that with masks and toyes
> Can make him fatt againe...
> But fooles are things for the pastime of kings
> ffooles still must be about them
> Soe must knaves too, where ever the[y] goe
> They seldome goe without them.[25]

David Norbrook

Buckingham aroused particular resentment because he was associated with the policy of selling off titles of honour, many of which were brought by members of his own family. The effect was to devalue traditional noble titles, creating a new brand of upstart nobles who came to seem, to those jealous of aristocratic traditions, no more than puppets in the hands of the king and his minion. In the words of one critic, James made 'the temple of honour a common theater, into which the basest were suffered to enter for their money'.[26] Unlike stage-plays, masques were meant to be exclusive aristocratic pursuits and not open to the public, but especially after the inflation of honours the court seemed to have become a corrupt theatre in which courtiers danced at the king's—or Buckingham's—bidding. The court masque had come to be a symbol of the dissolution, rather than the defence, of the traditional hierarchical order.

Buckingham's ascendancy was contested by an aristocratic 'opposition'. One of its leaders, the third Earl of Essex, had ample reason to dislike court masques. He had been humiliated when his wife, Frances Howard, divorced him for the king's new favourite, Robert Carr, Earl of Somerset. Jonson had celebrated Frances Howard's first marriage with a wedding masque, *Hymenaei*, in which he praised marriage as a mystical and indissoluble bond; somewhat inconsistently, he also wrote a wedding masque for her second marriage to the royal favourite. Not long after the wedding it began to be revealed that she had arranged for the murder of Sir Thomas Overbury, who had advised Carr against the marriage. It is not surprising that Essex tended to shun court festivities; his secretary Arthur Wilson later published a history of James's reign which drew a strong contrast between his patron's virtuous retirement and the idleness of a court that was a 'continued *Maskaradoe*'.[27] He did not share James's pacific values and after the outbreak of the Thirty Years' War he fought in defence of the Protestant cause in the Netherlands. He was to command the Parliamentary forces in the Civil War.

But Essex's personal and political disillusionment with the Jacobean court did not lead him to reject masquing altogether: on the contrary, when he retired to his country seats at the end of a season's campaigning he was regularly entertained with plays and masques.[28] These masques may, however, have been slightly different in content from the court festivities of this period. Only one text has survived; it describes a performance in honour of the marriage of Essex's sister Frances to Sir William Seymour in 1618.[29] Given Essex's family associations with Elizabethan chivalry—his grandmother, the widow of the first Earl of Leicester, attended some of these performances—it is interesting to find that the main masque was based on *The Faerie Queene*, that poetic embodiment of the political ideals of the Leicester and Essex circles. The male masquers took roles based on Spenser's characters, such as Arthur, Arthegall, Guyon, and Calidore. Though there was no direct reference to religious or foreign

policy, the Spenserian allusions did recall the values of Elizabethan chivalry which were no longer dramatised in the pacific masques of the court.
The performance ended with a compliment to Essex in which praise was
slightly more cautious and less hyperbolical than was becoming common
in court masques: instead of being celebrated as a deity Essex was praised
as 'Thou who greatnes does not swell thee,/To forgett, thou art a
man ...'.[30] Essex certainly took his commitment to personal and military honour seriously: he was soon to embark on his campaigns in the
Netherlands and he was one of the leaders, along with two other participants in the 1618 masque, of the aristocratic 'opposition' in the 1621
Parliament.[31]

When Charles I came to the throne in 1625 he tried to reform the royal
household and remove the grosser forms of waste and disorder. The
Puritan Lucy Hutchinson later commented that Charles's love of paintings
and sculptures was a marked improvement over James's enthusiasm for
'bawdry and profane abusive wit': she acknowledged the new king to be
'temperate and chaste and serious'.[32] The assassination of Buckingham in
1628 removed a major grievance, and in 1631 Jonson and Jones initiated
a new series of masques which celebrated the purity and chastity now
reigning at court and epitomised in the marital love of Charles and his
queen. (Jonson, it should be said, does not seem to have got on well with
Buckingham and wrote no Caroline masques until after his death.)[33] But
these reforms were accompanied by a religious reaction: Charles repudiated the Calvinist doctrine that had been part of the Anglican tradition
since the days of Elizabeth, and the High Church Laudian party gained
ascendency in the church.[34] After a brief phase of militancy Charles
reverted to a conciliatory foreign policy which seemed to his critics to
involve surrender to Spanish interests.

The response of William Prynne to this situation was to publish
Histrio-Mastix, indicating his hatred of the court's policies by indicting
its cultural preferences. But it would be misleading to generalise from
Prynne and expect to find a complete split between royalist 'court' and
Puritan 'country'.[35] The court was not monolithic: there were many
factional disputes. The queen disliked Laud, and some courtiers tried to
enlist her aid against the Archbishop.[36] Eager to cut down royal expendi-
ture, Laud himself was no great lover of masques. Some opponents of the
Laudians retained influential positions in the royal household. Weckherlin
was now one of the king's under-secretaries of state. He regarded the
Laudian bishops as 'Papists' and was to side with Parliament in the Civil
War: Milton was to succeed him in his secretarial post. But Weckherlin
was prepared to try to gain the Catholic queen's favour by writing a
masque for her. The draft of this masque, written in the late 1620s or early
1630s, is not particularly interesting: Weckherlin was imitating one of the
conventional themes of Caroline masques, the improvement in morality

brought about by the reign of Charles and Henrietta Maria. He did introduce a controversial note, however, by suggesting that two of the figures in his antimasque, Pride and Ambition, should be dressed as gentlemen or Spaniards. The French queen had no special love of the Spanish but the king would not have wanted them to be publicly insulted and Weckherlin's masque was not performed.[37]

Even the most spectacular Stuart masques, however, retained a certain margin for critical comment. While the antimasque of *The Triumph of Peace* satirised the hated monopolies, the main masque made the point that the king's peace had to be maintained with the aid of Law—a point that lawyers anxious about the king's constitutional position wanted him to remember.[38] This passage was reprinted in 1643 by a Parliamentarian pamphleteer who was urging the royalists to lay down their arms. The first part of the pamphlet parodied Shirley's antimasque, identifying the cavaliers with unruly figures like Fancy and Opinion. Like Shelley's old man, this writer may not have entirely understood the significance of Shirley's allegory but he inverted the relationship between masque and antimasque to make a political point.[39] For his part, the king may have failed to see the really very oblique criticisms of his policies in *The Triumph of Peace*, but participants in Caroline masques were not necessarily uncritical supporters of royal policy. Bulstrode Whitelocke, who organised the masque's music, was to be summoned before the council later in 1634 for being 'always wont to have a puritanical jerk at the Church'.[40]

It was in the same year that Milton wrote a masque to commemorate the installation of the Earl of Bridgewater as Lord President of Wales at Ludlow Castle. This was an important state occasion, and Milton provided his audience with many of the ingredients that would have been expected in a masque of the 1630s. The theme of chastity had a special relevance to the Earl's family: the Countess's brother-in-law, Lord Castlehaven, had recently been executed for scandalous sexual activities.[41] And the topic of the moral reformation of the court was a standard theme of masques in the 1630s. But Milton criticised these masques as well as imitating them, and took up many of the themes of earlier 'reformers' of the masque. Milton may have borrowed the figure of Comus from Jonson's *Pleasure Reconciled to Virtue* (1618), in which Hercules banished this riotous hedonist and hence implied the need for James to temper the disorder of his court. This was the first masque in which Charles appeared as Prince of Wales—a revised version was called *For the Honour of Wales*—and would thus have been an appropriate model for Milton's Welsh masque. But Milton went far beyond Jonson or Jones in his criticisms of masque conventions. Though *Pleasure Reconciled to Virtue* had condemned excessive disorder in revelry, it had also been a sustained defence of properly governed ritual in church and state.[42] Shortly before its performance, James had issued a proclamation defending the traditional Sunday sports in the countryside which Puritans were attacking as an incitement to irreligion. Jonson's masque implied that under a ruler as wise as James, ritual and godliness, pleasure and virtue, could be reconciled.

Sunday sports were newly topical in the 1630s. Charles had reissued his father's Book of Sports, and Laud was suppressing the lectureships which Puritans regarded as an essential means of combating the idolatry in superstitious 'dark corners of the land' like Wales and Northern England.[43] Prynne regarded Sabbath masquing and Sabbath sports as similar manifestations of a reversion to idolatry; the whole Calvinist tradition, which James had defended at least until the last years of his reign, now seemed in danger. In *Comus* Milton imitated certain features of Jonson's masques but introduced oblique allusions to traditions of low-church Protestant symbolism which Jonson had repudiated. Jonson's Comus was a cheerful Bacchic deity; Milton's Comus is the son of Circe, the wicked enchantress who had become associated in Protestant iconography with the Whore of Babylon. The scene in which he tempts the lady with an enchanted cup had many precedents in sixteenth-century Protestant drama, where representatives of the true faith were shown struggling with the magical temptations of idolatry. The lady's wanderings in the dark forest link her with the pure woman of *Revelation* who had appeared in the 1613 Aletheia masque, Middleton's civic pageants and in Spenserian poetry but not in most Stuart court masques.[44]

Like the 1613 apocalyptic masque project, *Comus* dramatises the difficulty of defeating evil without divine intervention: in conventional masques the heroes easily routed the forces of evil and even Jonson's Hercules, the symbol of a particularly strenuous form of heroic virtue, found it much easier to defeat Comus than Milton's Lady and her brothers. Jonson had made courtly dancing a central symbol of heroic virtue; in *Comus* the final dances are merely supplementary to the main action. The Lady's 'chaste footing' had disrupted Comus's unruly dance. The spirit's prologue and epilogue transpose the reconciliation between pleasure and virtue to a transcendental plane. As in the 1618 masque for Essex, the epilogue emphasises that the aristocratic audience are human beings, not deities.[45] The lady is freed from her imprisonment not by a spectacular display of courtiers in divine disguises but by the harmonious collaboration of music and poetry in the invocation of Sabrina. The recurrent emphasis on music rather than visual spectacle can be seen as a formal equivalent of Milton's suspicion of idolatry. Music appealed to many Puritans as an especially spiritual art, and in monodic songs like Lawes's the sound seemed to highlight the sense of the words rather than obscuring them with polyphony.[46] Music in *Comus* does not have the directly millenial associations of *On the morning of Christ's Nativity*—or the 1613 Aletheia masque—but it does offer the listener a promise of happiness, a 'sober certainty of waking bliss', which visual spectacle alone could not provide.

In some respects Milton was more radical than any previous 'reformer' of masques. Sixteenth-century apocalyptic poetry and drama had often combined calls for religious reform with social criticism: if the end of time was at hand it was essential that society should be justly ordered, and the nobility must distribute their surplus wealth amongst the poor. This vein of social criticism became muted in the Elizabethan and Jacobean periods, and the masque, which embodied the principle of conspicuous waste, was the last place where one would expect a serious call for austerity and economy. Jonson sometimes touched on the problem in his antimasques, only to set it aside: in *Love Restored* (1612) Plutus's attacks on courtly luxury are shown to be motivated by envy of the masquers' heroic virtue. Milton puts the defence of 'high solemnities' in the mouth of the anti-masque villain while his heroine calls for the redistribution of wealth. She does not explain exactly what a just distribution might be, and *Comus* itself, and its noble patron, are presumably felt to be sufficiently godly to avoid the charge of injustice. But Milton is questioning the conventional antithesis between envious, low-born antimasquers and magnanimous masquers.[47]

The examples of Milton, Whitelocke and Weckherlin show that there was no inherent incompatibility between Puritan sympathies and an interest in masques. The political upheavals of the 1640s certainly put an end to masquing in the Whitehall Banqueting House. But in the 1650s, as a certain degree of political stability returned under the Protectorate, masques began to be performed once more. In 1653 a masque by Shirley was presented on a semi-official occasion. The following year a masque by Thomas Jordan was given several performances. In 1656, with White-locke's encouragement, Sir William Davenant staged the first of several dramatic entertainments with musical accompaniments. Cromwell him-self was beginning to establish what amounted to a court—though it was more economically and efficiently administered than the Stuart royal households.[48] A masque-like entertainment was staged for the wedding of one of his daughters in 1657.

But these 'reformed' masques do not bear comparison with *Comus*; the devisers did not attempt to rethink masque conventions in the light of an apocalyptic Protestant ideology. On the contrary, these performances were symbols of a return to social normality after the disturbing events of the 1640s when radical sects had preached an apocalyptic egalitarianism in rather less abstract terms than Milton's Lady. When Whitelocke led an embassy to Sweden in 1653 he greatly impressed the queen by his elegant dancing at a ball. She told him that she had always believed the English regicides to be low-born 'mechanicals'; she could now see that some of them were gentlemen.[49] Davenant assured the audience of his first Commonwealth entertainment that the ruling classes would be less liable to popular envy if they displayed their wealth generously rather than hoarding it up. Milton had advocated a 'reformation' of plays and of popular recreations in the early days of the Long Parliament, but he had had in mind a new moral purity and integrity in art; by now 'reformation' was coming to imply little more than the inculcation of traditional aristocratic attitudes and the re-establishment of social distinctions.[50] Masques were, after all, better than anarchy.

NOTES

This is a revised version of a paper presented at the Modern Language Association Annual Convention, New York, 1981.

1 Shelley, *Poetical Works*, ed. Thomas Hutchinson (reset edition, London, 1943), pp. 488–92.
2 [George Ridpath], *The Stage Condemn'd* (London, 1698), pp. 12–31.
3 Stephen Orgel, *The Illusion of Power* (Berkeley, Los Angeles and London, 1975), pp. 38–44, 60.
4 See, for example, the collection of essays edited by Conrad Russell, *The Origins of the English Civil War* (London, 1973).
5 On Shelley's rejection of simpler Whig readings of the Caroline era see R. B. Woodings, ' "A Devil of a Nut to Crack": Shelley's *Charles the First*', *Studia Neophilologica*, 40 (1968), pp. 216–37; see also the same author's 'Shelley's Sources for *Charles the First*', *MLR*, 64 (1968), pp. 267–75.
6 On Shelley and the masque see Richard Cronin, *Shelley's Poetic Thoughts* (London, 1981), pp. 51–5.
7 *Biographia Britannica* (London, 1757), 4, p. 2400 (I owe this reference to John Pitcher). The idea of 'reforming' a traditional genre was common in the Renaissance: cf. the anonymous Puritan 'Christian Reformation' of Sir John Davies's *Nosce Teipsum*, British Library M.S. Royal 18A LXIX.
8 Anon. *Vindiciae contra tyrannos: A Defence of Liberty against Tyrants* (London, 1648), p. 121. The Latin text (Edinburgh, 1579, p. 196) reads 'ut palliatam quandam fabulam ludant'. 'Palliatus' was used by the Romans to describe actors wearing Greek cloaks, and hence had connotations of foreign decadence that the English translator associated with masques. On Sidney's politics see Richard McCoy, *Sir Philip Sidney: Rebellion in Arcadia* (Hassocks, Sussex, 1978).
9 Quoted by Blair Worden, 'Classical Republicanism and the Puritan Revolution', in *History and Imagination: Essays in Honour of H. R. Trevor-Roper*, ed. Hugh Lloyd-Jones, Valerie Pearl, and Blair Worden (London, 1981), p. 187.
10 See John Pitcher's essay. Daniel seems to be hitting at the new perspective stage which was used in Jones's masques in the preface to his play *The Queenes Arcadia* (initially titled *Arcadia Reformed*): Daniel, *Complete Works*, ed. A. B. Grosart (5 vols, London and Aylesbury, 1885–96), 3, p. 214. In a later verse epistle (probably to the Countess of Bedford) Daniel used

David Norbrook

imagery from masquing to describe the corruption of the Jacobean court: *Samuel Daniel: The Brotherton Manuscript. A Study in Authorship*, ed. John Pitcher (Leeds, 1981), p. 148.

11 I am reconstructing this episode from a letter in H.M.C. *Calendar of Hatfield Manuscripts*, 16, pp. 388-9. For protests against the extravagance of the Jacobean court in an early masque see David Lindley, 'Campion's *Lord Hay's Masque* and Anglo-Scottish Union', *HLQ*, 43 (1979-80), pp. 1-12.

12 This analysis is based on S. L. Adams, 'Spain and the Netherlands: The Dilemma of Early Stuart Foreign Policy', forthcoming in *Before the English Civil War*, ed. Howard Tomlinson. I am grateful to Dr Adams for letting me read his article in advance of publication and for reading an earlier version of this essay.

13 D. J. Gordon, 'Poet and Architect: The Intellectual Setting of the Quarrel between Ben Jonson and Inigo Jones', in *The Renaissance Imagination*, ed. Stephen Orgel (Berkeley, Los Angeles, and London, 1975), pp. 77-101. In *Threshold of a Nation: A Study in English and Irish Drama* (Cambridge, 1979), pp. 149-73, Philip Edwards forcefully argues that Jonson's relations with the court were rather more compromising than has sometimes been acknowledged.

14 Arthur Wilson, *The History of Great Britain* (London, 1653), p. 91. Jonson seems to have modified his opinions at a later date: see Anne Barton 'Harking Back to Elizabeth: Ben Jonson and Caroline Nostalgia', *ELH*, 48 (1981), pp. 706-31.

15 On the different public images of Prince Henry see Jerry W. Williamson, *The Myth of the Conqueror: Prince Henry Stuart, A Study of Seventeenth-Century Personation* (New York, 1978).

16 For a fuller account of this masque project see my article '*The Masque of Truth*', forthcoming in *Paideia*, Renaissance Issue. The text appeared in an account of the wedding festivities published by one D. Jocquet at Heidelberg in 1613.

17 William Prynne, *Histrio-Mastix* (London, 1633), pp. 320-1, 742, 451. For some suggestive comments on the political implications of attacks on plays see Stephen Foster, *Notes from the Caroline Underground: Alexander Leighton, the Puritan Triumvirate, and the Laudian Reaction to Nonconformity* (Hamden, Conn., 1978), pp. 20-4, 37-42.

18 *CSP Venetian 1619-21*, p. 390; *The Court and Times of James I*, ed. T. Birch, 2 vols (London, 1848), 2, p. 228.

19 Margot Heinemann, *Puritanism and Theatre: Thomas Middleton and Opposition Drama under the Early Stuarts* (Cambridge, 1980), pp. 121-33, 151-71.

20 Heinemann, p. 157.

21 M. A. E. Green, *Elizabeth Electress Palatine and Queen of Bohemia* (revised edition, London, 1909), pp. 320, 355. On Weckherlin see n. 35 below: and on Jonson's attitude to the Bohemian propaganda campaign see Sara Pearl's essay.

22 It is interesting that the Puritan lawyer Simonds D'Ewes was reading the *Arcadia* with enthusiasm at the same time as he was censuring court masques: *The Diary of Sir Simonds D'Ewes, 1622-1624*, ed. E. Bourcier (Paris, 1974), pp. 70, 76.

23 *H.M.C. Hastings*, 2, pp. 58-9. About this time Fletcher collaborated with Massinger on the topical anti-Spanish play *Sir John Olden Barnavelt*.

24 *Letters and other Documents Illustrating the Relations between England and Germany at the Commencement of the Thirty Years' War*, ed. S. R. Gardiner, 2nd series (London, 1868), pp. 132-4; *The Letters of John Chamberlain*, ed. N. E. McClure, 2 vols (Philadelphia, 1939), 2, p. 318. For similar complaints from Venetian sources see *CSP Venetian 1619-21*, p. 534, *1621-23*, p. 191.

25 Bodleian M.S. Malone 23, fols 20v, 21r.

26 Francis Osborn, 'Historical Memoirs', in *Secret History of the Court of King James the First*, ed. Sir Walter Scott, 2 vols (Edinburgh, 1811), 1, p. 256.

27 Wilson, *The History of Great Britain*, p. 53.

28 Arthur Wilson, 'Account of Arthur Wilson written by himself', in *The Inconstant Lady*, ed. P. Bliss (Oxford, 1814), p. 119.

29 The text was printed by R. Brotanek (*Die Englischen Maskenspiele*, Vienna, 1902, pp. 328-37), who attributed it to Jonson; G. E. Bentley, *The Jacobean and Caroline Stage*, 7 vols (Oxford, 1941-68), 5, 1311, suggests Richard Brome; but Arthur Wilson or Thomas Pestell are perhaps more likely candidates for authorship given their associations with Essex: Heinemann, *Puritanism and Theatre*, pp. 221-4, 240-1.

30 Though not drawing directly on Spenser's topical allegory, this masque did continue Spenser's exploration of sexual politics: the female masquers claimed to be superior to men and capable of living perfectly well without them, and at the end of the performance men and women recognised each other as equals.

31 Vernon F. Snow, 'Essex and the Aristocratic Opposition to the Early Stuarts', *Journal of Modern History*, 32 (1960), pp. 224-33.

32 Lucy Hutchinson, *Memoirs of the Life of Colonel Hutchinson*, ed. James Sutherland (London, 1973), p. 46.

33 It has been suggested that the only masque Jonson wrote for Buckingham, *The Gypsies Metamorphos'd*, in fact ingeniously satirised the favourite: Dale B. J. Randall, *Jonson's Gypsies Unmasked* (Durham, N.C., 1975). In the antimasque to *The Masque of Augurs* Jonson seems to be ridiculing the 'running masques' of Buckingham and his young friends, which seemed to Jonson to lack the appropriate aristocratic dignity.

34 Nicholas Tyacke, 'Puritanism, Arminianism, and Counter-Revolution', in Russell, *The Origins of the English Civil War*, pp. 119-43.

35 The split is perhaps exaggerated by P. W. Thomas, 'Two Cultures? Court and Country under Charles I', in Russell, *Origins of the English Civil War*, pp. 168-93.

36 R. M. Smuts, 'The Puritan Followers of Henrietta Maria in the 1630s', *English Historical Review*, 93 (1978), pp. 26-45.

37 Leonard Forster, 'Two Drafts by Weckherlin for a Masque for the Queen of England', *German Life and Letters*, 18 (1964-5), pp. 258-63; the drafts are now in the Trumbull Papers in the Berkshire Record Office. See further Leonard Forster, *Georg Rudolf Weckherlin: Zur Kenntnis Seines Lebens in England* (Basel, 1944).

38 Orgel and Strong, 1, p. 64, 2, pp. 539 ff.

39 Jean Fuzier, 'English Political Dialogues 1641-1651: A Suggestion for Research with a Critical Edition of *The Tragedy of the Cruell Warre 1643*',

David Norbrook

Cahiers Élisabéthains, 15 (1979), pp. 77-80; Lois Potter, '*The Triumph of Peace* and *The Cruel Warr*: Masque and Parody', *Notes and Queries*, N.S. 27 (1980), pp. 345-8.

40 Ruth Spalding, *The Improbable Puritan: A Life of Bulstrode Whitelocke 1605-1676* (London, 1975), p. 96.

41 Barbara Breasted, '*Comus* and the Castlehaven Scandal', *Milton Studies*, 3 (1971), pp. 201-24.

42 Leah Sinanoglou Marcus, 'The Occasion of Jonson's *Pleasure Reconciled to Virtue*', *SEL*, 19 (1979), pp 271-93: Jonson's masque had not yet been printed, but Marcus's study of Jonson's allegory strengthens the possibility that Milton had read it.

43 Christopher Hill, *Change and Continuity in Seventeenth-Century England* (London, 1974), pp. 3-47.

44 Prynne had had to acknowledge the existence of a tradition of Protestant drama in *Histrio-Mastix*, pp. 833-4; he argued that the performance of these plays under Henry VIII and Mary had been justifiable as a means of getting round censorship. On Milton's debt to these traditions see Alice-Lyle Scoufos, 'The Mysteries in Milton's *Masque*', *Milton Studies*, 6 (1974), pp. 113-42. Scoufos reads Comus as a representation of the Anglican episcopacy, but despite Prynne's hint about drama as a way of evading censorship it is unlikely that Milton would have risked this much in a masque performed before a royal official who cannot really be described as a 'Puritan'. Even if read as a more generalised warning against the dangers of a regression to idolatry, however, the masque is pointed enough.

45 These remarks merely sketch out some links between *Comus* and previous attempts to 'reform' the masque. See also the essays by Helen Cooper, Jennifer Chibnall, and John Creaser.

46 See Percy A. Scholes, *The Puritans and Music in England and New England* (Oxford, 1934).

47 There was a revival of apocalyptic ideas in the 1630s: see Charles Webster, *The Great Instauration: Science, Medicine and Reform 1626-1660* (London, 1975), Chapter 1.

48 Roy Sherwood, *The Court of Oliver Cromwell* (London, 1977), pp. 141 ff, 149.

49 Spalding, *The Improbable Puritan*, pp. 167-8, 186.

50 Lois Potter, 'Towards a "Reformed" Stage', in *The Revels History of Drama in English*, *vol. IV: 1613-1660*, ed. Philip Edwards, Gerald Eades Bentley, Kathleen McLuskie, and Lois Potter (London, 1981), pp. 294-304.

JOHN CREASER

'The present aid of this occasion': The setting of *Comus*

❖⊃◦⊂❖

MILTON'S *A Masque presented at Ludlow Castle, 1634* has long been celebrated as a text and patronised as an event. *Comus*, the now inescap- OCCASION able title foisted on to it by eighteenth-century adaptors, denigrates the occasion as much as it unbalances the moral poise of the work. The sublimity of the masque's verse and themes is well established, but it is too often thought to have been a small affair theatrically and socially, a 'diminutive' production,[1] with borrowed costumes, limited or no spec- tacle, and amateurish performers. W.R. Parker writes in the standard biography of the poet, a work of massive authority, that 'the masque was essentially a children's party' and 'a children's entertainment'; it was written 'without benefit of spectacle', and the antimasque costumes may have been 'left over' from Thomas Carew's *Coelum Britannicum*, one of the two great court masques of 1634.[2] For John S. Diekhoff, a meticulous student of *Comus*, 'the performance could hardly have been lacking in absurdity, even in an age of child actors'.[3]

It is my contention, however, that *Comus* was commissioned for a state event of some significance, and that new light is thrown on it by consider- ing how Milton responded to the demands and constraints of his com- mission.

What took place in Ludlow on 29 September 1634 is beyond exact reconstruction, but consideration of the performers or of the indications for performance in the text lends no support to the patronising view of the occasion. The masque was in the charge of Henry Lawes, who played the part of the Attendant Spirit and who, at thirty-eight, was one of the most celebrated composers of the age. As a leading court musician, he would have taken part in all or most of the six sumptuous Whitehall masques of the early 1630s. It was not in his interests to tolerate bungling amateurism, and the quality of his five surviving songs for *Comus* shows that he was neither giving second best himself nor expecting it from his aristocratic pupils.

Various children in the large family of Milton's client, the Earl of Bridgewater, had been performing in court masques for some years, and of the three youngest who took part in *Comus*, the fifteen-year-old Lady

Alice and eleven-year-old heir John, Lord Brackley, had taken part in
Aurelian Townshend's *Tempe Restored* two years earlier, while Lord
John and the nine-year-old Thomas had performed in *Coelum Britannicum*. In doing so, they would have survived weeks of rehearsal and been
exposed to and expected to attain very high standards of performance.[4]
The terms of Lawes's later dedication of some music to Lady Alice
suggest that she was an accomplished singer,[5] and the chromatic idiom
and exposed leaps of a seventh in the Lady's song to Echo do require a
sophisticated singer with a secure sense of pitch. It is a more demanding
song than the four Lawes wrote for himself to perform, and only a fine
singer could be expected to carry it off before an audience. It is highly
unlikely that Lady Alice would be allowed to make a fool of herself, all
the more so because young aristocratic ladies rarely sang in public.

There is no evidence that the antimasque costumes were borrowed
from the Revels Office, but if so, they would have been tokens of royal
munificence and splendour rather than 'left-overs'. Moreover, the Egertons, who were a literary and scholarly family, founders of a great library,
had commissioned a substantial text for the occasion from the most gifted
living poet, whose work was known to them from that exquisite entertainment, *Arcades*. Its unusual stature is all the more evident if it is
compared to the other surviving festivity for the new Lord President, a
genial but slight entertainment welcoming him to Chirk Castle in North
Wales, and this implies that *Comus* was written for a major occasion.[6]

The stage directions do not suggest that *Comus* was performed 'without
benefit of spectacle'. When Comus's rout entered 'like sundry sorts of
wild beasts, ... their apparel glistering, ... with torches in their hands'
(92), the costumes and the burst of light after the subdued opening in the
selva oscura must have been striking, especially for those in the audience
accustomed to court masques, where torch-bearers normally accompanied only the main masquers.[7] Visual splendour is crucial to the temptation scene: 'The scene changes to a stately palace, set out with all
manner of deliciousness: soft music, tables spread with all dainties' (658).
Sabrina, with her jewelled chariot and attendant nymphs, presents a
balancing, purified splendour. *Comus* cannot have matched the visual and
mechanical intricacies of Inigo Jones's current work for the court. Other
reasons apart, the space was probably not available, since the Ludlow
Hall, measuring sixty feet by thirty feet, was little more than half the area
of the smallest hall used for court masques.[8] Nevertheless, some simple
machinery must have been used, if only for Sabrina's chariot. It is probable, moreover, that a cloud machine was used for the Attendant Spirit's
arrival and departure. The performance began with a song, 'From the
heavens now I fly', adapted from Milton's epilogue, and this adaptation
suggests that the Spirit did indeed descend. Milton, too, had written in
the knowledge that the use of machinery was at least possible. The very

term 'stoop' used of Heaven in his closing line, for example, echoes masque descriptions of descending deities.[9]

A standard Renaissance perspective stage was almost certainly used: a proscenium arch, a few pairs of stationary, angled side-wings depicting woodland and focusing attention on a series of back-shutters: the wild wood, the stately palace, and the panorama of Ludlow. Allardyce Nicoll deduces from the word 'discovers' in the opening stage description, 'The first scene discovers a wild wood', that there was a stage curtain, and this strongly suggests that there was a picture-frame stage, since, as Nicoll says elsewhere, 'The presence of a curtain generally, if not universally, implies the framing of the stage by means of a proscenium arch.'[10] It would have been surprising if simple machinery had not been added to such a set.

Comus is likely, then, to have had the stage lay-out and some of the machinery of contemporary court entertainments such as *Tempe Restored*, Shirley's *The Triumph of Peace* (1634), and the French pastoral *Florimène*.[11] Quite apart from its visual impact, its very use at this date is an affirmation of courtliness. Such scenery was confined to plays at court or in the presence of royalty, or to masques, which by definition were royal or aristocratic occasions. Costumes might be passed on to common players, but not scenery.

Moreover, Milton enhances the courtliness of the occasion by having the final scene represent 'Ludlow Town and the President's Castle', a significant echo of recent court masques. It was rare for masque scenes to depict actuality, but after the main masque of *Albion's Triumph* (1632) by Townshend, 'The Scene is varied into a Landscipt, in which was a prospect of the Kings Pallace of *Whitehall*, and part of the Citie of *London*, seene a farre off, and presently the whole heaven opened.'[12] Similarly, *Coelum Britannicum* ended with a great revelation of the regal virtues, 'And in the lower part [of the final scene] was seene a farre off the prospect of *Windsor* Castell, the famous seat of the most honourable Order of the Garter.'[13] Windsor Castle is here, as Orgel and Strong argue, the 'centre and symbol of the monarch's power in the country', since Charles I had there installed the virtually re-created Order of the Garter and was enacting his moral and chivalric ideals in rituals of great splendour.[14] The climactic representation of the seat of government associates *Comus* with these extravaganzas of courtliness. The final scene is not a charmingly parochial touch, but a symbol of vice-regal authority.

Comus was, I believe, designed more as a vice-regal ceremony than as a children's party, and this is borne out by considering the occasion as well as the staging. The very title of the 1637 edition suggests an evening of official pomp: 'A MASKE/PRESENTED/At Ludlow Castle,/ 1634:/*On Michaelmasse night, before the*/RIGHT HONORABLE,/ IOHN *Earle of Bridgewater, Vicount* BRACKLY,/*Lord President of*

WALES, And one of / His MAIESTIES most honorable / Privie Counsell.'
The attendance was demonstrably not confined to the household, since
unpublished local records show that civic officials were invited.[15] Since
the town was represented, it is reasonable to assume that members of the
Lord President's Council in the Marches, with their families and other
local notables, were also invited. A large, formal gathering is suggested
by the Spirit's reference to 'your father's residence, / Where this night are
met in state / Many a friend to gratulate / His wish'd presence' (947-50).
It is sometimes assumed that the Earl had only limited funds at his
disposal, but he was among the richest men of the kingdom, with an
annual income of many thousands of pounds.[16] He was reported to have
offered Buckingham twenty thousand pounds to secure the Earldom
which had been promised his father. It is unlikely that he spared expense
on such an occasion.

The very date of *Comus* is significant. The Earl's sceptre was hardly
'new-entrusted' (36). He had been nominated to the Lord Presidency in
June 1631, had taken over at least some of the duties at once, and had
begun his first spell of official residence at Ludlow early in the July of
1634.[17] The household and private effects of his family were transported
to Ludlow from the main family residence, Ashridge in Hertfordshire, at
the beginning of that month.[18] *Comus* was not the first formal celebration
of their arrival, since the Chirk Castle entertainment took place in high
summer.[19] The major celebration must have been held back until 29
September not only to allow time for planning and rehearsal on site but
in order to exploit the associations of Michaelmas Day, the Feast of St
Michael and All Angels. The date was obviously chosen well in advance,
since Milton's text has its roots in the liturgy of the day, with the stress on
children and angels in the prescribed readings (especially Matthew xviii.1-
10 and Revelation xii.7-12). Michaelmas Day was, moreover, one of the
great events of the provincial year. Legal and administrative affairs were
brought together in the Quarter Sessions. The day was celebrated in many
towns with a period of saturnalian licence brought to a halt by the formal
institution of newly chosen civic officials. According to Robert Chambers
in his collection of popular antiquities, *The Book of Days*, magistrates
and other officials were appointed from St Michael's Day because of a
traditional association of magistrates with presiding angels. 'Local rulers
were esteemed as in some respects analogous to tutelar angels, in as far as
they presided over and protected the people.'[20] The date itself associated
government and divinity and, like the choice of Ludlow and its castle for
the final scene, is an affirmation of authority. The force of this will emerge
from consideration of the local and national context.

Bridgewater's appointment was made directly by Charles I as a reward
for years of faithful service. The Lord President ruled one of the main
organs of central government; it was in many ways a lesser Privy Council

and its procedures resembled those of the Star Chamber. According to its leading historian, Penry Williams, it had extraordinarily wide-ranging powers, greater in scope than those of any other court in the realm, with the possible exception of the Council of the North, and unlike that Council, it could try cases of treason.[21] Its power and prestige were associated with those of the royal prerogative, and when the Council came under attack from the common lawyers of Westminster in the early years of James I's reign, the argument turned in part upon that prerogative. The Council survived these attacks and was relatively secure during the 1620s, but in the years of Charles's personal rule it was gradually undermined, and with the coming of the Long Parliament it collapsed abruptly and ignominiously. It was associated with the hated Star Chamber and the other prerogative courts, and their abolition was to be one of the few areas of general agreement within that parliament and was the main achievement of its first year of existence.

Even though the Council was not in fact a political court like the Star Chamber, and although the unpopular policy of 'Thorough' seems to have been even less thorough in Wales and the Marches than elsewhere, and although its territory was to be overwhelmingly royalist in allegiance during the Civil War, the standing of the Council, and of Bridgewater with it, suffered through association with the centralist tendencies of the personal rule. Williams comments that Bridgewater and his predecessor Northampton 'found that royal policy brought the Council into increasing hatred and contempt.... These years saw growing discontent in Wales, whose gentry had once been loyal to the Council. The Puritan influence of merchants like Myddelton and Heylyn was beginning to provide an ideology of opposition for Wales, while Charles I, acting through Ludlow, brought home to the Welsh for the first time the disadvantages of Stuart rule.'[22] One consequence was the compilation in the late 1620s or early 1630s (most likely 1630-3) of a massive manuscript volume detailing the grievances of the Welsh at the alleged corruption, injustice, and harshness of the Council. A related consequence was Bridgewater's difficulty, as *ex officio* Lord Lieutenant for the border counties, in raising muster-master fees, an issue which here, as elsewhere, brought the rivalries of central and local government into the open. It was ominous that no one of substance in Shropshire publicly supported him in a dispute over the county's fee which began a few months after the performance of *Comus*, was seen as a threat to the prerogative of the crown itself, and led to Bridgewater's impeachment by the Long Parliament.[23]

In appointing Bridgewater during his personal rule, Charles was attempting to strengthen an organ of his prerogative government. The post of Lord President had been a distinguished one for most of Elizabeth's reign, but James appointed lesser men. According to A. H. Dodd, there was little sign of the old splendour under James, and the council became less a vice-regal court than a mere court of law.[24] As the son of Ellesmere the former Lord Chancellor, Bridgewater was a man of more standing than his Stuart predecessors. Moreover, the royal instructions on his appointment attempted to extend the prestige and support of the Council by substantially increasing its membership to over eighty, including twenty-four peers and eleven bishops, and by restoring to it control of the south-east counties of Wales which had long been disputed with the Earls of Worcester. Bridgewater, according to Dodd, 'determined to recover for Ludlow something of its former dignity as a viceregal court'.[25] *Comus*, in particular, was his reaffirmation of the glories of predecessors such as Sir Henry Sidney, who entered Shrewsbury for the St George's Feast of 1581 in a grand procession seven hundred yards long. Growing discontent in Wales may well have made that reaffirmation desirable.

A probable reason why the royalism as well as the splendour of the occasion of *Comus* has gone virtually unnoticed is that critics have stressed the supposed Puritanism of Bridgewater and his family.[26] The authority for this is John Collinges, *Par Nobile: Two Treatises* (1669), a hagiographical sketch of two daughters of the family, Frances, the first of the fifteen children, who was born in 1604 and married Sir John Hobart in 1622, and Katherine, who was born in 1611 and married Sir William Courten (or Courteen) about 1633. According to Collinges, Frances had a Huguenot governess, learned 'to be a *Calvinist* in point of *Doctrine*, and a *Presbyterian* as to Discipline' (p. 4), and later reflected sadly about having misspent 'part of many *Lords dayes*, in *masks*, and other *Court pastimes*, according to the fashion of others in her circumstances. This she would often *mention with bitterness*, and *honourably mention* and prefer before her self one of her *Noble Sisters* [Katherine], who in her youth had a just sense of that errour, and courage enough to resist the temptations to it. It was the only thing in which I ever heard her repent her obedience to, and attendance upon her *Mother*, whom yet she thought exceeding *pious*' (p. 6).

Evidence from Collinges (who became Frances's chaplain in 1646) should be treated with caution, since he is writing polemically in the Restoration out of a confessedly imperfect recollection of limited knowledge of his subjects' early lives half a century earlier. Even so, his statements merely suggest that *one* of this enormous family was a sabbatarian in youth. The rest of the family, it seems, was quite without such Puritan scruples at the time. Perhaps, too, the Huguenot governess was chosen for her language rather than her theology, since Lady Frances went to her as a toddler and 'learned French before she could distinctly speak English' (p. 3).

Against the eventual Presbyterianism of Lady Frances and Lady Katherine might be set the royalism and whole-hearted Anglicanism of Lady Alice and the future second Earl. Lady Alice was in 1652 to marry

Richard Vaughan, second Earl of Carbery, a former royalist general who seems to have made his peace with Cromwell but who was a royalist at heart. At the Restoration he was to be appointed Lord President of Wales. The Elder Brother of *Comus*, who in 1642 was to become son-in-law of the then Earl of Newcastle, one of Charles's most prominent supporters, was to write of his father: 'He was a dutiful son to his Mother the Church of England in her persecution as well as in her great splendour; a loyal subject to his sovereign in those worst times, when it was accounted treason not to be a Traytor.'[27] He was to write angrily in his copy of Milton's *Defensio: Liber igne Author furca dignissimi* (a book very worthy the fire and an author the scaffold). In the 1660s he was to harry Dissenters with ferocious zeal, including Milton's acquaintance the Quaker Isaac Penington, son of the Sir Isaac under whom Milton had served as an employee of the Commonwealth. It may well be significant that Milton removed all explicit reference to the Egerton family from the 1673 edition of *Comus* (as Jonson suppressed the occasion of *Hymenaei* after the Overbury scandal), whereas the headnote relating *Arcades* to the Countess of Derby was retained without change.

A picture of a household of strict piety does emerge from Collinges, and he twice makes the point (which critics have failed to cite) that Lady Frances honoured her father for having 'early prejudiced her against the *Arminian principles*' (p. 36). It will be recalled, however, that this refers to the early years of James's reign when the king was a zealous predestinarian, long before the rise of Arminianism under Charles, Buckingham, and Laud. Such 'prejudice' was simply the Anglican orthodoxy of the day, and tells us nothing about Bridgewater's allegiances in changed circumstances almost thirty years later.

The apparent readiness of almost all the family to participate in Sunday theatricals clearly distinguishes it from even that liberal wing of the Parliamentary Puritan movement which was prepared to enjoy, and exploit, the theatre, since, as Margot Heinemann has demonstrated, opposition to Sunday performances remained strong among those unpuritanical Puritans.[28] Furthermore, the giving of major speaking and singing parts to the Egerton children suggests an advanced attitude to theatricals. Not only was it rare for a young, high-born lady to sing in public, but *Tempe Restored* of 1632 (in which Lady Alice and Lord John performed) seems to have been the first occasion on which any woman singer appeared on the English stage.[29] The Court had only recently come to terms with aristocrats taking speaking parts in theatricals, and performances in plays by Queen Henrietta Maria had initially scandalised a good deal of English opinion. Few aristocrats other than Bridgewater's patron Buckingham had taken speaking parts in masques by 1634. It was rather daring that the children should have had such roles, and it was certainly part of the up-to-date courtliness of the occasion.[30]

Such courtliness is in keeping with Bridgewater if he is seen as a follower of Buckingham rather than falsely claimed for Puritanism, and this is what his career suggests. He was, for example, associated with Buckingham in defending Bacon in 1621; he joined the Privy Council in 1626; he supported unpopular actions of Charles and Buckingham such as the imprisonment of the Earl of Arundel and of Sir Dudley Digges and Sir John Eliot. Even in the 1640s, when he seems to have been at best a lukewarm supporter of the King, he retained what Charles L. Hamilton terms a 'residual loyalty', and when, after months of prevarication, he could no longer avoid taking the Solemn League and Covenant, he inserted a reservation that he accepted it in so far as it was compatible with his previous oaths of loyalty to the crown.[31] In 1634, there was not the slightest question of his allegiance to Charles.[32]

It is one of the more intriguing ironies of literary history that for this big occasion, his exercise in royalist public relations, this supporter of Buckingham should have commissioned work from a young man who was to be the defender of regicide and the most forthright opponent of king-worship in the period, a young man who happened to be the friend and admiring correspondent of the most notorious celebrant of Buckingham's assassination, Alexander Gill the younger. In November 1628, Gill had been savagely sentenced by the Star Chamber (although the sentence was later reduced); he had not only drunk a health in public to the Duke's assassin, asserted that King James and the Duke were reunited in hell and that Charles had only wit enough to keep a shop, but he had written a poem to express his feelings.[33]

The irony becomes the more intriguing if one considers that the work commissioned by Bridgewater was a masque, for this was *par excellence* the artistic form in which the early Stuarts embodied their absolutist claims, and during the personal rule masques at court were becoming ever more elaborate and assertive. As Orgel and Strong have demonstrated, masques were essential to the life and image of a Renaissance court, and more than any other, the Stuart court used the masque to foster an exalted conception of the divine right of kings.

The masquing hall crystallises an idyllic vision of the ruler as quasi-divine source of national power and unity, and its characteristic theme is the restoration of the Golden Age by virtue of his benign omnipotence. In the early 1630s, apologist and critic alike could see the quality of the court as epitomised in the masque. Thomas Carew, for example, turns to the masque in his verse epistle to Townshend declining to commemorate the death of Gustavus Adolphus of Sweden. Many felt the death of this brilliant Protestant leader as keenly as if he had been the national commander, since Britain's neutrality in the Thirty Years' War was thought by them to be deeply shaming. Carew wrote:

> But let us that in myrtle bowers sit
> Under secure shades, use the benefit
> Of peace and plenty, which the blessed hand
> Of our good King gives this obdurate Land,
> Let us of Revels sing ...
> ... These are subjects proper to our clyme.
> Tourneyes, Masques, Theaters, better become
> Our *Halcyon* dayes.　　　　　　　　　　　　　　(44–9, 94–6)

The lines chillingly epitomise the complacency which was to prove fatal to Charles and his supporters. *Histrio-Mastix*, William Prynne's massive compilation of puritanical extremity, was, on the other hand, not unreasonably taken as an attack on current court theatricals. Prynne himself was to explain that the work, which was published in November 1632, had been nine years in preparation. But the index, in which he dilates on his current obsessions, must have been written shortly before publication, and the Queen had been rehearsing Walter Montague's pastoral, *The Shepherd's Paradise*, since that September for performance in the January, and had anyway been active in court theatricals for some years. So entries in the index such as '*Kings* ... infamous for them to act or frequent Playes, or favour Players'; '*Women*, skill in dancing no good signe of their honesty'; and '*Women-Actors*, notorious whores' were at the least provocative.[34]

Milton was never to be a bigoted Presbyterian of the William Prynne stamp. His first published English verse was the sonnet on Shakespeare prefixed to the Second Folio—successor to that folio whose fine paper had so scandalised Prynne.[35] In 1642 of all years, he was to suggest that the theatre, as well as the pulpit, could be 'doctrinal and exemplary to a Nation', that the Song of Solomon 'affords us a divine pastoral Drama', and that 'the Apocalyps of Saint *John* is the majestick image of a high and stately Tragedy'.[36] Yet it remains intriguing that the future defender of regicide, *furca dignissimus*, whose later writings refer contemptuously to the masque form,[37] should have written a vice-regal masque. Although one cannot flatly impose the attitudes of the 1640s on the Milton of 1634 any more than one can on the nation as a whole, the seeds of discontent were already germinating in both.

The innovatory absolutism and Arminianism of Charles and Laud were beginning the transformation of mainstream Calvinists into heretical Puritan revolutionaries. The supplanting of communion-table by altar and the elevation of the altar above the pulpit, the stress on ritual, ceremony, and the sacraments, the attack on lecturerships and on doctrines of predestination, and the exclusion of Calvinists from high office in Church and state were all under way. Laud, especially since becoming Archbishop of Canterbury in 1633, was, with his 'demonic energy',[38] doing what he could to purge the Church. The influence of Henrietta

Maria and other active Catholics at court, and Charles's neutrality in the Thirty Years' War, made it the more difficult for many Calvinists to distinguish the new Laudianism of the Church from Roman Catholicism. Nathaniel Barnard's preaching of active resistance, the mutilation and imprisonment of Prynne and of that fanatical opponent of Laud, Alexander Leighton, the transformation through Charles's vindictiveness of the firebrand Sir John Eliot into a Parliamentary martyr after his death in the Tower, and the increase of emigration to New England were all tokens of a sense of division emergent even within the most successful years of the personal rule.

It is most unlikely that Milton did not share unease at such political and theological developments. His early education had been Low Church, and he was the former pupil and admiring friend and correspondent of the rigorous Presbyterian Thomas Young as well as of that irritant to authority, Alexander Gill. Young was to be one of the co-authors of the 'Smectymnuus' anti-prelatical tracts on whose side Milton entered the pamphlet war of the early 1640s. Milton's *Elegia Quarta* of 1627, addressed to Young in Hamburg as a chaplain there, describes him as a pastor driven out of his homeland for religion's sake. He is illustrious for his honouring of the primitive faith, *antiquae clarus pietatis honore*, and a bringer of glad tidings from heaven who has been cruelly deprived of a livelihood by his hard-hearted native land (ll. 17-18 and 87-94). In the sixth Prolusion, Milton praises Junius Brutus as 'that second founder of Rome and great avenger of the lusts of kings'.[39] Milton's Puritan earnestness is already evident in the seventh sonnet ('How soon hath time ...') and in the letter to an unnamed friend of around 1633 into which the sonnet was inserted; the stress in both on the parable of the talents is characteristic.[40] *Comus* was written midway between *Il Penseroso*, with its sympathetic portrayal of an Anglican sensibility, and *Lycidas*, which in the words given to St Peter brings the voice of radical criticism into the Anglican piety of *Justa Edovardo King*. The earlier entries in the Commonplace Book, those which are with confidence dated between *Comus* and the Continental journey of 1638-9, anticipate the distrust of the clergy and even the republicanism of the following decade. For example, Milton quotes with approval the statement of Sulpicius Severus 'that the name of kings has always been hateful to free peoples', and notes the early Christian view that 'willing service' is due to a king, but worship accorded to God alone. He says of nobility: 'From the spirit of God it must be derived, not from forefathers or man-made laws' and 'whoever serves Him, he is truly noble'.[41]

There was much in the court masques of the period to make a man like the young Milton uneasy. Masques characteristically defuse threat by reducing it to farce, and victories are won *sine sanguine sine sudore*,[42] whereas from the first in Milton the Christian life is conflict and 'that immortall garland is to be run for, not without dust and heat. Assuredly we bring not innocence into the world, we bring impurity much rather: that which purifies us is triall, and triall is by what is contrary.'[43] In *Comus* itself, it is the 'happy trial' which will prove 'most glory' (592).

Even at their most elevated, masques fostered a cult of excess. As Mercury says in *Coelum Britannicum*: 'we advance / Such vertues onely as admit excesse'.[44] In theory, the lavishing of vast sums on transient entertainment was a measure of royal liberality and magnanimity. But the Stuarts tended to brush aside the qualification, going back to Aristotle, that liberality ought to correspond to means and that a poor man could not be magnificent.[45] The fear that entertainment was imprudently lavish, 'rather spoyle then largesse', was often expressed even at court.[46]

Moreover, the persistent idealisation, and even deification, of royal personages and policies led to accusations of flattery, and to a sense, again shared by some courtiers, of political unreality. It cannot have been easy for the most dedicated of courtiers to see James, with his filthy personal habits, as Pan or Phoebus or the eye of the world, especially when he was liable to blurt out: 'Why don't they dance? ... Devil take you all, dance.' The central modern apologia for the masque—that the idealising of the king and court brought home not what they were but what they ought to be—is not entirely persuasive.[47] It owes much to Bacon's Essay 'Of Praise', yet Bacon does not apply the argument to such 'toys' as masques and triumphs. Similarly, a passage from Jonson's epistle to Selden (*Underwood*, xiv) which is often cited as evidence ("twas with purpose to have made them such') is deeply ambiguous, even evasive, in context, since he also acknowledges that this same over-praising is a crime to be confessed. His stated principle elsewhere is that praise should be matched to intrinsic worth. That the gulf between asserted ideal and mortal reality could merely cause cynical amusement in masque spectators is clear from many comments, of which Harington's account of a drunken performance at Theobalds is the most devastating. It is not easy, then, to take the masque 'as a kind of mimetic magic on a sophisticated level' where an attempt is made 'to secure social health and tranquillity for the realm by miming it in front of its chief figure'.[48] However exalted the attitudes of some masquers and authors may have been, it is clear from the popular drama alone that masques could also be viewed as 'tied to rules of flattery' and as scenes of licentiousness.[49]

Despite the didacticism of so many texts, there is indeed a pervasive sensationalism about the masque, in the conspicuous consumption, the ostentation of dress, the insistence on novelty of devices, scenic effect and costume and the flirting with indecorum. Dudley Carleton found the ladies' clothing in Jonson's *Of Blackness* 'too light and Curtizan-like for such great ones', and was surprised at how much of Queen Anne's legs he could see in Daniel's *Vision of the Twelve Goddesses*.[50] Presumably the risqué prominence of nipples and bare breasts found throughout Inigo Jones's designs—including some for Queen Henrietta Maria—was continued in the costumes actually worn. It is hardly surprising that, from the first, Stuart masques aroused Puritan hostility, on which the poets took revenge in a series of jibes and caricatures.

Was Milton able to match the absolutism and idealisation of the form and occasion with his Puritan leanings? William Haller goes so far as to say that *Comus* is as authentic an expression of the Puritan spirit on the eve of the revolution as anything from the hand of Prynne, while John Carey argues that it is a 'caustic masque', which snipes at the aristocratic children and their complacent audience.[51] Both views are implausible, Haller's because it depends on hindsight, Carey's because it attributes petty-minded duplicity to Milton, stupidity to the Egertons, and either or both of these to Henry Lawes. Bridgewater and his family were of literary and artistic interests, and had shown discrimination in re-engaging the unknown son of a scrivener when they might have called on any fashionable court poet. Lawes's dedication of the 1637 text reveals that *Comus* was popular with them and that manuscript copies were in demand. Sniping which might just have got by in a single performance would have been revealed when the text was read. Also, as Milton must have been working to instructions in writing major roles for the young aristocrats, it is difficult to believe that the text for such an occasion was not vetted before performance.

Nevertheless, it is most unlikely that Milton was simply working to a detailed brief, especially as *Comus* is far removed from the routine form and flattery of the Chirk Castle entertainment, even though this came from a household of markedly Puritan traditions.[52] The extreme views of Haller and Carey are salutary, especially as some authoritative recent studies present *Comus* as 'a masque that must be placed centrally in the Jonsonian tradition'.[53] It is evident that Milton wanted his audience and readers to approach *Comus* as 'A Masque', since that was his title throughout. It was old-fashioned by the 1630s to have a generic and occasional title instead of one emphasising theme or fiction, such as *The Triumph of Peace* or *Tempe Restored*. No English poet has a keener sense of genre than Milton; most of his works are the consummation of a mode, a drawing together of its resources in order to exploit and even exhaust them. 'A Masque at Ludlow' is no exception.

The court masque is essentially an occasional form which integrates fiction and reality by imitating the current life of the specific community from which not only the audience but also the leading performers are drawn. At the revels, when the masquers 'take out' members of the audience, fact and fiction become one. Furthermore, the life of the audience is celebrated in terms of 'ideal abstractions and eternal verities'.[54] There is a direct relation between the audience and the celestial.

This is why, in Enid Welsford's phrase, the opposition of good and evil 'is shown as a contrast rather than as a conflict' (p. 339). Conflict implies drama and suspense, while eternal verities are beyond all threat. So when Townshend created *Tempe Restored* out of Baltazar de Beaujoyeulx's highly influential *Circe* or *Balet Comique de la Royne*, he stripped the sorceress of all the considerable power she had in his original.[55] There Circe (who in part symbolised the horrors of civil war) was able by magic to transform a group of nymphs, one of whom was played by the Queen, into statues and was able to take even Mercury captive. It required a formidable concourse of deities and virtues to achieve, gradually, her overthrow. In Townshend, as in other masques for the Stuart court, we see not the exercise of evil, but the undoing of the prior work of evil. Indeed, his Circe has power only over those who surrender themselves to her:

> Tis not her Rod, her Philters, nor her Herbes,
> (Though strong in Magicke) that can bound mens minds; ...
> It is consent that makes a perfect Slave.   (p. 85)

Jonson's rapid evolution of 'antic' masque into antimasque made the absolute contrast of good and evil into the form's main structural principle. It represents a conscious exorcism of conflict, and it is fundamental that when the real-life threat figured in the antimasque actually was potent, then that threat is dismissed abruptly and imperiously by the main masque. In *The Vision of Delight*, for example, where the challenge enacted is slight, the transformation to the main masque permits some interaction. But in *The Masque of Queens*, *The Golden Age Restored* and—pathetically—*Salmacida Spolia*, the powers of darkness or the menace of civil war 'on a sudden are surprised and stopped in their motion' (*Salmacida Spolia*, l. 6), and 'the whole face of the scene altered, scarce suffering the memory of such a thing' (*Queens*, ll. 336-7).

Milton takes his masque inheritance seriously. Moral qualities are embodied in the dancing; the interaction of audience and performer is beautifully developed in the central device of the journey to the masquing hall, in the series of compliments to Lawes, and in the demonstrations of excellence he grants the young aristocrats (even in sitting still on the enchanted chair, Lady Alice would be manifesting her presence of mind).

In other ways, however, he is more probing and innovatory. Several recent masques had begun with the descent of a divine figure. In Jonson's *Chloridia* (1631), in which Lady Penelope Egerton had danced, Zephyrus appears on a cloud and sings:

> It is decreed by all the gods
> The heav'n of earth shall have no odds, ...
> Their glories they shall mutual make, ...
> Their honors shall be even.   (ll. 38-43)

The 'warmth of yonder sun' (49)—Charles himself—means that this matching of heaven and earth is already under way. In *Coelum Britannicum*, in which the Egerton brothers had danced, Mercury descends to announce that 'the high Senate of the gods' is to reform itself on the lines of Charles and his court: 'Th'immortall bosomes burne with emulous fires, / Jove rivalls your great vertues, Royall Sir' (ll. 68–9). By comparison, the dualism of the opening of *Comus* is striking: the Attendant Spirit emphatically distinguishes 'the starry threshold of Jove's court' from 'the smoke and stir of this dim spot / Which men call earth', and he expresses disdain for 'the rank vapours of this sin-worn mould'. The 'palace of eternity' firmly distinguishes heaven from the vice-regal court of Ludlow.

Moreover, the idiom has a marked biblical colouring, through phrases such as the 'mansion' before Jove's court, the 'just hands on that golden key', 'the crown that virtue gives' and 'the enthroned gods on sainted seats'. In court masques, the idiom of praise is overwhelmingly classical and pagan. Even though they were often performed on religious festivals such as Epiphany, it would have been unthinkable for, say, the sacred elements of the Eucharist to appear as stage properties, as they do in Spanish Corpus Christi plays of the period. The altar and marriage ceremonies of *Hymenaei* are Roman, even though the Anglican settlement is implicit. It was tactful to make the deification of royalty oblique: James could be represented as, say, Pan, who, through a popular etymology, was familiar as a type of Christian godhead, but one could not fuse the uncouth James into that godhead without blasphemy and manifest absurdity. When, uncharacteristically, the love of Charles and Maria is likened to the Word of God, 'gently moving on the waters' (*Love's Triumph through Callipolis*, l. 137), bringing the world to light out of chaos, their domestic content did provide a link, but some would have been uncomfortably aware that 'Charles's royal word was not worth a farthing, and everyone knew it'.[56] The dualism and the Christian idiom of Milton's prologue re-orient the audience's or reader's perspective, adjusting it from the danger of self-glorification towards traditional values and moral realism.

His closing lines make a similar qualification:

> Mortals that would follow me,
> Love Virtue, she alone is free,
> She can teach ye how to climb
> Higher than the sphery chime;
> Or if Virtue feeble were,
> Heaven itself would stoop to her.

The explicit moral strenuousness here is probably anticipated in Stuart masques only by the ending of Jonson's then unpublished *Pleasure Reconciled to Virtue*, the exception proving the rule. Nothing could be less typical of the masque than the way Milton's Spirit, like Jonson's Daedalus, separates high rank from virtue. Virtue alone is free (used partly in the older sense of nobly born), as for Daedalus "Tis only [Virtue] can make you great, / Though place here make you known.'[57] Moreover, by addressing the assembly as 'mortals', the Spirit returns his distinguished audience and fellow performers to 'the smoke and stir of this dim spot'. While it is not rare for a masque to include a *memento mori*, this is invariably softened by death's being made remote, or by its becoming the merited entrance into heavenly life, or by expectations of a glorious dynasty to follow, or by affirmations of undying fame, or by flattering hopes that the king may live on for generations yet.[58] Milton's authoritative reminder of the imperfect and uncertain condition of humanity is virtually unprecedented. When Momus enters in *Coelum Britannicum* with 'By your leave, Mortalls' (l. 108), the term merely shows, as Mercury says, that he is impertinent and scurrilous.

In Milton, however, the term epitomises the masque. We have witnessed the freedom of virtue in the impregnability of the Lady's mind at Comus's palace. But we have also seen her trapped and have witnessed Heaven's stooping to her in the guise of the Spirit. By implication, then, we have also witnessed the 'feebleness' of her virtue. It has certainly not been feeble by everyday standards, but its strength has become relative rather than absolute. Milton's point is that she necessarily shares what Comus, with his characteristic misappropriation of orthodoxy, magnificently terms 'the unexempt condition / By which all mortal frailty must subsist' (685-6). She may not have shown moral frailty, but she cannot lack mortal frailty.

Within masque assumptions, the import is momentous. The good are no longer ideal, and the powers of darkness *are* powers. In other masques, innocent victims are always trapped before the action begins; on the night, only the sovereign power of virtue is exercised, and the victims are released. But Comus is seen deluding the Lady, and the release of his new victim is hard to achieve. His previous, corrupted victims remain untransformed, and he himself is a threat to the very end: 'Let us fly this cursed place, / Lest the sorcerer us entice / With some other new device' (939-41).

The action tests, and proves wanting, the masque-like expectations of the elder children, expectations which the title and occasion of the work also arouse. The Lady overcomes her fear of darkness and isolation by asserting that 'he, the Supreme Good ... Would send a glistering guardian if need were / To keep my life and honour *unassailed*' (217-20, my italics). The Elder Brother begins with some awareness that his sister may be in real danger, but is carried away into asserting a magical conception of chastity: 'She that has that, is clad in complete steel. ... No savage fierce, bandit, or mountaineer / Will *dare* to soil her virgin purity; / Yea there, where very desolation dwells ... She may pass on with unblenched majesty' (421–30, my italics). Meanwhile the audience is already aware that Comus is at work. The Elder Brother imagines that the response of evil to chastity is 'blank awe' (452), but this is undercut by Comus's pretence at line 301 that he was 'awe-struck' at the sight of the brothers. He knows the 'proper' response to virtue—indeed he can feel it—but he has the resilience of Antaeus and he returns to the offensive whether he has been deeply moved, as by the Lady's song, or deeply disturbed, as by her speech on virginity. The Elder Brother continues protesting too much even after the arrival of Thyrsis, since he asserts that he will retract nothing of his earlier affirmations (586), though he does now admit that 'Virtue may be assailed' (589).

There is, therefore, implicit criticism of some of the elder children's exalted conceptions of virtue. There is even explicit criticism of the brothers: 'What, have you let the false enchanter scape?/O ye mistook, ye should have snatched his wand/And bound him fast' (814–16). This must imply that they could have been more successful (and perhaps the criticism is necessary if the brothers are not to overshadow their elder and dramatically more important sister).

This does not mean, however, that Milton is mocking his clients' children, even supposing he would have been allowed to commit such gross discourtesy. He is tactfully exploiting the almost unprecedented fact that his central masquers are children. He can point to immaturity without insult, because in them it is only natural. His criticism of them is muted, as the speeches which are exposed to irony are reactions to states of anxiety. Those who find the children priggish,[59] are failing to respond to this fear, as well as to the keen sensibility and lovable moral idealism manifest in passages such as the Elder Brother on Diana, 'Fair silver-shafted queen for ever chaste' (441–5) or on the glory of trial (589–94), or the 'thousand fantasies' (205) or 'flame of sacred vehemence' (784–99) of the Lady. The audience's reaction is suggested by the response of the Spirit to the Elder Brother's most impressive speech: 'Alas good vent'rous youth,/I love thy courage yet, and bold emprise,/But here thy sword can do thee little stead' (609–11). One can still recover the feelings of mingled delight and tenderness which the children acting out their parts in Ludlow Castle must have aroused. Their speeches are at once uplifting and amusing; their fear is poignant, their idealistic eagerness is enchanting, and the unreality of some of their expectations arouses a saddened protectiveness as does Miranda's 'O, brave new world'.[60] They have, after all, only been 'nursed' (34) in princely lore; the plot itself represents their initiation into the labyrinth of the spiritual life, and more subtle tests lie ahead. What they have to assimilate is the central Christian paradox that while it is possible to resist any single temptation, it is impossible to resist all temptation. In the words of I Corinthians x.13: 'God is faithful, who will not suffer you to be tempted above that ye are able'; nevertheless, 'All we like sheep have gone astray', and 'all our righteousnesses are as filthy rags' (Isaiah liii,6 and lxiv.6).

When the Lady, after her encounter with the feigned shepherd, prays that providence may 'square my trial/To my proportioned strength' (329-30), she is moving beyond the unreal assumption that she will be unassailed towards the truth expressed in Corinthians. When the Elder Brother, after meeting the Spirit, asserts that the 'happy trial' shall prove 'most glory' (592), he echoes the Geneva gloss on Corinthians: 'Hee that led you into this tentation . . . will turne it to your commodity, and deliver you'. Both retain some of their naive assertiveness, but they are beginning to leave behind the fundamental assumption of the court masque: the invulnerability and self-sufficiency of virtue.

In this way, *Comus* hovers between the opposed modes of masque and drama, qualifying idealised 'princely lore' with the 'unexempt condition' of mortal frailty. Formally, this is reflected also in the lack of a decisive 'hinge'. There is instead a series of thwarted, imperfect or ironic pivotal moments. The Lady's approach scatters and silences the antimasquers, but only so that she can be waylaid; the stage actually becomes darker. When the scene does change from the wild wood to the brilliant and stately palace, the palace is the tempter's. In the printed text, the Lady brings a masque transformation to mind when she says she might shatter the tempter's magic structures into heaps over his head, but although her words daunt him for a while, the palace remains standing. When the brothers rush in, the antimasquers are driven away, yet the Lady is still trapped in the chair. When, thanks to Sabrina, she is able to rise, there is still no scene-change; the palace of evil has to be escaped, and is not destroyed. When at last the young masquers are presented to the audience and fact and fiction unite, this does not coincide with the final, triumphant scene-change. The visual impact of the panorama of Ludlow has gone to reinforce the benign antimasque of country-dancers. Ruler and ruled have come together, related by indebtedness to Sabrina, the spirit of the place.

It is important that the Earl is in no way called upon to release the Lady from the chair. In other courtly masques and entertainments, the mere presence of royalty or nobility undoes the enchantments of evil: 'It is but standing in his eye/You'll feel yourselves changed by and by' (*The Irish Masque at Court*, ll. 161-2). In *Comus*, however, release is effected by Sabrina, whose part cannot have been taken by an aristocrat, since her name is not recorded on the title-page. The suggestion that she was played by Lady Penelope Egerton fails to do justice to Milton's originality: here decisive power is no longer wielded by social eminence, and a commoner brings about what would normally have been the prerogative of the king's representative.[61] One might compare Jonson's *Love Freed from Ignorance and Folly*, since this masque is uncharacteristic in the degree of power

John Creaser

given to the vices. Before the action begins they have captured not only Love but the Daughters of the Morn, who were played by Queen Anne and her ladies, and within the action Love is in fact on the point of death. But a glance at 'the brightest face here shining' (l. 237), at the king's, is enough to save him.

The climax of Milton's action disturbs masque assumptions in another way. When the Lady says that courtesy 'oft is sooner found in lowly sheds ... than in tap'stry halls / And courts of princes' (324–5), it would seem little more than an indirect compliment to the audience, since Comus takes her to a mere perversion of their courtliness. But she defends the 'holy dictate of spare Temperance' in terms which move remarkably beyond the exclusive world of masquing:

> If every just man that now pines with want
> Had but a moderate and beseeming share
> Of that which lewdly-pampered Luxury
> Now heaps upon some few with vast excess,
> Nature's full blessings would be well-dispensed
> In unsuperfluous even proportion.   (768–73)

In 1634 this must even have been the climactic argument against Comus, since the following passage on 'the sage and serious doctrine of Virginity' does not occur until the 1637 edition. Its egalitarianism belongs with the early Church of Acts (ii.44 and iv.32), with More's *Utopia*, with certain speeches of moral agony in *King Lear* (III.iv and IV.i), and even with some of the persecuted Anabaptists, rather than with the strictly hierarchical world of the masque, where degree determines one's place on the 'degrees'.[62] Milton's democratic sentiments are expressed tactfully—not all the poor are 'just' and the possibility is left floating that not all the rich are luxurious—but again he reminds his audience of their common humanity. Here Milton's voice of traditional moral authority is also radical enough to anticipate the 1640s.[63] Little could be further from the conventional homage of the Chirk Castle entertainment.

Milton may seem to pay such homage when at line 18 the Spirit begins to describe his task, yet even here he pays a handsome and patriotic compliment to the 'noble peer of mickle trust and power' without deviating into routine flattery. The concept of Britain as an empire, ruler of the seas, and a world of itself, *divisus ab orbe*, was important to her Reformation rulers. Consequently, masques often celebrate James or Charles as 'lord of the four seas, / King of the less and greater isles' (*The Vision of Delight*, ll. 199–200), or as 'King of the ocean and the happy isles' (*The Masque of Augurs*, l. 276). James is identified with the god of the sea in *Neptune's Triumph* and *The Fortunate Isles*. Mercury characteristically opens *Coelum Britannicum* with an address to Charles and Maria 'Before whose Throne three warlike Nations bend / Their willing knees, on whose

Imperiall browes / The Regall Circle prints no awfull frownes / To fright your Subjects' (ll. 49–52).

In *Comus*, Neptune has 'imperial rule of all the sea-girt isles' and is given stature equivalent to both 'high and nether Jove', his brothers; Britain is specifically isolated as just one isle (l. 27) and assigned to Neptune's 'blue-haired deities'. The Variorum editors find a magnificent compliment to Charles here, identifying him with Neptune and setting him above two orders of lesser rulers, the 'blue-haired deities' and the 'tributary gods', implying that 'other maritime rulers acknowledge his supremacy and reign by his sufferance'.[64] But if we identify Charles with Neptune, then he is imagined to be ruler of *all* islands, not just the British Isles, the Fortunate Isles. This goes far beyond the concept of Britain as an *imperium*, which was 'essentially limited to the micro-empire of the islands of Britain', as *divisus ab orbe* implies.[65] It seems that the 'noble peer' is also to be identified with one of the Tritons, the 'blue-haired deities', as he takes power directly from Charles. This again is implausible, firstly because it implies that the Lord President is to be set above rulers of foreign powers, since the Tritons rank higher than the 'tributary gods'; secondly because the Lord Presidency was not a maritime post; and thirdly because the lack of modulation between 'blue-haired deities' and 'a noble peer' leaves them emphatically in different orders of being. One might more plausibly place Charles below Neptune and absorb him, with other British monarchs, into the Tritons. These attendant deities are minor figures in masquing terms,[66] and here are merely the more eminent of the 'tributary gods', who have been given leave, in a slightly deflating phrase, 'to wield their little tridents'.

The passage evokes yet eludes the idiom of royalist deification. Characteristically, Milton maintains a decent independence and reserve, complimenting but not flattering. This is anticipated even in his much slighter and more straightforward work for the family, *Arcades*. There the Genius of the Wood, the artist figure, celebrates the music of the spheres, which he can hear, but

> which none can hear
> Of human mould with gross unpurgèd ear;
> And yet such music worthiest were to blaze
> The peerless height of her immortal praise,
> Whose lustre leads us, and for her most fit,
> If my inferior hand or voice could hit
> Inimitable sounds, yet as we go,
> Whate'er the skill of lesser gods can show,
> I will assay. (72–80)

In Marston's entertainment for the same Countess of Derby years earlier, the audience did hear what was said to be the music of the spheres.[67] *Tempe Restored* paid its audience the same high compliment, as *Salma-*

cida Spolia was to do. But Milton implies the common humanity of his hearers even after celebrating the Countess in conventional terms as 'a goddess bright', though their ears are, of course, 'gross' and 'unpurged' only in the sense that the Lady's virtue is 'feeble'. They share fallen man's 'unexempt condition'.

Departing from courtly norms towards moral orthodoxy, Milton inserts human limitation into *Arcades* and *Comus*. But he does this tactfully, without insulting the children before the assembly, or their father or the Countess on their seats of state. The absence of the masque's extreme idealisation means that Milton is no longer 'tied to rules of flattery', and the unconventionality of his work makes the praise it does contain all the more discriminating. The children, for example, are portrayed *becoming* masquers. This is why they do not rejoice together at the release of the Lady. Having earned the role, they lapse into the distinguished silence of masquers, and their function is to dance in triumph before their parents and the assembly in a culminating manifestation of aristocratic presence.

This rapprochement with masque norms in the closing section remains heavily qualified in ways I have been suggesting. Nevertheless, *Comus* is not, as John Carey says (p. 50), 'a masque against masquing'. It is an emergent Puritan's recuperation or, as David Norbrook says elsewhere in this volume, reformation, of the masque.[68]

NOTES

This is a revised and expanded version of part of a lecture from a series of lectures and a conference on drama in society at the Shakespeare Institute, Birmingham and Stratford, 1981.

1 John G. Demaray, 'The Thrones of Satan and God', *HLQ*, 31 (1967), p. 27. Demaray's limiting judgement is significant, because in *Milton and the Masque Tradition* (Cambridge, Mass., 1968) he makes a higher claim for *Comus* as an event than any other critic to date.
2 William Riley Parker, *Milton: A Biography*, 2 vols, (Oxford, 1968), I, pp. 142, 132, 129, respectively.
3 Introduction to *A Maske at Ludlow: Essays on Milton's Comus*, ed. John S. Diekhoff (Cleveland, Ohio, 1968), p. 3.
4 For the intricacy of children's dancing, see John Finet quoted by Enid Welsford, *The Court Masque* (Cambridge, 1927), p. 189.
5 David Masson, *The Life of John Milton*, revised edition, 6 vols (London, 1881), I, p. 590.
6 The text is printed by Cedric C. Brown in 'The Chirk Castle Entertainment of 1634', *Milton Quarterly*, 11 (1977), pp. 76–86.
7 Allardyce Nicoll, *Stuart Masques and the Renaissance Stage* (London, 1937), p. 213.
8 Nicoll, pp. 33–4.
9 For example, *Hymenaei*, l. 227 in *Ben Jonson: The Complete Masques*, ed.

Stephen Orgel (New Haven, Conn., 1969). All quotations from Jonson's masques are taken from this edition.

10 Nicoll, pp. 104 and 44.

11 Nicoll, pp. 91-2, 97 and 112.

12 E. K. Chambers, ed., *Aurelian Townshend's Poems and Masks* (Oxford, 1912), p. 72.

13 Lines 1084-6 in Rhodes Dunlap, ed., *The Poems of Thomas Carew* (Oxford, 1957), p. 183.

14 Orgel and Strong, 1, pp. 69-70.

15 The Ludlow Bailiffs' Accounts for 1633-4 in the Shropshire Record Office contain these two adjacent entries:

Itt*em* for a sugerloafe to Ed: Berry beinge one of those was presented to the Countesse _ _ _ _ _ _ _ _ _ _ _ _ _	00-16-7
Itt*em* to some of the officers when wee were invited to the maske _ _ _ _ _ _ _ _ _ _ _ _ _ _ _ _ _ _	00-2-6

These annual accounts run from Simon and Jude (28 October) and the appearance of these entries late in 1633-4 places them at exactly the right time for *Comus*. The first entry refers to a civic presentation, since gifts of sugar were often made to visiting dignitaries and local magnates, who would most certainly include the Countess of Bridgewater. Together they suggest that *Comus* took place during a period when the town and the castle were ceremonially greeting one another (presumably because of the arrival of the Earl's family that summer), and they also indicate that *Comus* was a civic as well as a family occasion. These entries were kindly drawn to my attention by Professor J. A. B. Somerset, who is editing the Shropshire dramatic records for the series *Records of Early English Drama*.

16 Bernard Falk, *The Bridgewater Millions* (London, 1942), p. 55, and Charles L. Hamilton, 'The Bridgewater Debts', *HLQ*, 42 (1979), pp. 217-29.

17 I owe this information to Cedric C. Brown whose forthcoming book, *John Milton's Aristocratic Entertainments*, adds enormously to our knowledge of the Earl of Bridgewater in this period.

18 The Lady Alix Egerton, *Milton's Comus: Being the Bridgewater Manuscript with Notes and a Short Family Memoir* (London, 1910), p. 29.

19 Brown, 'The Chirk Castle Entertainment', p. 78, is tentative about the time of year of the performance, but the climatic change which so amazes the speaker of the opening lines makes no sense unless he is speaking during the dog-days. Early or mid August seems the most likely time.

20 *The Book of Days*, 2 vols (London, 1862-4), 2, p. 389. On the significance of the date, see James G. Taaffe, 'Michaelmas, the "Lawless Hour", and the Occasion of Milton's *Comus*', *ELN*, 6 (1969), pp. 257-62, and William B. Hunter, Jr, 'The Liturgical Context of *Comus*', *ELN*, 10 (1972), pp. 11-15. M. S. Berkowitz, 'An Earl's Michaelmas in Wales', *Milton Quarterly*, 13 (1979), pp. 122-5 adds a little to Taaffe. On the relationship between drama and religious festivals, see R. Chris Hassel, Jr, *Renaissance Drama and the English Church Year* (Lincoln, Neb., and London, 1979).

21 My discussion of the Council in the Marches is heavily indebted to the studies of Penry Williams, notably *The Council in the Marches of Wales Under Elizabeth I* (Cardiff, 1958); 'Government and Politics in Ludlow, 1590-1642', *Transactions of the Shropshire Archaeological Society*, 56 (1957-60), pp. 282-94; 'The Activity of the Council in the Marches under the

Early Stuarts', *Welsh History Review*, 1 (1961), pp. 133–60; 'The Attack on the Council in the Marches, 1603–42', *Transactions of the Honourable Society of Cymmrodorion* (1961) part 1, pp. 1–22; and incidental details in *The Tudor Regime* (Oxford, 1979). I have also consulted Caroline A. J. Skeel, *The Council in the Marches of Wales* (Cambridge, 1904), and 'The Council in the Marches in the Seventeenth Century', *EHR*, 30 (1915), pp. 19–27.

22 'Attack on the Council', p. 17. For an evaluation of such charges, see 'The Activity of the Council'. On Sir Thomas Myddelton and Rowland Heylyn, prominent London citizens of Welsh background who used their wealth to further the spread of Puritanism into Wales, see n. 52 below and Christopher Hill, 'Puritans and "the Dark Corners of the Land" ', *Change and Continuity in Seventeenth-Century England* (London, 1974), ch. 1.

23 Charles L. Hamilton, 'The Shropshire Muster-Master's Fee', *Albion*, 2 (1970), pp. 26–34. Bridgewater's difficulties are seen in a broader context in Robert Ashton, *The English Civil War: Conservatism and Revolution 1603–1649* (London, 1978), pp. 55 ff.

24 *Studies in Stuart Wales*, second edition (Cardiff, 1971), p. 59.

25 *Studies in Stuart Wales*, p. 61.

26 For example, Parker, *Biography*, 2, p. 792; Christopher Hill, *Milton and The English Revolution* (London, 1977), p. 43; Alice-Lyle Scoufos, 'The Mysteries in Milton's *Masque*', *Milton Studies*, 6 (1974), pp. 113–42, especially 135; John D. Cox, 'Poetry and History in Milton's Country Masque', *E L H*, 44 (1977), pp. 622–40, especially 629; P. W. Thomas, 'Two Cultures? Court and Country under Charles I', in Conrad Russell, ed., *The Origins of the English Civil War* (London, 1973), p. 188.

27 Alix Egerton, *Milton's Comus*, p. 12.

28 *Puritanism and Theatre: Thomas Middleton and Opposition Drama under the Early Stuarts* (Cambridge, 1980), pp. 30, 261, 279.

29 Orgel and Strong, 2, p. 479.

30 Orgel and Strong, 1, p. 25; Kenneth Richards, 'Queen Henrietta Maria as a Patron of the Drama', *SN*, 42 (1970), pp. 9–24.

31 'The Earl of Bridgewater and the English Civil War', *Canadian Journal of History*, 15 (1980), p. 366. My account of Bridgewater's career is indebted to Hamilton. On his prevarication, see Alfred Kingston, *Hertfordshire during the Great Civil War* (London, 1894), pp. 45 and 160–1.

32 The argument of Cox, 'Poetry and History' (see note 26), that by moving to Ludlow Bridgewater joined the 'Country' opposition to Charles, is a bizarre misreading of the situation.

33 Masson, 1, pp. 207–13.

34 P. W. Thomas ('Two Cultures') similarly juxtaposes Carew and Prynne, pp. 179 ff.

35 *Histrio-Mastix*, preliminary address 'To the Christian Reader': 'Shackspeers Plaies are printed in the best Crowne paper, far better than most Bibles'.

36 Don M. Wolfe *et al.*, eds., *Complete Prose Works of John Milton* 8 vols (New Haven, Con., 1953–83), 1, p. 815.

37 *Complete Prose Works*, 3, p. 342 and 7, p. 425; *Paradise Lost*, iv, 768; 'To Mr Cyriack Skinner Upon his Blindness', l. 13.

38 H. R. Trevor-Roper, *Archbishop Laud, 1573–1645*, second edition (London, 1962), p. 104.

39 *Complete Prose Works*, I, p. 267.

40 *Complete Prose Works*, I, pp. 318–21.

41 *Complete Prose Works*, I, pp. 440, 437, 471–2, respectively. On the Commonplace Book's anticipation of Milton's later attitudes, see James Holly Hanford, 'The Chronology of Milton's Private Studies', *PMLA*, 36 (1921), pp. 251–314, especially 293–4.

42 'Without blood, without sweat' (quoted from *Salmacida Spolia*, l. 60, in *A Book of Masques in Honour of Allardyce Nicoll*, ed T. J. B. Spencer and Stanley Wells (Cambridge, 1970), p. 348).

43 *Complete Prose Works*, 2, p. 515.

44 Lines 659–60. Jennifer Chibnall quotes more of the passage on p. 92.

45 *Nicomachean Ethics* IV.ii. See also Roy Strong, *Splendour at Court: Renaissance Spectacle and Illusion* (London, 1973), p. 72.

46 N. E. McClure, ed., *The Letters of John Chamberlain*, 2 vols (Philadelphia, 1939), 2, p. 127.

47 Ernest William Talbert, 'The Interpretation of Jonson's Courtly Spectacles', *PMLA*, 61 (1946), pp. 454–73. For reservations about this and other recent defences of the masque, see Philip Edwards, *Threshold of a Nation* (London, 1979), pp. 131–73. More recently still, Leah Sinanoglou Marcus has been developing a powerful case for the tolerated expression of limited criticism within the Jacobean masque: ' "Present Occasions" and the Shaping of Ben Jonson's Masques', *ELH*, 45 (1978), pp. 201–25; 'The Occasion of Ben Jonson's *Pleasure Reconciled to Virtue*', *SEL*, 19 (1979), pp. 271–93; 'Masquing Occasions and Masque Structure', *RORD*, 24 (1981), pp. 7–16.

48 Jonas A. Barish, *Ben Jonson and the Language of Prose Comedy* (Cambridge, Mass., 1967), p. 244, in a passage which, through Orgel, has deeply influenced recent views of the masque.

49 See Strato in the opening lines of *The Maid's Tragedy*, and Inga-Stina Ewbank, *A Book of Masques*, p. 424.

50 Herford and Simpson, 10, p. 448; E. K. Chambers, *The Elizabethan Stage*, 4 vols (Oxford, 1923), 3, p. 280.

51 William Haller, *The Rise of Puritanism* (1938, reprinted Philadelphia, 1972), p. 317; John Carey, *Milton* (London, 1969), p. 41.

52 Chirk Castle and its Denbighshire estate had been bought by the financier Sir Thomas Myddelton (or Middleton) (1550–1631), Lord Mayor of London, 1613–14, an ardent Puritan propagandist in his native Wales. In 1630, he and Rowland Heylyn financed the first Welsh translation of the Bible to be available cheaply. In 1634, Chirk Castle had long been the home of his son, the second Sir Thomas (1586–1666), deputy lieutenant of Denbighshire, a member of the Council in the Marches, and perhaps the largest landowner in north Wales. He was to become the centre of opposition to Charles in North Wales, to work in 1641 for the downfall of the Council, and to become a Parliamentarian general. He seems, however, to have been less zealously Puritan than his father, and in the 1650s he was to work for the restoration of the monarchy. See Heinemann, *Puritanism and Theatre;* Dodd, *Studies in Stuart Wales*, and 'Mr Myddelton the Merchant of Tower Street', in S. T. Bindoff *et al.*, eds., *Elizabethan Government and Society* (London, 1961), pp. 249–81; Anon., *A Memoir of Chirk Castle* (Chester, 1859); and Gwyn R. Thomas, *Sir Thomas Myddelton II, 1586–1666* (unpublished University of Wales M.A. thesis, 1967). The tone of the Chirk text is suggested by G. E.

John Creaser

Bentley's comment: 'Certainly the words of the entertainment assume a royal audience' (*The Jacobean and Caroline Stage*, 7 vols (Oxford, 1941–68), 5, p. 1305).

53 Demaray, p. 96. See also his pp. 2–3; Stephen Orgel, *The Jonsonian Masque* (Cambridge, Mass., 1965), p. 102; Rosemund Tuve, *Images and Themes in Five Poems by Milton* (Cambridge, Mass., 1957), pp. 112–61. The contrary view that *Comus* is antipathetic to the masque is most influentially stated in Enid Welsford, *The Court Masque*, pp. 316 ff.

54 Orgel, *Jonsonian Masque*, p. 73.

55 There is an account of the performance of this work in 1581 in Demaray, pp. 13 ff., and a translation by Carol and Lander MacClintock (American Institute of Musicology, 1971).

56 J. P. Kenyon, *The Stuarts: A Study in English Kingship* (London, 1958, reprinted 1970), p. 68.

57 See Marcus, 'The Occasion of *Pleasure Reconciled to Virtue*' for the circumstances which made such a reminder from Jonson politic.

58 *The King's Entertainment at Welbeck*, ll. 334–41 (Herford and Simpson, 7, pp. 802–3) is representative of the *memento mori* turned to flattery. See David Norbrook's essay, p. 103, for a tellingly unrepresentative masque conclusion. This was addressed to the Earl of Essex, an 'opposition' peer who scorned the court, and the masque, written for a private occasion, remained unpublished. The conclusion is, moreover, a compliment to him on his humanity rather than a warning of his mortality.

59 For example, Carey, *Milton*, p. 51; Roy Daniells, *Milton, Mannerism and Baroque* (Toronto, 1963), p. 28; Gale H. Carrithers, Jr, in *Critical Essays on Milton from ELH* (1969), pp. 109–10 (from volume 33, 1966); J. B. Broadbent in Julian Lovelock, ed., *Milton: Comus and Samson Agonistes* (Casebook series, London, 1975), pp. 71–5.

60 See C. L. Barber, 'The Masque as a Masque', reprinted in Lovelock's Casebook, p. 96, for a similar response.

61 The suggestion is made by Marjorie Hope Nicolson, *A Reader's Guide to John Milton* (London, 1964), p. 69, and by Demaray, pp. 77 and 101.

62 Saad El-Gabalawy, 'Christian Communism in *Utopia, King Lear*, and *Comus*', *UTQ*, 47 (1978), pp. 228–38.

63 For example in *Of Reformation Touching Church Discipline* (1641), Milton applies a similar argument to inequality within the Church (*Complete Prose Works*, 1, p. 590).

64 A. S. P. Woodhouse and Douglas Bush, eds., *The Minor English Poems* (London, 1972), p. 861, (vol. II.iii of *A Variorum Commentary on the Poems of John Milton*, general editor Merritt Y. Hughes).

65 Graham Parry, *The Golden Age Restor'd* (Manchester, 1981), p. 260.

66 Compare Jonson, *Of Blackness*, ll. 24–9, and Daniel, *Tethys' Festival*.

67 Arnold Davenport, ed., *The Poems of John Marston* (Liverpool, 1961), p. 200.

68 Since Barbara Breasted, '*Comus* and the Castlehaven Scandal', *Milton Studies*, 3 (1971), pp. 201–24, much has been made of the alleged influence of this scandalous episode on the theme and text of *Comus*. I have omitted discussion of this influence here, since I believe it to be negligible; see my article 'Milton's *Comus*: The Irrelevance of the Castlehaven Scandal', forthcoming in *Notes and Queries*.

HELEN COOPER

Location and meaning in masque, morality and royal entertainment

✺⊃∘⊂✺

ONE OF THE GREATEST differences between drama and royal entertainment or masque lies in the interpretation given to the acting area and its relationship to the audience. A Shakespearean play begins when the first characters walk on to the stage: 'I thought the King had more affected the Duke of Albany than Cornwall.' There are no visual indications of where the scene is supposed to take place.[1] The opening speeches of each scene, or the action itself, give us all the information we need: from the first line of *King Lear* we learn that we are at a royal court, in England but otherwise unlocalised. Stage locality has no significance independent of the characters and the action. If the figures on the stage do not need to have their location specified, it will remain uncertain, as happens throughout most of *King Lear*. Locality in the Elizabethan theatre is fluid; Shakespeare and his contemporaries rarely specify particular settings, and modern editorial practice has belatedly caught up with them.

One thing is, however, consistently important: the stage represents somewhere different from the spectators. It stands for Elsinore or Venice or ancient Rome; or if it stands for London, as happens in the city comedies, it stands for the London whose literal reality the audience has left behind on entering the theatre. There is an imaginative divide between audience and playing area; and the presence of spectators on stage, or the use of a chorus or a prologue whose function is to link the two worlds, only serves to sharpen the distinction. A chorus will redefine the empty stage as somewhere else, whether 'In Troy there lies the scene' or 'Our scene is London'; or he will stress the inadequacy of 'this wooden O' to represent 'the vasty fields of France'. A play such as *The Knight of the Burning Pestle*, in which actors playing members of the audience not only comment on the action but intervene in it and alter it, is not an exception to this division between the worlds of the play and the theatre itself so much as a highly sophisticated exploitation of it, for Beaumont is focusing attention on precisely how curious it is that one should normally give imaginative credence to the autonomy of the staged action.

The Stuart masque starts from a very different set of assumptions. There, the acting area functions as a particular place, landscape or seascape or even skyscape, and the elaborate scenery is set up before ever the audience, or the characters, enter. The start of the masque is marked not by the appearance of the actors on stage but by the arrival of the chief spectator, the King. Thomas Campion's account of *The Lord Hay's Masque*[2] opens with the declaration that 'the first, and most necessary part is the discription of the place'. He describes the seating arrangements, the placing of the musicians, and the scenery itself (probably designed by Inigo Jones). There was a 'double vale' with a green valley in the middle, and 'nine golden trees of fifteene foote high'. Hidden by the vale were two hills, one representing the bower of Flora, decorated with 'all kinds of flowers, and flowrie branches with lights in them', the other representing the house of Night, on the turrets of which 'were plac't on wyer artificial Battes and Owles, continually moving'. After some pages of initial description, Campion reaches the point where things actually begin to happen:

> As soone as the King was entred the great Hall, the Hoboyes (out of the wood on the top of the hil) entertained the time till his Majestie and his trayne were placed, and then after a little expectation the consort of ten began to play an Ayre, at the sound whereof the vale on the right hand was withdrawne, and the ascent of the hill with the bower of Flora were discovered, where *Flora* and *Zepherus* were busily plucking flowers from the Bower, and throwing them into two baskets, which two *Silvans* held, who were attired in changeable Taffatie, with wreathes of flowers on their heads.[3]

'In this manner,' as Campion says at the start of another of his masques, 'was the eye first of all entertayned.'[4] Spectacle takes precedence over dramatic action, or it can in itself constitute the action.[5] The first action in this masque is the entry of the King; and that is the signal for music and for a change of spectacle before anything at all has happened in terms of drama.

There is a basic paradox in this contrast of masque and play settings. In the theatre, there is little or nothing apart from the raised stage itself to distinguish acting area from audience, but the stage locality represents something unequivocally different from the audience locality. In the masque, enormous effort goes into transforming one end of the hall into somewhere as different as possible. The literal indoor setting is disguised as landscape, and cut off from the rest of the hall by a proscenium arch; and yet it is crucial to the masque that there should be no sharp imaginative division between the audience and the acting area. The masquers come down to dance with members of the audience, and they can do so partly because they belong to the same social world as the spectators. If a masque text gives a list of *dramatis personae*, it is a list of the people who take part in the piece: Campion lists nine for *The Lord Hay's Masque*, starting with two sons of the Earl of Suffolk and working down in social order through the other participants. A list of the characters in the masque, if it is given at all, almost always comes in second place.

Illusionist settings were first developed not for stage plays but for the masque; but the action of a masque is not literal or naturalistic, as such detailed settings and use of perspective would suggest, but allegorical or mythical. Moreover, while the action of drama is confined to the unlocal-ized stage, the action of a masque moves outwards from its setting to focus on the chief spectator: 'through the use of perspective the monarch, always the ethical centre of court productions, became in a physical and emblematic way the centre as well'.[6] It was not only the crush of spectators that meant that the King alone was able to see the masque properly: the perspective was correct only when viewed from his seat. The action emanates from the chair of state—it begins when the King takes his place, and describes the conditions brought about by his presence; and it is also presented to him, in terms of dramatic focus and as a kind of homage.

Despite the illusionist scenery, then, the masque is designed to break down the division between the fictive world of the action and the real world of the audience. The playing area is symbolically as well as physi-cally continuous with the floor of the hall where the King sits. Such a definition of the acting space aligns the masque much more closely with older dramatic forms, especially the morality play, than with contem-porary drama. The affiliation between dramatic allegory in morality and masque has long been recognised; but the allegorical nature of the action also has repercussions on the relationship between action and audience, stage and 'auditorium'.

Few of the morality plays were staged with any degree of elaboration, and the lack of scenery and properties—of anything that would mark out the stage as representing 'somewhere else'—functioned to emphasise the literal and symbolic integration of playing-space and audience. The acting area in a morality most commonly stands for middle-earth, between Heaven and Hell: the underlying principle is not that 'all the world's a stage', but that the stage is all the world. The human race is represented not only by the characters—especially the central character, Mankind or Everyman—but by the audience as well. The spectators literally inhabit the same world that the playing space represents in epitome; the two are not only physically continuous but allegorically co-extensive. The inter-play between actors and spectators therefore becomes much more than a theatrical device: it serves to underline the unity of the two worlds. In *Mankind*, Mercy addresses mankind as represented by the audience and Mankind as represented on stage in a way designed to obliterate the distinction between the fictional world and the real, and the figure of mankind answers for both.[7] Vices and devils and tempters of various sorts customarily run about among the audience for similar reasons. The morality play is a means of giving a local habitation to moral or spiritual abstractions. The habitation is the playing area, and its extension into the audience is a reminder of the real existence of the abstract qualities concerned: Mercy, or the devil, corresponds to something real in the spiritual world, and allegorical drama allows their physical realisation.

Spectacle may not be present in moralities as it is in the masque, but the visual effect of the plays is none the less very important in giving visible substance to the conflicting forces of good and evil. In this respect at least, masques are the direct descendants of the morality, and their nature as spectacle a logical extension of their allegorical or symbolic function. The setting of masques is, however, generally something rather more specific than middle-earth. To dramatise the world precludes any need for the paraphernalia of scenery: the earth is there, and the people are there, and to add anything further would be counter-productive. The playing-space is in a sense a literal representation of middle-earth—an epitome, but not an allegory. The few moralities that require more elaborate stage settings, such as the *Castle of Perseverance*, are generally more fully allegorical, and so the symbolic identity of the playing-space with the audience area is broken. The *Castle* is located not on middle-earth but in the soul of man, set between the world, the flesh, and the devil, who are arranged on scaffolds around the main acting area.[8] In so far as the action is still co-extensive with the audience, it extends from their souls rather than their bodies, so the sense of physical continuity is lost. The stage now represents an abstraction, and so requires a greater elaboration of visual form to make its point. The more allegorical the action, the greater the need for its interpretation in concrete shape. Many masques contain very precise allegories, and the spectacle becomes correspondingly elaborate.

Other forms of early drama exploit the fluidity of meaning of the acting area to an even greater degree. In the cycle plays (which died out only in the second half of the sixteenth century, and so overlapped with the rise of the masque), the stage stands primarily for middle-earth, occasionally with a Hell or Heaven to prove the point; and its function as epitome of the secular world means that it can also stand for both ancient Israel and contemporary England. In the Towneley *Second Shepherds' Play*, for instance, the acting area represents the fields outside Bethlehem, and also medieval Yorkshire, as the shepherds search familiar named localities for their lost sheep.[9] It can encompass not only the fields but Mak's house and the stable, and the action moves freely from one to the other without any necessity for a cleared stage.[10] The scene at Mak's house, and the antics of the vice figures in the moralities, carry something of the same structural and thematic function as the anti-masque; and the change of locality to the stable, or to Heaven at the end of the *Castle of Perseverance*, corresponds to the masque movement from disorder to order.

The masque stage attempts to keep something of the same fluidity through scene changes; and these too are as likely to represent a change of allegorical function as a shift of location. The impulse towards the final harmony is represented in this way, and the crucial metamorphosis is often contained in a change of scene.[11] On occasion, the final scene change will be used to emphasise the topical significance of the allegory. Campion's *Somerset Masque*[12] consists largely of a semi-allegorical narrative about knights transformed to pillars while on their way to celebrate Somerset's marriage; there is a disordered dance, of the antimasque variety, in which Error, Rumour, Curiosity, Credulity, and the four winds, elements, and continents take part; and then there is a 'sudden' scene change and 'London with the Thames is very artificially presented' in place of the sea-coast that has constituted the previous setting. It is at this point that the action of the masque comes together with the event it celebrates, as the knights are released to pay homage to the King and to the bride and groom. The gulf between action and audience is bridged in terms of narrative; it is physically abolished, as the masquers dance with the ladies; and the scene now represents the same place where the masque itself is literally happening. The same thing occurs at the end of *Comus*, when 'the scene changes, presenting Ludlow Town and the President's Castle',[13] and the Lady and her brothers are presented to their parents. Racan's *Artemice*, the first masque of Charles I's reign, and Townshend's *Albion's Triumph* use the same device at the end to bring together the allegorical and the literal,[14] and to dissolve the stage illusion into the real world.

The extension of the action in masque to involve the audience in more than just dancing, its moving out from the playing area to the chief spectator, owes much to the development of royal pageants and entertainments in Elizabeth's reign. These most typically took place outdoors, as street shows or later as more elaborate entertainments to welcome her on her progresses. The earliest shows in her honour were simply street pageants of the traditional kind, such as greeted her on her first entry into London or contributed to her coronation procession. These normally consisted of an emblematic tableau with either written verses or a presenter, or both, to explain the meaning, which was usually designed to urge some act of policy. They had an encomiastic function too, of course, but the impulse behind them belongs as much or more to mirror-for-princes literature as to government propaganda or simple eulogy. The monarch was normally a passive, though it was hoped also a receptive, spectator at such shows; but Elizabeth varied the pattern by insisting on playing a more active role. When the city of Worcester, which had supported the Yorkist cause, welcomed Henry VII in 1486, it had in readiness a show in which a figure representing Henry VI eulogised the princeliness and general desirability of mercy.[15] London arranged a pageant for Elizabeth's coronation procession which showed two hills, one barren, representing 'a decayed Commonweal', the other green, representing 'a florishyng

Commonweal', and in which Time led forth his daughter Truth carrying an English Bible. Such a show contains a broad policy hint—Protestantism, economic recovery, and good government all go together—but Elizabeth was not content to be advised or preached at. She not only accepted the Bible offered to her but 'kissed it, and with both her handes held up the same'—a gesture that made a deep impression on the onlookers.[16] She was never content to be the passive recipient of such tributes; she dominated them, and turned their symbolism from an expression of hope offered from below into a declaration of goodwill. She insisted, in other words, on her own symbolic function, and made sure that pageants of this kind extended outwards to make her part of their action.

The Queen's insistence on participating in such shows brought about a substantive change in the nature of royal entertainments in the course of the reign. Before that, it had not made very much difference whether a pageant used a lay figure to represent the monarch or gestured outwards to the sovereign himself. Once the sovereign became an actor, the entertainment had to be differently shaped: it had to be designed around her, not directed at her. The early tableaux had offered an allegory representative of the real political world but spatially independent within it. The later Elizabethan entertainments made the Queen herself part of the action, so that the borderline between drama and audience dissolved.

'Entertainment' is a misleading term for these shows for several reasons. For one thing, they were rarely, if ever, staged purely as pastimes; they were not disinterested. There was always some matter of deeper import lurking behind the innocent surface. Secondly, Elizabeth rarely sat back and watched. James I, at the focal centre of court masques, did not usually in fact have to do anything. Elizabeth worked for her entertainments. Those organised for her later in her reign tended to give her an increasingly important role to play within them.

Elizabeth's reign was the golden age of outdoor entertainment. Her summer progresses in particular called for something of the kind, to welcome her on her arrival at each successive nobleman's house and to entertain her during her stay. These shows required neither imaginative participation to supply the setting, nor illusionist scenery: their location was the actual landscape. This could be interpreted literally, emblematically, mythopœically, or in terms of romance, but all the interpretations provided interesting variations on bringing together the literal and symbolic. They were rarely fully allegorical. The typical characters were not the personifications of the Jacobean masque—Truth, Opinion, Fame, Heroic Virtue—but rural denizens, shepherds or foresters, or the gods and demi-gods of the countryside. The landscape itself is figuratively brought alive by these means, so that setting is given a fuller realisation than the merely literal countryside could achieve. Lakes could be classicised and filled with nymphs and tritons, or turned into an Arthurian romance setting filled with ladies of the lake. In Jean Wilson's words, 'Satyrs and Wild Men lurked behind every tree, ready to address her in Poulter's Measure. Shepherds and Shepherdesses infested the hills, singing pastoral ditties, and demanding that she arbitrate in their disputes.'[17] The effect is not one of fantasy, for these landscapes are not being re-interpreted as fictions. Like the morality play stage, location here is both literal and symbolic. 'The Elizabethans are not dealing with play worlds. What they are doing is transforming the real one.'[18] Just as the Queen's participation served to change street pageants from the functional to the dynamic, so the use of literal landscape in the summer entertainments helped to bridge the gap between myth and reality. There is no need in these entertainments to introduce an artificial London, or Ludlow: further meanings are perceived in the countryside itself. Elizabeth's reign established itself as mythopœic even before her death partly because of the way the celebrations of her could transform the actual.

The simplest, and rarest, use of landscape in these entertainments was to make a piece effectively locationless except as an excuse for introducing rural characters; the countryside is simply countryside. Sidney's *The Lady of May* was ostensibly of this kind, but more layers of significance emerge from it before the end. It was presented to the Queen in May 1578 as she walked by the grove in the garden of the Earl of Leicester's property at Wanstead.[19] The May Lady runs out from the woods with her rival suitors, a shepherd and a forester, with their companions, and asks the Queen to judge between them. On the surface, only the month of May and the Queen's presence serve to link the dramatic action with the real world; but Elizabeth was apparently being asked to judge a genuine cause, not a fictional play. The shepherd Espilus and the forester Therion are probably figures for Sir Christopher Hatton and Leicester, and Elizabeth herself was often presented as the May Lady, the incarnation of a perpetual spring.[20] The actors of the piece were presumably not aristocrats, as masque actors were (Leicester was not even present, though both he and Hatton apparently knew about the entertainment); instead, they *represent* aristocrats while acting the parts of countrymen. Elizabeth has to locate the real cause within the fictional, and that her judgement was at odds with the tenor of the text may indicate her success.[21] At the end of the piece Sidney brings together the dramatic setting and the real: 'In this our city we have a certain neighbour, they call him Master Robert of Wanstead.'[22] The unlocated action returns to the garden where the Queen is walking, and to its owner.

The entertainments Leicester had organised for the Queen at Kenilworth on her visit there a few years earlier, in 1575, were altogether more elaborate, and the landscape was put to the fullest possible use. The difference between the use of setting here and at Wanstead is apparent from the accounts of the two pieces. The opening words of *The Lady of May* are, 'Her most excellent Majesty walking in Wanstead garden': as in a masque, the presence of the monarch initiates the action. Robert Laneham's account of the Kenilworth entertainment[23] opens with a lengthy description of the castle itself and its immediate surroundings—park, pool, bridge, groves and so on. In this entertainment, the landscape comes alive for Elizabeth, but the origins of the action supposedly go back long before her arrival. The castle, according to the Lady of the Lake who floated to welcome her on a moving island, had long belonged to the earls of Leicester, and the lake had been her own since King Arthur's day. The arrival of the Queen causes new things to happen in this ancient landscape, the first of them being that the Lady of the Lake hands over her domain and her power to Elizabeth. 'It pleased her Highness too thank this lady, and too add withall, "We had thought indeed the Lake had been ours, and do you call it yourz now?"'[24] At Kenilworth, Elizabeth refused to accept the fiction wholeheartedly. In the overlap between drama and reality, she was going to demand more of reality. She would play her own part, not the one Leicester assigned to her.

The distance between entertainment and mere pastime is everywhere apparent in the Kenilworth revels. Leicester had designed them with one aim in mind: to encourage Elizabeth to marry him. A literal local brideale was presented to her as part of the propaganda. The pieces specially written for the days' entertainments could come dangerously near being explicit, as in the dialogue between a wild man, who inhabited the woods where she had been hunting, and Echo:

[WILD MAN]	Gifts? what? sent from the Gods, as presents from above?
	Or pleasures of provision, as tokens of true love?
ECHO	True love.
[WILD MAN]	And who gave all these gifts? I pray thee (Eccho) say;
	Was it not he who (but of late) this building here did lay?
ECHO	Dudley.
[WILD MAN]	O, Dudley, so methought: he gave himselfe and all,
	A worthy gift to be received, and so I trust it shall.
ECHO	It shall.[25]

Further devices included a romance sequence in which Elizabeth was cast as the rescuer of distressed damsels, with the landscape again made Arthurian; and a playlet in which Diana claimed to have lost her nymph Zabeta. This ended with Iris recommending the substitution of Juno's virtues for Diana's, and including the line, 'How necesserie were for worthy Queenes to wed.'[26] This play was in fact never performed: 'being prepared and ready (every Actor in his garment) two or three days together, yet never came to execution. The cause whereof I cannot attribute to any other thing than to lack of opportunity and seasonable weather.' George Gascoigne, the author, is being disingenuous: it was not rain that was the chief hazard. The Queen had had quite enough. She left several days earlier than expected, and Gascoigne hastily had to devise a parting speech and dress up as 'Sylvanus, god of the woods', so that the spirit of the place could give her an appropriate farewell that combined eulogy, apology, and justification in roughly equal measures. Elizabeth, finally, was not the principal spectator but the principal actress and the principal character, and Leicester had to rewrite his script to fit.

The entertainments of the 1590s marked the high point of the use of landscape as setting. The most elaborate of these entertainments—and after Kenilworth probably the most spectacular of Elizabeth's reign—was laid on for her stay at Elvetham in 1591. It was meant to be a surprise visit, but surprise was a comparative term on these occasions. The house and park were small, so small that the owner, the Earl of Hertford, had to build a range of temporary additional quarters, and hunting, the Queen's favourite pastime, was out of the question. Outdoor entertainment was, however, essential; so shows were rapidly devised using the landscape available. The simplest of these were emblematically perfunctory in their use of setting, as when six virgins representing the Graces and Hours diligently removed some highly allegorical blocks 'supposed to bee layde there by the person of Envie' out of the Queen's literal-symbolic path.[27] The spectacular centre-piece of her stay, by contrast, was constructed in elaborate detail around the topographical layout of the grounds. The contemporary account opens with a description of the setting; as at Kenilworth, the landscape determines the nature of the action.

There was a crescent-shaped lake at Elvetham, presumably designed in Elizabeth's honour, though it may have been constructed in anticipation of a visit rather than specially for this occasion.[28] In it were three islands, shaped like a ship, a fort, and a snail. The contemporary woodcut of the scene shows them as illusionist constructions, but the written account makes it clear that they were features of the landscape: 'The first was a Ship Ile, of a hundred foot in length, and four-score foote broad, bearing three trees orderly set for three masts. The second was a Fort twenty foot square every way, and overgrown with willows. The third and last was a Snayl Mount, rising to foure circles of greene privie hedges, the whole in height twentie foot, and fortie foote broad at the bottom.'[29] An entertainment had to be devised to fit this highly particularised setting. The lake, ship, and fort presented no problem, and an appropriately complimentary show of sea-gods and such (some armed with water-pistols) took place in and around them. The snail remained something of an embarrassment; but it was accommodated by having fireworks attached to its 'horns' and being re-cast as a kind of dragon tamed and metamorphosed by the Queen's presence:

Yon ugly monster creeping from the South
To spoyle these blessed fields of Albion,
By selfe same beams is chang'd into a snaile,
Whose bullrush horns are not of force to hurt.[30]

Jacobean masques sometimes strain to produce a text that will justify spectacular settings, but even Queen Anne's demand for blackamoors cannot have presented quite so intractable an obstacle as a forty-foot snail.

The Elvetham shows, like those at Kenilworth, devised a background story to explain the action presented. Many of the entertainments presented to the Queen on her progresses did not attempt to make a romance out of the landscape; instead they mythologised it, so that its deities and semi-deities could come and pay homage to her through encomium. Her own role was most likely to be as goddess to be worshipped, a part she was always graciously pleased to accept. These later entertainments have moved generically a long way from the *tableaux vivants* of her coronation procession with their didactic mirror-for-princes function, but the eulogies are held back from becoming flattery by their deliberate grounding in political reality. The entertainment that welcomed her at Bisham in 1592 had a cast list of shepherdesses (played by the daughters of the household, in an unusual early move towards the masque), a Sybil, Pan, and Ceres and her nymphs; but they spoke not only as rural deities worshipping the greater sovereign Cynthia, but with a consciousness of how fully the countryside was literally dependent on her for its well being: 'By her it is (Pan) that all our Carttes that thou seest are laden with Corne, when in other countries they are filled with Harneys; that our horses are ledde with a whipp, theirs with a launce; that our Rivers flow with fish, theirs with bloode; our cattel feed on pastures, they feed on pastures like cattel.'[31] As in the morality play, the acting area is being re-interpreted literally, as an epitome of the larger world. The point of the setting here is that it does not represent somewhere else. In the first instance, it is Bisham, newly blessed with the Queen's presence; in the second place, it is a part of her realm. The setting is not a function of the action; the action is made possible by the landscape itself. The peace and plenty brought by the Queen does not depend on her physical presence (though it became a commonplace to declare that the summer departed with her). The setting here transcends the specific occasion. The landscape emanates from the Queen; the state, epitomised in the countryside, is her second body, and they reflect each other. She embodies in herself the order displayed at large in the setting. She is the principal actor in a masque-like display of order and peace that is co-extensive, spatially and temporally, with her realm and her reign.

Outdoor entertainments were less common in James's reign, and make less use of landscape. It seems as if the removal of landscape to within the banqueting-hall neutralised much sense of its literal possibilities; and the King's reluctance to participate inevitably altered things considerably. On his entry into London he never took over the drama, as Elizabeth did—he never extended the symbolism outwards to insist on his own personal role in it. Jonson's outdoor entertainments written for him or Queen Anne in the early years of the reign assign the monarchs a more passive function than Elizabeth had been given. They are presented *at* the sovereign: satyrs and fairies pay respects,[32] Pan and Mercury welcome them on May morning,[33] but the close integration of countryside and sovereign, the sense of the Queen as creator and good genius of her own realm, is gone.

One of the few entertainments designed to fit a specific landscape was Campion's *Caversham Entertainment*, composed for Queen Anne on her visit there after she had said farewell to her daughter Elizabeth after her marriage in 1613. Campion's account again opens with a description of the house and its setting, and his entertainment is devised in several parts appropriate to welcome her on her approach. The first part is presented on the outskirts of the estate, the next as she gets nearer to the house, another when she reaches the garden, and so on, and continuing after supper in the hall and at her departure. Despite the careful spatial transitions, there is still less coherence between landscape and action than in some of the entertainments for Elizabeth—or, rather, landscape is at something of a discount. The Cynic, one of the first characters to speak, refers to the (literally) furrowed earth; but the emphasis is on the increasing civilisation as one approaches the house. Silvanus and his semideities do not appear where they belong, in the woods, but inside the house: the sense of a mythologised landscape is lost. Instead, the settings successively moving nearer, and into, the house parallel the use of scene changes in masque to indicate increasing order.

It was left to Milton, with his deep sympathy for Elizabethan traditions, to restore the sense of wholeness between masque and landscape, and even he, paradoxically, is working for an indoor setting. Both *Arcades*[34] and *Comus* contain landscape descriptions of a fullness and vividness associated more with the bare Elizabethan stage, where setting could only be created verbally, than with masque spectacle. *Comus* was elaborately staged with several scene changes, but neither piece will have been able to draw on the resources available to court masques, so there may have been more room for such extensive verbal scene-painting.

Comus—'A Masque presented at Ludlow Castle, 1634'—is unique in many ways, not least because Milton is so highly conscious of the different levels of reality on which the masque can work (differences epitomised by the alternative titles). The relationship between the stage action and the ostensible occasion of its presentation is particularly complex, and interesting. The piece celebrates the arrival at Ludlow of the Earl of Bridgewater, President of the Council of Wales and Lord Lieutenant of the country. The action of *Comus* in one sense emanates from him and is directed to him, as court masques were focused on the king: the Earl's children, the Lady and her brothers, are on their way to greet him when they encounter Comus, and the masque ends after their presentation to their father. The primacy of the social identity of masquers and spectators over the dramatic action is given unusually sharp expression here, as the Earl's children play themselves. This is not allegory—scarcely even fiction; and the children stepping out from the acting area to greet their father have no imaginative divide to cross. On another level, however, the action is completely divorced from the immediate circumstances. In the full development of its text, *Comus* has often been likened to play rather than masque; as dramatic fiction, it is not about the Earl or his family, but about a Lady, an Attendant Spirit and the wicked Comus. On this level, story is paramount, and the occasion comes second. Playing area and audience may come together at the end, but for most of the time they are as sharply separated as on the Elizabethan stage.

There is also a strong moral, almost allegorical, level to the piece which relates it less to plays, or even to masques with their personifications, than to morality plays, for the moral implications are much more universal than royal encomium allows. *Comus* is about innocence and experience, chastity and temptation, the encounter of virtue with vice: 'Heaven hath timely tried their youth, / Their faith, their patience, and their truth' (969-70). The setting becomes a moral epitome, where temptation can be enacted. The tangled woods come to stand for moral disorder; but for the virtuous Lady, the 'tufted grove' is lit by the moonlight lining 'a sable cloud', with obvious symbolic implications. The landscape thus becomes man's soul, scene of every psychomachia; and also middle-earth, where men have to live morally, and where 'if Virtue feeble were, / Heaven itself would stoop to her' (1021-2).

The setting is also, as at Bisham, a topographical epitome, though not a literal one. It represents the actual locality—the countryside around Ludlow—and perhaps also in miniature the country of which the Earl has charge, so that the piece also has political implications of civil order and disorder. Paradoxically, this may be why the crucial role of healer is given to Sabrina, the nymph of the Severn, where from royal entertainment or masque one would expect it to be given to the Earl, in person or symbolically. Resolution lies not in the political acts of a Royalist government but at a deeper level, in the harmony of man and countryside. Sabrina helps the shepherds, they in turn honour her:

> The shepherds at their festivals
> Carol her goodness loud in rustic lays,
> And throw sweet garland wreaths into her stream. (847-9)

The regenerating, mythic powers of the earth in the territories for which the Earl bears responsibility work on the side of political order and stability. Myth informs middle-earth, and the scene of one's physical and moral life. The final scene change, when the ideal of masque order is reached, shows Ludlow itself.

Milton exploits the multiple possibilities of masque setting to create a richer and more complex image of life—of moral action, good government, the symbolic and mythic dimensions of everyday living—than any other single piece encompasses. The Stuart masque, with its substitute landscape shut off from the larger world, peopled with aristocrats and personified virtues, and focused on the king, can come dangerously close to self-congratulation. In *Comus*, the identification of the stage with the immediate locality, and of both with the scene of moral temptation, gives the piece an undertone of tough moral realism such as the fantasy associated with the masque form rarely achieves. The *Masque presented at Ludlow Castle, 1634* transcends the limitations of the circumstances for which it was written by exploiting its topicality to the full.

NOTES

1 Sign-boards had a limited use, and were probably not changed during performance; see Clifford Leech, 'The Function of Locality in the Plays of Shakespeare and his Contemporaries', in *The Elizabethan Theatre*, 1 (1969), pp. 103–4.
2 *The Works of Thomas Campion*, ed. Walter R. Davis (London, 1969), pp. 203–30; also in Orgel and Strong, 1, pp. 115–20. It was presented in Whitehall on Twelfth Night, 1607.
3 Davis, p. 214.
4 *The Somerset Masque*, ed. Davis, p. 269.
5 See Stephen Orgel, 'To Make Boards Speak: Inigo Jones's Stage and the Jonsonian Masque', *Renaissance Drama*, N.S. 1 (1968), p. 123.
6 Orgel and Strong, 1, p. 7.
7 *The Macro Plays*, ed. Mark Eccles (Early English Text Society 262, London, 1969), e.g. *Mankind*, 188, where Mankind prays for God's mercy on 'this whole congregation'.
8 *The Macro Plays*, frontispiece and p. 1, where a full description of the staging is given.
9 *The Wakefield Pageants in the Towneley Cycle*, ed. A. C. Cawley (Manchester, 1958), *Secunda Pastorum* 455.
10 It is possible that the properties representing Mak's house doubled for the stable, but not enough is known about the staging to make that clear.
11 Orgel gives examples in 'To Make Boards Speak', p. 124.
12 Davis, pp. 263–76.
13 *Milton: Complete Shorter Poems*, ed. John Carey (corrected edition, London, 1981), *A Masque Presented at Ludlow Castle, 1634*, stage direction 956–7.
14 Orgel and Strong, 1, pp. 25, 60, 69; 2, p. 457.

15 John C. Meagher, 'The First Progress of Henry VII', *Renaissance Drama* N.S. 1 (1968), p. 63. The show was in fact never performed (p. 61).

16 *The Progresses and Public Processions of Queen Elizabeth*, ed. John Nichols, 3 vols (1823; reprint New York, n.d.), 1, pp. 48–51, 60. The pageant is discussed by Jean Wilson, *Entertainments for Elizabeth I* (Woodbridge, 1980), p. 6. Henry VII, by contrast, did not attempt to build royal response into emblematic pageant: his reactions were reserved for a separate, non-dramatic occasion (see Meagher pp. 69–72).

17 Wilson, p. 42.

18 Wilson, p. 43.

19 The full text, including the recently-discovered ending, is in *Miscellaneous Prose of Sir Philip Sidney*, ed. Katherine Duncan-Jones and Jan van Dorsten (Oxford, 1973), pp. 21–32.

20 Helen Cooper, *Pastoral: Mediaeval into Renaissance* (Ipswich, 1977), pp. 148–50, 196–206.

21 S.K. Orgel, 'Sidney's Experiment in Pastoral: *The Lady of May*', *Journal of the Warburg and Courtauld Institutes*, 26 (1963), pp. 198–203.

22 Duncan-Jones and van Dorsten, p. 31.

23 Nichols, 1, pp. 426–84.

24 Nichols, 1, p. 431.

25 George Gascoigne, *The Princely Pleasures at the Courte at Kenelworth* (Nichols, 1, p. 496).

26 Nichols, 1, p. 514.

27 Wilson, pp. 105–6.

28 The account says, 'There had been made in the bottom, by handy labour, a goodly Pond, cut to the perfect figure of a half moon' (Wilson, p. 100).

29 Wilson, p. 100; the woodcut is reproduced as the frontispiece. There is, however, also a less well known woodcut that shows the snail more naturalistically, reproduced by Bruce R. Smith in 'Landscape with Figures: The Three Realms of Queen Elizabeth's Country-house Revels', *Renaissance Drama*, N.S. 8 (1977), p. 90.

30 Wilson, p. 110.

31 Wilson, p. 45.

32 *The Entertainment at Althorp*, Herford and Simpson, 7, pp. 121–31.

33 *The Entertainment at Highgate*, Herford and Simpson, 7, pp. 136–44.

34 On the staging of *Arcades*, see Cedric C. Brown, 'Milton's *Arcades*: Context, Form and Function', *Renaissance Drama*, N.S. 8 (1977), pp. 264–8.

JOHN PEACOCK

The French element
in Inigo Jones's masque designs

THE ITALIAN ORIGINS of Inigo Jones's designs for the court masques have been progressively recognised, and especially his relationship to the work of the Florentine stage-designers who were his contemporaries, Bernardo Buontalenti and Giulio and Alfonso Parigi. It has been surmised that some experience of the court festivals of Florence, acquired during his Italian travels round the turn of the century, helped to equip him for his début as a masque designer for Queen Anne in 1605.[1] This is supported by his very earliest costume designs, which place the figures on a miniature 'terrain' appropriate to their character: verdure, sea, cloud—a quintessentially Buontalentian mannerism.[2] And his interest in imitating the set-designs of Giulio Parigi is evident early in his career, not just in the 1630s as Orgel and Strong have suggested.[3] The idea that Jones's formation as a masque-designer owes most to Florence was canonised in the recent Medici exhibitions where he was presented as an honorary Florentine: 'Inigo Jones "Fiorentino"'.[4]

In fact this is far from the whole story. However much Jones learnt from Florence, and from Italy, about the practice of scenography, we have to remember that for him the scenographic art was not an end in itself. It became a means to a larger end, the naturalisation of the entire tradition of Renaissance art in England.[5] This explains why so many of the masque designs are based on non-Italian sources.

Even before the arrival of Henrietta Maria in 1625, and her advocacy of her native culture, there is a persistent French influence in Jones's designs. It comes from the school of Fontainebleau, from sixteenth-century architecture, and from the *ballets de cour*. These are very different areas of artistic endeavour, but all together they highlight one crucial question: what, in this historical context, might 'French' influence be? What, during the late Renaissance period, *is* 'French' art? The school of Fontainebleau was headed by two Italians, Rosso and Primaticcio. The greatest French architect of the century, Philibert de l'Orme, had trained in Italy. And the *ballets de cour* were the province of both Italian and French designers.

In other words, the French element in Jones's masque designs some-

[*Illustrations at end of chapter, between pp. 168/9*]

times has a pronounced Italianate character. This does not mean that it lacks a distinguishable identity. Italian art mediated by the historical circumstances of the French Renaissance is very different from Italian art received directly, and Jones's procedures in composing his more complex designs from their various sources imply a recognition of this kind of difference. Rather than arriving at cordial eclectic compromises the designs tend to work through an interplay of their differing components. So even before the advent of a French Queen forced Jones's willing hand French art is a distinct presence in his work.

It can be seen as early as 1609, in Anne of Denmark's *Masque of Queens*. Both the costumes and the *mise en scène* show the influence of engravings after Rosso Fiorentino. Jones's design for the House of Fame draws on Giulio Parigi's *Palazzo della Fama* for a Florentine *intermezzo* of the year before, but its use of caryatids and of a round-headed proscenium arch enclosing the structure derive from an engraving of a tabernacle after Rosso.[6] And the poses of Rosso's caryatids (Fig. 1) reappear in Jones's costume designs, in the figure of Candace with her upraised right hand,[7] and that of Camilla with her downcast eyes and the fingers of her left hand curiously pointed and splayed (Fig. 2). Rosso is followed here as an international mannerist, a master of mannerist figuration; more specifically French are the headdresses which Jones has derived from Rosso masquerade headdresses for French court festivals (Figs. 3 and 5). The mask-like faces of most of these drawings, with their stereotyped profiles, vacant eyes, and open mouths, reveal their origins. Those for Lady Derby as Zenobia and for Anne of Denmark as Bel-Anna, Queen of the Ocean (Figs. 4 and 6), show how Jones has used Rosso's inventions, adapting them to his own practical purposes while retaining something of the quality of abstract fantasy peculiar to the engravings.[8]

Soon after the production of *The Masque of Queens* Jones made a short visit to France on business for James I.[9] He seems to have taken the opportunity to study modern French architecture, and the fruits of this study can be seen in the designs for *Oberon* about eighteen months later. He must also have become acquainted with the aesthetic ambience of the court in Paris; and probably visited the palace of Fontainebleau, which in this period was coming to be seen as a spectacular museum of French Renaissance art. A drawing of the next year, 1610, seems to show signs of such a visit. It is a design for a pageant used by Lord Dingwall in the Accession Day Tilt, in the form of an elephant and castle (Fig. 7). Elephant pageants were common enough in sixteenth-century festivals, but the affiliations of this particular image suggest something of Jones's use of French art in its Italian Renaissance context.

The image of the elephant derives ultimately from Raphael,[10] although Jones took it from an engraving after Raphael's pupil Giulio Romano (1, p. 177, Fig. 21). Behind the engraving lies one of Giulio's designs for a series of tapestries on the life of Scipio commissioned for Fontainebleau in 1532.[11] It is quite possible that Jones saw the Scipio tapestries at Fontainebleau and made a mental cross-reference between Giulio's elephant and a similarly striking image of an elephant, the enigmatic fresco known as *L'Elephant fleurdelysé* in Rosso's *Galerie Francois Ier*, where the animal is caparisoned and decorated and surrounded by spectators. As in the case of Giulio, there was a reproduction of Rosso's elephant available, an etching by Fantuzzi.[12] The possible Fontainebleau connection of Jones's design is reinforced by the forms of the scrolled terms round the 'castle', which seem to be derived from another etching by Fantuzzi of a decorative scheme by Primaticcio (Fig. 8) (used again by Jones for the proscenium of *Albion's Triumph* in 1632).[13]

Jones's reworking of a monumental image of Raphaelesque origin in a spirit of hyperdecorative stylisation (note, for example, his deliberate multiplication of the scroll motif over the whole design) implies an appreciation of how Italian High Renaissance forms were revised in the art of Fontainebleau. The primacy of these aesthetic considerations, perhaps stimulated by the French visit of 1609, is underlined by the failure of Lord Dingwall's elephant pageant to work very well; in the event it turned out to be 'long a coming ... and then as long a creeping about the Tilt-yard' (1, p. 147). The practical aspects of the design were lost sight of in the laborious elaboration of its aesthetic economy.

The architectural impact of the French visit can be gathered from the set-design for *Oberon*, Prince Henry's masque presented on New Year's Day, 1611. It has been shown that in Jones's first design for Oberon's palace he copies the sculptural group over the gateway of Philibert de l'Orme's chateau of Anet (1, pp. 210, 212, Fig. 25). However the structure on which he places it has little in common with the solidity and volumetric complexity of Philibert's architecture, consisting as it does of a domed upper storey suspended over a virtual void and supported on a few slender columns (Fig. 9). It gains cohesion and structural credibility from a careful system of proportions reinforced by a network of precisely plotted notional lines traced across the structure by the gestures of the extra figures which Jones has added into the sculptural population. The design is an experiment, a translation into architectural terms of the fountain designs of Salomon de Caus, the French engineer and garden designer who was Jones's colleague in Prince Henry's Works.[14]

We may wonder what prompted Jones to make this apparently heterogeneous connection between the gateway of Anet and de Caus's fountains. One answer lies in the fact that the figures of a stag and hounds above the Anet portico were automata.[15] Now de Caus was an expert on automata, which played a crucial part in the grottoes and fountains of his garden designs. It may be that he collaborated with Jones on this project for *Oberon*, and that the figures on the palace were actually intended to make sounds and move just as those at Anet did. This would have made Jones's architectural paraphrase of his ideas less abstract than it seems from the drawing.

A second connection emerges when we realise that Jones's design derives not only from the portico of Anet but from one of its fountains. This is illustrated in a book by the Florentine antiquarian and traveller Gabriele Simeoni (Fig. 10). It is a hexagonal structure with Corinthian columns supporting a dome around which are putti with bows and arrows—all features found in Jones. This may not be an accurate rendering of any of the fountains at Anet, since the view of the chateau in the background is very approximate, but that is immaterial. Even if it is topographically inaccurate Simeoni's image is perfect as a fantasia on themes from the iconography of Anet, the mythology of Diana as applied to its owner Diane de Poitiers; and as such it would have interested both Jones and de Caus.

For a final connecting factor is their mutual interest in the work of Philibert de l'Orme, de Caus's compatriot. When the latter came to design the gardens at Heidelberg for the Elector Palatine, brother-in-law of the by then deceased Prince Henry, he made extensive borrowings from de l'Orme's architecture.[16] One of these is the monumental garden gateway known as the Elisabethentor after Henry's sister, the Electress. This is closely derived from a gateway designed by de l'Orme for a *salle de triomphe* in 1559, a temporary structure for the festivities at the Hôtel des Tournelles during which Henri II met his death in a jousting accident.[17] The same gateway had influenced the design of Jones, or of Jones and de Caus, for Oberon's palace, which is essentially a grand portico through which the Prince and masquers are meant to make their entrance. De l'Orme's design, illustrated in his treatise *Le Premier Tome de l'Architecture*, uses the Corinthian order, which he says permits a greater richness of ornament,[18] and accordingly above the cornice it carries a group of decorative–allegorical figures, as does Oberon's palace, which also has the Corinthian order. His text gives detailed advice about proportions, and if we make some measurements on Jones's careful drawing we see that this has been taken to heart.[19] Moreover de l'Orme's illustration is on the very next page to his illustration of the gateway of Anet, and both have exactly the same idiosyncratic scrolled pediment which recurs on Oberon's palace—and which appears earlier on Jones's Cotton monument[20] and later on de Caus's Elisabethentor. Evidently de l'Orme repeated this motif from his regular oeuvre on a piece of festival architecture because he thought it succeeded as a decorative effect, and the interchange suggests the nature of his appeal to two such different artists as Jones and de Caus, whose interests partly overlapped. His inventiveness appeals to de Caus (who in the *Hortus Palatinus* draws consistently on the more decorative tendency in his work) and to Jones the masque designer, while his knowledge of the rules of classical architecture appeals to Jones the nascent Palladian architect. An artist who concerns himself with the correct proportions of a piece of festival architecture is the ideal exemplar for Jones at this stage; and de l'Orme's work, considered as design, lies along a spectrum between theory and fantasy which is not matched by any Italian, depending as it does on his unique context in the French Renaissance.

Jones's second design for Oberon's palace, the one which was actually used in the production, has a different relationship to Philibert's architecture and to French architecture in general. It is in a romantic, hybrid style, partly medieval and partly Italianate classical, which expresses the dual character of Oberon as a figure of native Arthurian legend who is also a classical hero[21] (the design for his costume expresses the same duality). Certain details are derived from Jacques Androuet du Cerceau's *Plus excellents bastiments de France*, which had been republished in 1607, and which Jones may well have used as a guide when looking at buildings in 1609. The scheme of the elevation, beginning with a basement of rock and heavy rustication and ascending through various stages of refinement to the shapely forms on the skyline, also owes much to the sixteenth-century chateaux depicted in du Cerceau. The aspects of Anet which have influenced this second design are much more to do with 'solid architecture', in Jones's phrase. The twin turrets marking the corners of a two-storey central block are derived from du Cerceau's illustration of Anet. More generally, de l'Orme's architecture is an ideal point of reference for Jones's expressive purpose in this masque because of its dynamically contrived relationship between native and classical forms.[22]

It would be wrong to think that Jones's sights were always fixed exclusively on Italy, or that his architectural career was an inevitable advance towards Palladian purism. The period we are considering was one of transition, marked by two turning points, the French visit of 1609 and the departure for Italy in 1613. Its central phase is that of the Surveyorship to Prince Henry between 1610 and 1612. Curiously, Jones was not employed on major building projects, and so his chief creative opportunities were offered by the Prince's masques. Here the necessity of fabricating a mythological identity for the Prince, compounded of Arthurian and neo-antique elements, coincided with an interest in experiments in architectural design, attempts to relate traditional and neo-classical forms. The exemplar for such relationships would have seemed to be French architecture *par excellence* (Italian being too advanced and English still too retrograde). As well, of his two eminent colleagues in Prince Henry's Works, Jones was certainly closer to the Frenchman Salomon de Caus than to the Florentine Costantino de' Servi, who was a rival and, as we learn from Campion, an impossible collaborator.[23]

The death of Prince Henry dissolved the personal and creative complexities of this situation. Soon Jones was on his second, definitive visit to Italy, to become on his return Surveyor of the King's Works. It is worth reminding ourselves that his journey home lay through France.

In the decade between Jones's return in 1615, and Charles I's marriage in 1625 the masque designs begin to show some influence from the *ballets de cour* which were becoming increasingly popular at the Bourbon court. Two unidentified drawings described by Orgel and Strong as 'Anti-Masque Characters *c*. 1615' have affinities with designs for the famous *Ballet de la délivrance de Renaud*, performed and published in 1617. No. 86 *Lady in a farthingale* with the upper part of her body surrounded by reeds recalls the illustration of a water demon,[24] and No. 87 *Lady in a cloud* the *esprit aérien*[25] with clouds round his head, neck, shoulders and waist. In *Pleasure Reconciled to Virtue* (1618) the stage curtain, 'painted to represent a tent of gold with a broad fringe, the background of blue canvas flecked all over with golden stars' (1, p. 283), sounds as if it derived from the last scene of *Renaud*, where the decor is a fringed pavilion of cloth of gold seen against a starry sky;[26] just as the pyramidal figure in which the masquers danced exactly recalls the formation of the '*danse générale et dernière*' in the ballet.[27] In *Neptune's Triumph for the Return of Albion* (1624) Jones's design for the floating island of Macaria with the masquers sitting in their 'archèd arbour' recalls in part the last scene of *Renaud*, with Godfrey and his knights grouped in their pavilion, and in part the previous scene showing Godfrey's soldiers in a wood which moved forward, like the island, on a mobile pageant car.[28] This design was eventually used for *The Fortunate Isles and Their Union* (1625), the masque for Prince Charles's betrothal to Henrietta Maria, so its French derivation became accidentally appropriate. But in the years that followed there was to be nothing accidental about French influence on the masques.

The fact that suddenly the Queen of England was a Frenchwoman put Jones in a curious situation. Although at first her personal and political position was insecure and variable, in cultural and aesthetic matters she evidently had a mind of her own. She was used to court entertainments in which royalty and the nobility took a more histrionic role than was thought decorous at the Stuart court; hence her decision to appear on the stage, and its notorious consequences; Jones's part in this was an awkward one, as we shall see. For the interior decoration of her residences she employed French designers, and Jones was sometimes obliged to execute their work almost literally;[29] for an artist who broke decisively with his most talented collaborator over the issue of 'invention' this must have been ironically embarassing. A hint of the stress in their relationship emerges in a note written by Jones on his design for the Queen's costume in *Chloridia* (1631): 'This design I conceive to be fit for the invention and if it please her Majesty to add or alter anything I desire to receive her majesty's command and the design again by this bearer. The colours also are in her majesty's choice; but my opinion is that several fresh greens mixed with gold and silver will be most proper' (2, pp. 439, 445, No. 181). No doubt such deference about royal masquers' costumes was conventional, and the phraseology is formulaic, but the tone in which Jones virtually insists that the costume falls within the province of the designer's conception, not the royal taste, comes across to us, especially as we know with hindsight the force of the word 'invention'—it was over this very masque that the quarrel with Jonson about 'invention' flared up. In a previous draft of his note Jones has crossed out the phrase 'but I should humbly' and substituted 'but my opinion is' (2, pp. 439, 441, No. 180). He too had a mind of his own.

It may well have been one thing to explore French art in a spirit of creative curiosity and experiment, quite another to deal with it by royal command. Unfortunately there are few surviving masque designs from the first five years of the reign, and so we cannot trace the story of how Jones came to terms with the Queen as an exigent mediatrix of her native culture. For the designs of the 1630s show that there was a coming to terms, a new richness of content and stylistic development which show further signs of French influence.

However there is one strand of change which can be followed through the visual record. We have designs for all three of the Queen's pastoral plays—*Artenice* (1626), *The Shepherds' Paradise* (1633), and *Florimène* (1635)—and the changes over the lapse of time between the first and the later two are revealing. Jones's design for the standing scene of *Artenice* is a stiff, awkward composition, its heterogeneous parts not at all combined into a unified stage-picture (1, pp. 386-7, No. 135). Its only resolute feature is its uncompromisingly Italian style, which seems perversely chosen for a French play. There is a sense of inhibition and intransigence about Jones's response to the commission. Perhaps, like others whose opinions are known to us, he disapproved of the Queen acting in a play.

But there may be other reasons for the unsatisfactory quality of the design. It may, for example, represent an initial attempt to combine several of the locales of the play together in one scene. The basis is the village where the characters of the play live. On the left is what appears to be the house of Artenice's father, the 'logis de Silène' described by Cléante in Act IV Scene iv,[30] which he speaks of as a substantial dwelling. Beyond it is the ruined chateau where Artenice goes to meet the magician Polistène.[31] The temple on the right (not that of Diana, which the text indicates is elsewhere) with its Corinthian portico and stepped dome like the Pantheon appears to be a temple of all the gods, 'les dieux' whom the druid Chindonnax refers to repeatedly.[32] The Christian ambience of the play would support this hypothesis.

Evidently Jones read the play carefully, even if his attempt to rationalise its settings does not work. His Italianate style may be expressing a recognition that it is an Italianate play, a naturalisation of Tasso and Guarini. As well, it could be a means of bringing out the essential qualities of the play in 'the classical language of architecture'. The Doric entablature and rusticated basement of the proscenium are exactly right for pastoral, and the stylistic contrast of the vernacular 'logis' opposite the Corinthian order of the temple may be trying to capture the primitivist, *dévot* quality of the play's ethical and religious atmosphere. It is an atmosphere which is recognisably and peculiarly Catholic, not with the extroverted Catholicism of baroque Italy but with the spirituality of St François de Sales. Here perhaps was another stumbling-block for Jones, who could only respond with a certain kind of scholarly Anglo-Saxon puritanism.

Seven years later, in the designs for *The Shepherds' Paradise*, we find him infinitely more relaxed, even though the play has some features in common with *Artenice*. It was supposed to give the Queen an opportunity to practise her English, a reason which has the air of a pretext, especially as Salvetti reported that she spoke her dialogue extremely competently.[33] It was written by Walter Montagu, a member of her circle who was to convert to Catholicism, and the play has an inward-looking quality which suggests the self-preoccupation of a special group. The 'Shepherds' Paradise' is a sort of state within a state, an enclave within the imaginary kingdom where the action is set, 'a Sanctuary for distressed virtue'. Its virtuous refugees must join a quasi-religious order and take a vow of celibacy. Every year they elect a queen, the qualifications being youth and beauty. Bellesa, the queen in the play, was acted by Henrietta Maria and is obviously an idealised version of the Queen herself, just as the Shepherds' Paradise is an idealised version of her court.

The religious tone of this celebration of persecuted virtue is decidedly Catholic. The characters spend time off-stage at their 'private devotions'. When the High Priest describes the yearly commemorative service at the tomb of the foundress of the order, he receives the reply: 'This is so heavenly a tradition, as it becomes best our delivery.'[34] The action is punctuated by numerous ceremonies: the commemorative service, the election of the queen, various admissions of postulants to the order. These sometimes occur between acts, and have the effect of pseudo-sacred intermezzi.

None of this seems to disconcert Jones in the least. For the scene of 'the Ceremony of the devotion to the tomb' (2, pp. 512–13, No. 249) he resorts straight to the imagery of papal pomp and adapts a view of the interior of St Peter's on the occasion of the canonisation of S. Carlo Borromeo,[35] although he reworks the architecture, altering the scale and especially the proportions in accordance with his own architectural principles. Similarly with the proscenium design: pastoral calls for Doric, but instead of the puritanically severe Doric order of the *Artenice* proscenium he uses an enriched version of Doric which is much more attractive but still perfectly correct on grounds of scholarship (2, p. 510, No. 245). The use of consoles instead of triglyphs in the frieze is justified by the precedent of a frieze fragment among the Arundel Marbles (and Jones followed the same precedent in the Doric order for the Royal Closet screen in the Queen's Chapel at Somerset House).[36] He is able to satisfy his own standards of design, decorum, and scholarship while giving sympathetic expression to the aesthetic pretensions of Montagu's play. The designs suggest an aesthetic rapprochement between Jones and the Queen.

Some of his drawings for *The Shepherds' Paradise* show a French influence which must surely be associated with her. The setting of the play is the Pyrenean kingdoms between Spain and France. The two principal female characters, Bellesa (Henrietta Maria) and Fidamira turn out to be Princesses of Navarre, and although none of the action actually takes place there it is the locale most stressed. Clearly there is an allusion to the homeland of the Bourbon dynasty (Henrietta was literally a Princess of Navarre), and the geography of the play has both a literal and a romant-ically allusive dimension. Jones's costume designs reflect this range. For Fidamira who does not know she is a Princess of Navarre and thinks she is Castilian by birth he provides an exact version of Spanish court dress, copied literally from a portrait as Orgel and Strong have shown (2, p. 529, No. 261 and Fig. 91). Other costumes have a French flavour which fits the allusive aspect of the play. Votorio the High Priest could come straight out of an illustration to a contemporary French romance,[37] and Prince Basilino, even though his costume is partly *à l'antique*, resembles the young French aristocrats illustrated in Abraham Bosse's *Jardin de la noblesse française* (from which Jones copied a scene for *Florimème*).[38]

When Jones provides a scene of a garden it is an unmistakably French garden. He has used Callot's etching of the 'Parterre du palais de Nancy' which combines a literal view with nostalgic reminiscences of Tuscany (2, pp. 518–19, No. 252 and Fig. 90). In adapting it Jones cuts out the Tuscan features and all the figures too, but reproduces the minutest details of the garden, created in fact by one of the designers of Henri IV, Henrietta's father. In an identical scene for the King's masque *Coelum Britannicum* (1634) Jones shows an Italian garden (2, pp. 586–7, No. 281 and Fig. 95); here, with his French garden, he is obviously responding to the Queen's own preferences and the special ambience of her production. Gardens were very much in her mind, as she had recently brought over André Mollet from France to lay one out at St James's Palace.[39]

The last of the Queen's pastorals was *Florimène*. As before, a garden scene ('The Second Intermedium: Spring'; Fig. 11) is taken from a French source, the title-engraving of Abraham Bosse's *Jardin de la noblesse française* (Fig. 12). Also the design for the proscenium and standing scene is markedly French in inspiration, and is Jones's most successful compo-sition of this type. Both the proscenium and the set-design are derived from a variety of different sources but each makes a unified whole, and together, as stage-picture and frame, they are beautifully coordinated (Fig. 13).

The set is derived from various etchings by Callot.[40] The proscenium, where the Doric order is now subtly implied rather than stated, displays the figures of a shepherd and shepherdess habitually found on the title-pages of French pastoral romances of this period;[41] the putti on the frieze come from the *Livre de la toison d'or* (Fig. 14), one of the most important suites of engravings to emerge from the school of Fontainebleau, by Rosso's pupil Léonard Thiry.[42] Thiry was a crucial influence on Jones's proscenium designs of the 1630s, just as Callot was on his sets and costumes, and there will be more to say about both of them. Here, one simply notes how much at ease Jones is working for the Queen in a French idiom.

Her appreciation of his work is on record. Sir Henry Herbert reports her comment on the costumes of *Coelum Britannicum* the year before, some of which were very much in the style of Louis XIII's designer Daniel Rabel: 'Pour les habits, elle n'avait jamais rien vu de si brave' (2, pp. 570). How had their aesthetic relationship reached this happy state? We cannot say for certain, but Jones's break with Jonson may well be a factor to consider. The first masque designed by Jones for the Queen after the break was *Tempe Restored*. Like the corresponding King's masque, *Albion's Triumph*, which has figures of Theory and Practice on the proscenium, it starts with a programmatic assertion of Jones's principles—the figures here are Invention and Knowledge—announcing a new order of things (2, p. 480, l. 34). But the elimination of such a potent collaborator as Jonson, however exasperating their relationship became, must have left a vacuum for Jones which minor figures like Townshend could not fill. Stephen Orgel has suggested that 'Jones's chief collaborator, after 1630, was the King himself' (1, p. 52); we might add to this 'and the Queen too'. The noticeable French influence in the designs for *Tempe Restored* may well be due to the Queen's prompting and Jones's new receptiveness.

Knowing that the text is based on the *Balet comique de la reyne* we are not surprised to discover that the Queen's costume is based on that of the Cardinal Virtues from the same ballet (Figs. 15 and 16). The costumes for both choruses of musicians are in the manner of Daniel Rabel.[43] And the proscenium, although no drawing of it survives, is given such a detailed description in the text that we can trace its provenance to three of the engravings in the *Livre de la toison d'or*,[44] which Jones used repeatedly in this period.

Of course all these sources could have been known to Jones without any recommendation from the Queen. There is a possibility he was using the *Livre de la toison d'or* as early as 1621.[45] The *Balet comique* is just the sort of book he would have sought out for himself, since festival books of every kind and especially records of theatrical productions at foreign courts were grist to his mill. He could have received copies of Rabel's designs through normal diplomatic channels, just as he requested designs from Florence through the Tuscan minister.[46] But the coincidence of all these in one masque for Henrietta Maria, together with the text of the *Balet comique* as well, strongly suggests an intervention by the Queen herself.

This is especially probable in the case of Daniel Rabel's costume designs. The album of nearly a hundred drawings which survives in the collections of the Louvre displays not only their aesthetic charm and theatrical verve but also a high degree of idiosyncracy, a powerful repetitiveness of effects, motifs, and mannerisms, which must have formed a compelling taste in someone who, like Henrietta Maria, was brought up on them. We know that copies were made,[47] presumably not only as records of the productions but for dissemination to other European courts: for example, the court ballets at Turin, where the Duchess was another sister of Louis XIII, show Rabel's influence.[48] So when this influence appears in Jones's masques we can be almost certain that copies after Rabel are being put into his hands by Henrietta Maria.

The closest parallels are in *The Temple of Love* (1635), the Queen's masque next after *Tempe Restored*. Here the 'Anti-masque of the Spirits' is a *ballet à entrées* in the French fashion, and Jones has derived two of the costumes from designs by Rabel for similar ballets. The costume for a 'watery spirit, with a fish's head and fins and scales all over' (Fig. 17) is taken from a design for an unspecified 'monstre' which however is obviously an aquatic monster (Fig. 19). And the first version of an 'earthy spirit' (Fig. 18) is based on an 'Entrée des gelés' from the ballet of the *Douairière de Billebahaut* (Fig. 20). As well, the costume for Henrietta Maria as Indamora, with its curling plumes on the skirt, sleeves, and headdress, is recognisably in Rabel's most characteristic manner—such plumes are one of his obsessive visual signatures.[49] Once again it looks as if the Queen has intervened.

If we survey the Caroline masques from this point of view we see a new upsurge of French influence, with the Queen as the moving spirit. But Jones's collaboration with her interests was by no means docile and passive. The classic problem for the court artist, of creating 'by order' or 'by authority', he negotiated with ingenious integrity. His independent, long-standing interest in French art was not to be pre-empted, and the Queen's demands became the occasion for a new effort of research which advanced his work as a designer on all fronts.

One outcome was the development of a personal style of ornament, which could be applied both to interior decoration and to the design of proscenium arches for court masques and plays. A sheet associated with the proscenium for 'The Tragic Scene', which also contains what look like sketches for wall or ceiling decoration (Fig. 24), suggests a connection in Jones's mind between these two fields, given that in practice they posed different problems. In proscenium design, 'picture qualified with moral philosophy' in his own phrase (2, p. 730, l. 67), there needed to be a special balance between decorative abstraction and allegorical content. A proscenium was both frame and picture. For prototypes in this ambivalent genre Jones looked back to a group of artists who had already exerted their fascination on him—the school of Fontainebleau.

An example will indicate how he used their work. In the frieze of the proscenium for *Albion's Triumph* the children sleeping on festoons are copied from an etching after Primaticcio (Fig. 8), as John Newman has shown.[50] In the original the images look quite shamelessly decorative. Jones has given them a specific meaning of his own: in a masque much concerned with sculpture they allude to the famous statue of a sleeping Cupid, supposedly by Michelangelo, which was coming to Charles I in the Mantua collection.[51] He has also enclosed them in clearly defined compartments which fit into an overall scheme of compartmentalisation, so they now exist in a precisely realised space. Jones's rationalising revision of Primaticcio adumbrates a personal recapitulation of the history of French ornament from the school of Fontainebleau to the *style Louis XIII*. Instead of simply copying the current style he goes back to the beginning and works over the ground for himself.

Such examples can be multiplied. Preliminary designs for the figures on the proscenium of 'The Tragic Scene' are also taken from Primaticcio, this time from van Thulden's engravings of the *Galerie d'Ulysse* published in 1633.[52] A drawing for Hercules is taken from a figure of Polyphemus (Figs. 21 and 22), and another for Truth from one of Penelope (Figs. 24 and 23). In the final version Truth is adapted from another print after Primaticcio, of Diana (Figs. 25 and 26). This kind of experimental derangement of Primaticcio's oeuvre, turning figure-painting into ornament, again suggests an urge to re-enact along different lines the historical evolution of which he forms a part. Here Jones has produced for Henrietta Maria (who may have presented the van Thulden volume to him) an individual version of the *style Louis XIII* from first principles.

However the main artist who figures in Jones's Fontainebleau revisions is not Primaticcio but Rosso. He does not figure *in propria persona* but is unmistakably present by proxy through the medium of the *Livre de la toison d'or*. These engravings designed by Léonard Thiry, Rosso's most able assistant, and executed by René Boyvin, who became the leading interpreter of Rosso's work, are a brilliant pastiche of his major project—the *Galerie François Ier*. Since the prints by Fantuzzi which reproduce parts of the *Galerie* literally are sparse and unsatisfactory, Thiry's pastiche offers the most suggestive record of what is undoubtedly the capital achievement of the school of Fontainebleau.[53]

Jones used the *Livre de la toison d'or* in no less than five of his proscenium designs—those for *Albion's Triumph, Tempe Restored, The Triumph of Peace, Florimène,* and *Luminalia.* It was his breviary of the Fontainebleau style. It offered not only a dazzling repertory of ornament but also a versatile demonstration of Rosso's great contribution to monumental art, his striking problematisation of the relationship between picture and frame. Jones's response was to detach the ornamental repertory from Rosso's subversive 'system' and reconstitute it on the matrix of a rational classicism, a new synthesis based on the High Renaissance values which Rosso had undermined. We can see this happening, for example, with the motifs Jones has excerpted from Thiry's designs and included in his *Florimène* proscenium: he retains their decorative qualities while working them into a rational pictorial and architectural scheme which is far from their original context (Figs. 13 and 14). So what looks from the Queen's point of view a beautifully relaxed exercise in the French taste is at the same time, more pertinently, part of Jones's classicising revision of the stylistic evolution of French ornament.

The advantage Jones took of his position vis à vis the Queen was extensive. His inexperienced colleague Aurelian Townshend, apologising courtier-like for his supposed reluctance to provide the text of *Albion's Triumph,* writes 'But my excuse and glory is, the King commanded, and I obeyed' (2, p. 458, ll. 453–4). How little of the story this tells in Jones's case we have already seen. Rather like Felix the artist in James's *The Europeans* who advises Mr Brand to look on life not as a duty but an opportunity, Jones, remarkable artist that he is, reaches always towards creative maximisation.

Occasionally his eloquently tacit opportunism is set off by a hinted gleam of resistance. It is difficult to explain the neo-antique, Roman style of the ceiling decoration in the Bedchamber of the Queen's House;[54] a tempting surmise is that Jones, obediently using the *style Louis XIII* elsewhere in the interiors, meant this as a stylistic riposte. A similar moment is the antimasque of the 'mock *romansa*' in *Britannia Triumphans.* Davenant writes this as pseudo-demotic medieval burlesque, but the set which Jones designs for it belongs in quite a different context, the world of those contemporary French literary romances which were very much a part of the Queen's cultural ambience. In fact his drawings closely resemble an illustration in Mouchemberg's *La Suite et continuation de l'Argenis,* which was dedicated to Henrietta Maria.[55] They hint at a different sort of burlesque, aimed against that self-image of the Queen's circle which *The Shepherds' Paradise,* seven or eight hours in performance, had conveyed with all the indulgent prolixity of romance.

The Queen had no monopoly on Jones's dealings with the French tradition. French influence in the proscenium design for the King's masque *Albion's Triumph* has already been noted, and it is even more apparent in the proscenium for *The Triumph of Peace*, commissioned by the Inns of Court (2, pp. 554-5, No. 267). Orgel and Strong discuss the failure of this masque to get across its critical message to the King; and they give part of the reason: 'it represents the only instance we have of Charles's critics retaining Inigo Jones in an attempt to speak to the King in his own language' (1, pp. 63-6). The implications here need to be drawn out. The visual 'language' in question is not only a symbolic language, as they acknowledge, but a stylistic one too. As soon as the King looked at the proscenium of *The Triumph of Peace* he would have recognised the decorative style which Jones had been developing for the royal masques over the last few years. Although far from an exclusively French style—it could best be described as Franco-Italian—it had a strong French flavour and was a close relative of the *style Louis XIII*, the style inseparably associated with the triumphalistic tone of the French monarchy. A tell-tale sign appears on the cartouche in the top right-hand corner: the symbol of crossed palm branches. Whatever new meaning Jones meant this to have it was instantly recognisable as a motif associated with the glory of the French monarchy, stretching back to the days of Henri II but more immediately germane to the Bourbons and their binary symbology of the twin kingdoms of France and Navarre.[56] In the same vein the pairs of crossed torches in the frieze are uncannily reminiscent of the crossed sceptres in the frieze of a design for a gateway in Francini's *Livre d'Architecture* of 1631, a rich pattern-book of French royalist ornament.[57] There is here a stressing of kinship with the *style Louis XIII*, the ornamental vocabulary of nascent absolutism. From the very beginning of the masque the French affinities of Jones's stylistic language help to neutralise the lawyers' critique of royal policy.

We are verging on two crucial but difficult questions: how does the French element in Jones's work relate to the other important strands, especially the all-important Italian influence? and how far are there intelligible political overtones in his synthesis of the arts and styles of different 'national' cultures? These are complex topics, but a modest start can be made on them by turning to the final theme in this examination of the 'Frenchness' of Jones's masque designs: the influence of Jacques Callot.

Apart from Giulio Parigi, Callot was the artist to whose work Jones turned most often during the 1630s. He turned to him for inspiration, and that was exactly what he found. Callot was clearly one of the most accomplished and fascinating artists among the galaxy of Jones's continental contemporaries, and since the print was his medium his work was easily accessible at first hand. These facts alone constitute a reason for Jones's interest, although no doubt there were more circumstantial reasons as well. Perhaps he first heard of Callot through his Roman acquaintance Francesco Villamena, with whom Callot may have been associated while an apprentice engraver in Rome.[58] He must certainly have been aware of him as the etcher of many designs by Giulio Parigi for Florentine court festivals. And he may have finally started copying and adapting his work in 1631 (for *Love's Triumph through Callipolis*) at the prompting of Henrietta Maria, since around this time Callot, having previously worked for Louis XIII, was giving drawing lessons to her other brother Gaston who had fled from France to the court of Lorraine at Nancy.[59]

These criss-crossing connections suggest how complex Callot's formation as an artist was and how equally complex any perception of his work necessarily had to be. Brought up at the court of Lorraine in a Francophile culture which deferred to Paris, he was trained by the French engraver Thomassin in Rome, then employed at the Medici court in Florence for ten years, the happiest of his life. His later years back at Nancy were punctuated by significant intervals in Paris, working for Louis XIII.[60]

Essentially there are three vital points on Callot's creative itinerary: Nancy, Florence, Paris. Nancy was his birthplace, his home, in practical terms his centre of gravity. Florence was his ideal city, the centre of his imaginative life. Paris was the magnetic pole of his cultural formation and the centre of political power, power which, with the French invasion of Lorraine, became destructive and hateful. We see Callot in his maturity precariously established at Nancy, looking with unsettling nostalgia towards Florence in one direction and with ambivalent, constrained attentiveness towards Paris in the other. The interaction between these creative *loci* constitutes one of the central dynamic principles of his work and the motive which makes it important for Jones.

The perception of Callot which Jones's drawings suggest has several aspects. He fits into the context of the Medici court theatre which Jones drew on repeatedly in the 1630s, and so can be seen alongside Giulio and Alfonso Parigi and also Antonio Tempesta (one of his masters) whose engravings, much used by Jones, have something of the spirit of the Florentine festival tradition. As well he figures as a festival designer in his own right in the *Combat à la Barrière* of 1627 from which Jones borrows the design for the Furies in *Salmacida Spolia*,[61] possibly knowing quite well that the Duchesse de Chevreuse in the audience had seen exactly the same characters attending 'her' knight M. de Couvonge in the original *Combat* at Nancy.

But the essence of Callot's contribution to Jones's art of festival design lies not in any reproduction of detail but in the communication of a certain attitude. In one of the final etchings of the *Combat* entitled 'Entrée de son Altesse à pied'[62] Callot gives a view of the entire hall where the jousting is taking place, with a line of spectators, their backs to us, placed in the foreground right along the lower edge of the print. The *whole* scene is shown as a spectacle, with the spectators just as much a part of that spectacle as the fête they are watching. This is a nostalgic variant of one of Callot's best known Florentine prints, showing an intermezzo in the Uffizi theatre in 1616,[63] where the spectators themselves are presented as the most beguiling part of the spectacle. A similar work is the etching known as 'The Fan' where spectators watching a distant river pageant on the Arno lounge and sit on the grotesque ornamental border which encloses the scene.[64]

As a foreigner from Lorraine Callot is able to express his love of Florence and of the Grand Duke's festivals in an intensely fascinated, self-conscious way, using the festivals as a metaphor for the whole of Florentine life. What he imparts to Jones's work is that self-conscious delight in Italy which only an artist from a different culture can realise; and a sense of the theatricality of existence, a sense in which populism and refined connoisseurship are compatible. This is a side of Jones's masques which has received little stress and perhaps should receive more.

The sense of theatricality, in that it derives from Callot's role as a rapt spectator of Italian life, is ultimately based on a feeling of division in his experience, of benign alienation. Jones's drawings also intimate a perception of more explicit divisions in Callot's work. An example is the drawing of 'A Garden' for The Shepherds' Paradise, adapted from the 'Parterre du palais de Nancy' (2, p. 252 and Fig. 90).[65] This large etching of 1625, produced several years after Callot's return to Nancy from Florence, combines a faithful view of the French garden behind the ducal palace with an idealised architectural surround featuring an imaginary villa in an unmistakably Tuscan style. It is based on drawings made both in Nancy and earlier in the Boboli Gardens.[66] This is an ideal topography, an attempt to synthesise the disparate locales of Callot's imaginative experience. Jones, needing a scene appropriate for Henrietta Maria's play, excerpts the parterre à la française and omits the whole element of nostalgic toscanità which would be out of place. His adaptation has the force of an analysis of the original, deftly distinguishing between its French and Italian aspects, and implying an understanding of their coexistence in Callot's work. For Jones's scenography Callot the mediator between France and Italy was just as important as Callot the quintessential artist of the theatre.

In perceiving Callot as an artist for whom, like himself, the synthesis of different cultures and different artistic traditions was vital Jones could not fail to perceive also the negation within the enterprise of synthesis, Callot's increasing preoccupation with the dichotomy between peace and war. One of Jones's most Callotesque designs is an Italianate architectural collage whose parts are excerpted both from etchings made in the palmy Florentine days—'The Fair at Impruneta' and the large commedia dell' arte figures—and from depictions of suffering—a scene from the 'Small Passion' and 'The Punishments', a print associated with the two series of

'The Miseries of War'. The apparent indifference to provenance is compounded by the fact that Jones's design, inscribed 'Forum of Peace' is for a masque entitled *The Triumph of Peace*. Similarly, the rustic cottages in the peaceful pastoral set for *Florimène* are adroitly abstracted from prints in the 'Small Passion' and the first 'Miseries of War'.[67]

It is possible to explain these disconcerting misrepresentations. The mythology of peace had a central place in the Caroline masques. Jones's procedures here reveal it being formulated with a certain coercive deliberation. His revision of war as peace suggests that, aesthetically, there shall be peace at any price: *fiat pax*. In so far as Jones's scenographic art was an art of synthesis, Callot was at once a very inviting and a very difficult artist to come to terms with. Finding him irresistibly useful Jones had to pacify the contradictions in Callot's work, or at least restate them in aesthetic terms only, so that in his Caroline version of Callot the miseries of French wars dissolve into earlier, happer scenes of peaceful Tuscany, and the insoluble dichotomy of war and peace into the cultural disparity of France and Italy, a problem which makes a feasible challenge to Jones's method of aesthetic synthesis.

Jones's dealings with Callot help to sharpen the focus of our view of the French element in his masque designs. From seeing it as one principal strand in his revision and reordering of the Renaissance tradition we move in closer to observe how problematically it may consort with the Italian art from which it originates. French art figured differently in Jones's work at different stages in his long career. Some of its diverse forms and phases were gradually incorporated into his increasingly confident recapitulation of the history of Renaissance art, but the more masterful the assimilation the more of a kind of oblique definition is given to aspects of difficulty and conflict in the whole enterprise.

NOTES

I am grateful to the British Academy for financial support from their Small Grants Fund in the Humanities for my research towards this study.

1 John Summerson, *Inigo Jones* (Harmondsworth, 1966), p. 17.
2 See, e.g., the designs reproduced in the exhibition catalogue *La Scena del Principe* (Florence, 1980), pp. 359–63.
3 Orgel and Strong, 2, pp. 41–2.
4 *La Scena del Principe*, pp. 375–82.
5 John Newman, 'The Inigo Jones Centenary', *Burlington Magazine*, 115 (1973), p. 561; John Peacock, 'Inigo Jones's Stage Architecture and Its Sources', *Art Bulletin*, 64 (1982), p. 195.
6 Peacock, p. 199, fig. 10.
7 Orgel and Strong, 1, p. 147, No. 24. Future references to this book, by volume and page number, are given in the text.

8 A more literal copy is the drawing inscribed 'Lady Blanch', Orgel and Strong, 1, pp. 150, 152, No. 30; cf. A.P.F. Robert-Dumesnil, *Le Peintre-graveur français*, 11 vols (Paris, 1835-71), 8, pp. 53, 89, ii. Much later, in the 1630s, some designs for headdresses are again based on Rosso e.g. Orgel and Strong, 2, p. 564, No. 273 'Masquers: the Sons of Peace' (top sketch on the sheet), cf. Robert-Dumesnil, 8, pp. 52, 87, ii.

9 J.A. Gotch, *Inigo Jones* (London, 1928), pp. 51-2.

10 See Charles Hope, *Titian* (London, 1980), p. 57, pl. 25.

11 *Jules Romain. L'Histoire de Scipion. Tapisseries et Dessins. Grand Palais, 1978* (Paris, 1978), pp. 5, 95-7.

12 Exhibition catalogue *L'Ecole de Fontainebleau* (Paris, 1972), p. 261, No. 309.

13 See below p. 160.

14 For a fuller discussion see John Peacock, 'Inigo Jones's Stage Architecture and its Sources', *Art Bulletin*, 64 (1982), pp. 199-202.

15 *Le Premier Tome de l'Architecture de Philibert de l'Orme* (Paris, 1568), fol. 246v; Anthony Blunt, *Philibert de l'Orme* (London, 1958), p. 34.

16 Blunt, p. 118, n. 3.

17 *Le Premier Tome*, fol. 247r. Orgel and Strong, 1, p. 210 refer to the Venetian Ambassador's report that Henry wanted *Oberon* to take the form of an equestrian pageant or joust but the King refused. It could be that discussions about the design of the masque revived memories of Henri II's death.

18 *Le Premier Tome*, fol. 246v.

19 John Peacock, 'Inigo Jones's Stage Architecture and Its Sources', p. 201.

20 John Harris, Stephen Orgel, and Roy Strong, *The King's Arcadia: Inigo Jones and the Stuart Court* (London, 1973), pp. 33-4. The scrolled pediment appears on the tomb as executed (fig. 33) and not on the preparatory drawing.

21 Stephen Orgel, *The Illusion of Power* (Princeton, N.J., 1975), p. 67.

22 John Peacock, 'Inigo Jones's Stage Architecture and Its Sources', pp. 202-3.

23 *King's Arcadia*, p. 43; W.R. Davis, ed., *The Works of Thomas Campion* (London, 1969), p. 268. H.R. Hitchcock, *German Renaissance Architecture* (Princeton, N.J., 1981), p. 319, suggests that the Englischer Bau at Heidelberg was jointly designed by Jones and de Caus.

24 *Discours au vray du Ballet dansé par le roy le dimanche XXIXe jour de Janvier 1617* (Paris, 1617), pl. 2.

25 *Discours*, pl. 5.

26 *Discours*, pl. 12, reproduced by Margaret M. McGowan, *L'Art du ballet de cour en France 1581-1643* (Paris, 1963), pl. XIV. John Webb used the same design from *Renaud* in 1656 for *The Siege of Rhodes:* see Roy Strong, *Festival Designs by Inigo Jones* (Washington, 1967), No. 110.

27 *Discours*, pl. 13.

28 *Discours*, pls. 11 and 12 (McGowan, pls. XIII and XIV).

29 John Harris, 'Inigo Jones and His French Sources', *Metropolitan Museum of Art Bulletin*, 19 (1961), p. 256; *King's Arcadia*, p. 153, Figs. 277-8.

30 Honorat de Bueil, Sieur de Racan, *Les Bergeries*, ed. L. Arnould (Paris, 1937), IV.iv.2180-90.

31 *Les Bergeries*, I.iv.435-44.

32 *Les Bergeries*, IV.v *passim*.

33 John Orrell, 'Productions at the Paved Court Theatre, Somerset House, 1632/3', *Notes and Queries*, 221 (1976), p. 224.

34 Walter Montagu, *The Shepherd's Paradise* (London, 1659), p. 27.

35 Engraving by Girolamo Rainaldi, reproduced by Maurizio Fagiolo dell' Arco and Silvia Carandini, *L'Effimero Barocco*, 2 vols (Rome, 1977-8), 1, p. 30.

36 John Harris, 'The Link between a Roman Second-century Sculptor, Van Dyck, Inigo Jones and Queen Henrietta Maria', *Burlington Magazine*, 115 (1973), p. 529.

37 See e.g. A.-M. de Mouchemberg, *La Suite et continuation de l'Argenis* (Paris, 1626) (dedicated to Henrietta Maria), p. 301 where the illustration shows the priestesses of Pallas (Votorio was played by a woman).

38 *Le Jardin de la Noblesse Francoise* (Paris, 1629), pls. 5 and 6.

39 Roy Strong, *The Renaissance Garden in England* (London, 1979), p. 188.

40 John Peacock, 'New Sources for the Masque Designs of Inigo Jones', *Apollo*, 107 (1978), p. 104.

41 See Diane Canivet, *L'Illustration de la poésie et du roman francais au XVIIe siècle*, Figs. 8, 9, 11, 13, 14 (Paris, 1957).

42 *Livre de la Conqueste de la Toison d'or, par le Prince Iason de Tessalie: faict par figures avec exposition d'icelles*, (Paris, 1563).

43 See, e.g., the drawing 'Musique servant du récit au Grand Ballet' (Cabinet des Dessins du Louvre, No. 32 652) reproduced by Henry Prunières, *Le Ballet de Cour en France avant Benserade et Lully* (Paris, 1914), pl. 12.

44 John Peacock, 'Inigo Jones and the *Livre de la Conqueste de la Toison d'Or*', *Gazette des Beaux Arts*, forthcoming.

45 See Peacock, 'Inigo Jones and the *Livre de la Conqueste*'.

46 R. M. Smuts, *The Culture of Absolutism at the Court of Charles I* (Princeton University Ph. D. thesis), University Microfilms (Ann Arbor, Mich., 1976), p. 189.

47 McGowan, p. 347, n. 1.

48 Compare, e.g., the drawing of 'Winter' reproduced by Allardyce Nicoll, *Stuart Masques and the Renaissance Stage* (London, 1938), Fig. 118 with Fig. 20 in this chapter.

49 Compare the plumed costumes in M.-F. Christout, *Le Ballet de cour de Louis XIV* (Paris, 1967), pl. 2.

50 'The Inigo Jones Centenary', *Burlington Magazine*, 115 (1973), p. 561.

51 See P. F. Norton, 'The Lost *Sleeping Cupid* of Michelangelo', *Art Bulletin*, 39 (1957), pp. 251-7.

52 This means that 'The Tragic Scene' must be dated 1633 or later, not 1629-30 as suggested by Orgel and Strong, 1, p. 397.

53 For a fuller treatment of this topic see John Peacock, 'Inigo Jones and the *Livre de la Conqueste*'.

54 See G. H. Chettle, *The Queen's House, Greenwich* (London, 1937), frontispiece and pls. 77-82.

55 *La Suite et continuation de l'Argenis*, p. 174.

56 See Henry Martin, *La Grammaire des styles. Le Style Louis XIII* (Paris, 1924), p. 30; Alessandro Francini, *Livre d'Architecture* (Paris, 1631), Gregg Press facsimile (Farnborough, 1966), pls. IX, XXXIX; also XVI, XXIV, XXX, XXXII, XXXIII, XXXIV, XXXVII, XXXVIII, XXXX.

57 Francini, pl. IX.

58 Georges Sadoul, *Jacques Callot miroir de son temps* (Paris, 1969), pp. 28-9.

59 Félibien, quoted in Sadoul, p. 281.

60 Summer and Autumn 1629, March–April 1630, January–April 1631; see the detailed chronology in Sadoul, pp. 391–3.

61 *Combat a la Barriere Faict En Cour De Lorraine Le 14. Febvrier, En L'Année presente 1627* (Nancy, 1627), pp. 24–30; Orgel and Strong, 2, pp. 757, 763, No. 416 and Fig. 126.

62 *Combat a la Barriere*, pp. 50–1, reproduced by Howard Daniel, *Callot's Etchings* (New York, 1974), pl. 208.

63 Daniel, pl. 6.

64 Daniel, pl. 89.

65 Orgel and Strong's reproduction of only part of Callot's print (No. 252 and Fig. 90) obscures the point of Jones's selective use of it; for the entire etching see Daniel, pl. 196.

66 Sadoul, p. 201.

67 John Peacock, 'New Sources for the Masque Designs of Inigo Jones', *Apollo*, 107 (1978), pp. 102, 104.

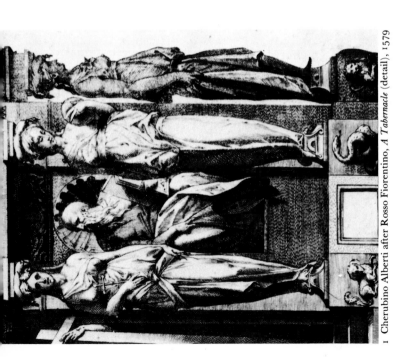

1 Cherubino Alberti after Rosso Fiorentino, *A Tabernacle* (detail), 1579

2 Inigo Jones, *Camilla* for *The Masque of Queens*, 1609

3

4

3 René Boyvin after Rosso Fiorentino, *Masquerade headdress*
4 Inigo Jones, *Zenobia* for *The Masque of Queens*, 1609
5 René Boyvin after Rosso Fiorentino, *Masquerade headdress*
6 Inigo Jones, *Bel-Anna, Queen of the Ocean* for *The Masque of Queens*, 1609

5

6

Shi non fa serva la bottica ꝑ

7 Inigo Jones, *Elephant Pageant* for the Accession Day Tilt, 1610

8 Antonio Fantuzzi after Francesco Primaticcio, *Jupiter Sending the Three Goddesses to the Judgment of Paris*, 1543

9 Inigo Jones, *Palace within a Cavern* for *Oberon*, 1610

10 *Fontaine d'Anet*, woodcut illustration from *Les Illustres Observations Antique Du Seigneur Gabriel Symeon Florentin*, Lyons, 1558

11 Inigo Jones, ?Act II: The Second Intermedium: Spring for Florimène, 1635

12 Abraham Bosse, Title-engraving for Le Iardin de la Noblesse Françoise, 1629

13 Inigo Jones, *Proscenium and Standing Scene* for *Florimène*, 1635

14 René Boyvin after Léonard Thiry, *Le Livre De La Conqueste De La Toison D'Or*, 1563, plate 13

15 Inigo Jones, *Divine Beauty* for *Tempe Restored*, 1632

16 *Entry of the Cardinal Virtues* from *Le Balet Comique de la Reyne*, 1581

17, 18 Inigo Jones, *A Watery Spirit* (left) and *An Earthy Spirit* (right) for *The Temple of Love*, 1635

19 Daniel Rabel, *Entrée des Sorcières et des Monstres* from *Le Ballet du Château de Bicêtre*, 1632

20 Daniel Rabel, *Entrée des Gelés* from *Le Ballet de la Douairière de Billebahaut*, 1626

21 Inigo Jones, *Hercules* for *The Tragic Scene*, after 1633

22, 23 Theodoor van Thulden after Francesco Primaticcio, *Les Travaux
d'Ulysse*, 1633, plate 9 (above) and plate 50 (below)

25 Inigo Jones, *The Tragic Scene* (detail), after 1633

26 Master L. D. after Francesco Primaticcio, *Diana*

PAUL HAMMOND

Dryden's *Albion and Albanius*: The apotheosis of Charles II

⟨⟩○⟨⟩

> May you not neede the art to multiply
> Joyes, in the fancies unsafe flattery,
> But may your pleasures be still present, pure,
> Diffusive, great, and in their trueth, secure.[1]

THE ANXIETY discernible in Sidney Godolphin's compliment to Charles I and his Queen was all too prophetic. The fancy of the court artists in the reigns of James and of Charles did indeed help to ensnare the monarch in an unsafe flattery which offered comforting reflections whose truth was insecure. The masque was one of the chief forms in which a distorting mirror was held up to a complacent court, and the form, for the most part, died with its audience. In 1649 the 'Royal Actor' played his last scene at the Banqueting House in Whitehall, where many masques had been staged, and where the spectacular ceiling by Rubens depicted the apotheosis of James I. But this time the scene was designed by men unconvinced of the King's focal place in a divinely ordered world; the harmonious order fabricated in the court entertainments gave way to what Marvell, depicting the fate of the young Charles II in his poem *The Unfortunate Lover*, called 'This masque of quarrelling Elements'.[2] During the Interregnum the tradition of court entertainment was much attenuated, and after the Restoration Charles II found himself unable to stage a masque since (as he told his sister in 1663) there was not one man at court 'that could make a tolerable entry'.[3]

Though the masque as court entertainment perished, features of it persisted in the lavish drama of the Restoration, and Dryden's *Albion and Albanius* (1685) is a late scion of this tradition. It is also an example of the curious short-lived English opera, a hybrid form which occasioned much debate.[4] This essay will leave on one side the problem of the form and nomenclature of the piece, and the relationship of Dryden's words to the music by Grabu, and will consider instead how Dryden adapted the iconography of the early Stuarts to the task of strengthening the position of Charles II and his luckless brother James. As we shall see, Dryden took up features of the pre-war masque—the definition of the monarch–hero's qualities by mythological figures, and the challenge to his authority by the subversive denizens of the antimasque—but he cast them into a different form. In his hands these elements take on a new dramatic relationship to each other, and the whole has an altered, more polemical, relationship with its audience.

One preliminary point which needs to be recognised is that *Albion and Albanius* has an ambiguous place in the public domain. Late in 1684 it was played two or three times before Charles II, who particularly enjoyed the first and third acts.[5] It was not exclusively a court entertainment: public performances were planned for early 1685, though as the seats were to be at double the normal prices the audience would be select. But on 6 February 1685 Charles died, and some revision in the third act was needed before it was staged on 3 June. Even then only a few performances were possible before news of Monmouth's landing reached London on 13 June and the work foundered.

Dryden's revision to accommodate the piece to the death of Charles was the second alteration which he had been forced to make. He tells us in his preface that he originally intended it to be 'a Prologue to a Play, Of the Nature of the *Tempest*;[6] which is, a Tragedy mix'd with *Opera*; or a *Drama* Written in blank Verse, adorn'd with Scenes, Machines, Songs and Dances' (10). Then some 'intervening accidents' deferred the performance of the main play, and so Dryden added two further acts to his prologue, and turned it into an entertainment in its own right. The main play eventually saw the light in 1695 as *King Arthur*, though it had been heavily revised in the interim. Dryden's choice of an Arthurian subject suggests that the exaltation of the Stuart monarchy was originally to have been the aim of the main play as well as of the prologue, for the Arthurian legends had been laid under contribution for the glorification of the early Stuarts. Jonson used the fact that 'Charles James Stuart' may be anagrammatised as 'Claimes Arthurs Seate',[7] and this fits so neatly with Dryden's celebration of the two brothers in the prologue that he may have intended it to be the theme of the whole entertainment, and designed an enthronement as its climax. In any case, we know from Dryden himself that his original draft was so explicitly celebratory of the Stuarts that it had to be heavily revised after 1688 in order not to give too much offence to William III. In originally designing a political allegory to be a dramatic prologue to a play, Dryden may have had in mind the prologue to John Crowne's 'masque' *Calisto*, which was performed at court in 1675. Here Augusta (the City of London), who is 'inclin'd to fears', is comforted by 'The Genius of England' and two martial figures. But prologues of this kind were also fashionable in France, as may be seen from three plays by Philippe Quinault which were performed before Louis XIV. In the prologue to *Cadmus et Hermione* (1672) the figure of Envy rouses the serpent Python and the winds; Python is then struck down by the sun-god. As this was staged in front of the sun-king the symbolism is obvious. The prologue to *Proserpine* (1680) represents the defeat of discord, and the subtitle of the play is close in phrasing to Dryden's description of his intended work: 'Tragedie en Musique. Ornée D' Entrées de Ballet, De Machines et de Changemens de Théatre'. Thirdly, in *Phaëton* (1683) the prologue depicts Saturn and Astraea accomplishing the return of the golden age.

Albion and Albanius in its final form begins with a prologue which establishes the polemical tone of the piece. Drawing upon the Restoration tradition of prologues which tease and bully the audience into approval, Dryden makes a direct—indeed, an insulting—challenge to any who consider their loyalty to be to the City of London rather than the King; they are not citizens but cits:

> Cits and Citesses, raise a joyful strain,
> 'Tis a good Omen to begin a Reign:
> Voices may help your Charter to restoring;
> And get by singing, what you lost by roaring. (15)

Dryden's gibe requires a brief explanation. Tension between court and city had a long history. Parliament had found a fairly secure base of power in London during the Civil War and Commonwealth; the Popish Plot of 1678-9 (an anti-Catholic movement which was particularly suspicious of the Queen and the Duke of York) found more gullible and virulent adherents there than in the provinces; and during the Exclusion Crisis of 1680-1 Londoners gave such vociferous support to the Earl of Shaftesbury's attempt to remove James from the succession that Charles summoned his Parliament to meet in Oxford instead. Nor did troubles end there. In November 1682 the city's sheriff, Thomas Pilkington, was successfully sued for slander by James and incurred damages of £50,000. Charles eventually decided that the city should forfeit its charter and receive a new one, under which key civic appointments would be in his control. A writ of *Quo Warranto* was issued in November 1681, but judgement was not given against the city until June 1683, and the charter was compulsorily surrendered in October. This was a controversy in which Dryden himself had been involved. His play *The Duke of Guise* (1683) had implicitly ridiculed the city sheriffs, and drew several rejoinders. So Dryden's onslaught on the city of London in *Albion and Albanius*, and especially his exaltation of James, probed wounds which had scarcely healed.

Dryden's challenge to the city is reinforced by the frontispiece to the opera. When the curtain rises the audience sees 'a Woman representing the City of *London*, leaning her Head on her Hand in a dejected Posture (shewing her Sorrow and Penitence for her Offences)'; opposite her is 'a Figure of the *Thames* with his Legs shakl'd, and leaning on an empty

Urn'. Behind them are represented the King and Queen, with Pallas ('or Wisdom, and Valor') who offers the city a new charter, while the King raises her head (17-18). By using these traditional figures Dryden points to the change which has come over the relations between London and the monarchy. Queen Elizabeth had participated with enthusiasm and ready wit in the pageantry which the city laid on for her coronation and at other festivities; James I had suffered his inaugural entry with bad grace, but had been greeted by the joyful figure of the Thames at the Fenchurch arch.[8] Charles I shunned such public demonstrations altogether, but when his son rode to his coronation in 1661 he too was welcomed by the figure of Thames at the naval arch.[9] Furthermore, Dryden's frontispiece introduces the figures of Peace and Plenty as attributes of monarchical government, whereas these blessings had been celebrated annually in the Lord Mayor's show as benefits won by the city itself as a proud trading capital. Even in *Calisto*, performed at court, Peace and Plenty are Augusta's natural supporters. Dryden, however, turns back to earlier assertions, such as the embrace of Peace and Plenty in the panel of the ceiling in the Banqueting House which depicts the characteristics of the reign of James I. It is also from the monarch, once again, that the arts spring: the frontispiece shows Poetry, Painting, and two Muses with musical instruments.

The first act opens with the curtain rising on a set which features the Royal Exchange, London's commercial centre; but this is boldly flanked by equestrian statues of Charles I and Charles II: the equestrian statue, revived in the Renaissance from classical Rome, is a forceful assertion of imperial power. Mercury (who is both the messenger of the gods and the god of merchants) descends in a chariot drawn by ravens, the birds of augury. He approaches Augusta and Thamesis. The figure of the Thames is familiar from the coronation arches; Augusta is the ancient name for London, which had been revived by Dryden in *Annus Mirabilis* (1667) and adopted by Crowne in *Calisto*.[10] On the side of Augusta's couch are painted falling towers, which are a standard emblem of the ruined commonwealth which awaits restoration: similar pictures greeted Elizabeth and Charles II on their coronation entries, and the *topos* was aired in the opening speech at *Prince Henries Barriers* (1610). Mercury begins with the words: 'Thou glorious Fabrick! stand for ever, stand' (20). We know that for Dryden a 'fabric' was more than a physical construction; for him architectural patterns and harmonic patterns betokened social and universal harmony.[11] And yet this image is left in abeyance, and, in spite of its prominence at the opening of the opera, is to play little part in its conceptual ordering—which is doubly surprising, given its potential for organizing and deepening this particular form.

Mercury discovers the reason for Augusta's mourning: 'Speak! did'st not Thou / Forsake thy Faith, and break thy Nuptial Vow?'. Here Dryden re-employs an image which he had used in *Astraea Redux* (1660), where

England was represented as the faithless bride who greeted the return of her lord in penitence. Augusta explains that she has been beguiled by Democracy and Zeal. These characters now appear, attended by Archon (a Greek term for a chief magistrate). Democracy, a man, and Zeal, a woman, demand money from Augusta, but, as Thamesis remarks, no amount of gold will 'suffice for Pious uses, / To feed the sacred hunger of a Saint!'(23). These figures of course express Dryden's distrust of the anarchic tendencies of the London mob, particularly when spurred on by religious fanaticism; but it is perhaps worth pausing over the figure of Zeal. Writing with the Civil War and Exclusion Crisis in mind, Dryden sees Zeal as destructive, but it had not always been so: though Ben Jonson had ridiculed puritan excess in the character of Zeal-of-the-Land-Busy (in *Bartholomew Fair*, 1614), Thomas Middleton could depict Zeal fighting for Truth against Envy in *The Triumph of Truth*, his Lord Mayor's Show for 1613. However, by 1685 Zeal has become tyrannical, and prepares to assist Democracy to rape Augusta. At this point Archon intervenes, and we see that he represents General Monck, who led his army from Scotland in January 1660 and secured the restoration of Charles II. Dryden employs here his favourite technique of transforming, and thus correcting, an image created by an opponent, for Lord Archon was the idealised Cromwell-figure in James Harrington's republican treatise *Oceana* (1656). Mercury gives Archon a wand with which he charms Democracy and Zeal asleep, though both mutter that they will wake again. The two fall asleep on a pedestal representing Hypocrisy and Fanaticism, which then sinks below the stage.

The significance of Mercury's action is not clear. Since he is the god of eloquence and learning, Dryden may be saying that Monck's wise persuasion won over the mob; if so, it is only a half-truth, since it was chiefly Monck's very silence about his intentions which played such an important part in the preparation for the Restoration. On the other hand, Dryden may simply be adopting a convenient image without pursuing its implications; for on the ceiling of the Banqueting House Mercury is shown vanquishing the enemies of the throne, though there he does it as the ally of Minerva-Pallas (regal wisdom), and he strikes down discord with the caduceus of concord.[12]

Juno now appears in a machine drawn by peacocks—as in Jonson's *Hymenaei*[13]—and enjoins Augusta to be faithful to the bed of Albion. Iris reports that Albion has returned and has been greeted by his people, and Juno then announces the return of the golden age: ''Tis time to mount above / And send *Astraea* down, / The Ruler of his Birth, / And Guardian of his Crown'(29). Astraea, the goddess of justice, left the earth when mortals grew degenerate, but was to return with Saturn to inaugurate a new golden age. Thus Virgil in Eclogue IV, writing in praise of the settlement of the state by Augustus after the civil wars. It was Elizabeth who was most frequently identified with *Astraea*,[14] but the image was also applied to James I at his coronation entry, and in Jonson's *The Golden Age Restor'd*, and this myth fitted so well with the Augustan precedents in 1660 that several writers invoked it again, notably Dryden himself in *Astraea Redux*.

At this point part of the scene disappears, and the four triumphal arches erected for Charles's coronation are seen. These had been depicted and explained by John Ogilby, who with a wealth of antiquarian learning showed how many of the details had precedents in Roman practice.[15] Albion and Albanius now appear. Dryden took his name for Charles from the old name of England; 'Albanius', as Earl Miner has suggested, is probably an adaptation of James's title, Duke of Albany. One precedent for this quasi-Roman setting may be found in Aurelian Townsend's masque *Albion's Triumph* (1632) in which Albanactus and his queen Alba stage a Roman-style triumph in the city of Albipolis. Dryden's first act is concluded with the four parts of the world rejoicing at the restoration of Albion; these figures had also been present in the coronation entry and in *Calisto*.

Act II moves the time forward from 1660 to 1678, and changes the scene to hell. Theatrically, hell has strong spectacular possibilities, but it probably also appealed to Dryden as an appropriate setting because of its traditional use in pamphlet literature: writers who described conspiracies often depicted their origin in a debate in hell.[16] But if Dryden seems to be using the tactics of the propagandist, and inclining towards cheap theatricality, this is not all that is to be said about this setting. Powerful scenes in Cowley's *Davideis* had described satanic plots against the young David, who became a standard image for Charles. Dryden himself would have agreed with the figure of Rebellion at Charles's coronation entry when she acknowledged her infernal origin:

> I am Hell's Daughter, *Satan's* Eldest Child,
> When first I cry'd, the Powers of Darkness smil'd,
> And my Glad Father, Thund'ring at my Birth,
> Unhing'd the Poles, and shook the fixed Earth.
> My Dear *Rebellion* (that shall be thy Name,
> Said He) Thou Emperours, and Kings shalt tame,
> No Right so good, Succession none so long,
> But thou shalt vanquish by thy Popular Throng.[17]

But by 1685 these had become party rather than national sentiments.

In hell, Pluto and Alecto (imported from *Aeneid* VII) select one egregiously wicked soul—Titus Oates—who will wreak havoc on earth. The second scene of Act II then returns us to London at the time of the Popish Plot. Augusta is possessed by jealousy, despairing both of her repentance and of Albion's love. To her enter Democracy and Zelota in the guise of a Patriot and Religion. They argue that Augusta should restore the golden age herself by deserting Albion; to this end they oppose to the nuptial bond arguments reminiscent of the rakish ethos of Restoration comedy:

> A King is but a King on Tryal;
> When Love is lost, let Marriage end,
> And leave a Husband for a Friend. (36)

Albion and Albanius enter, and Albion laments that 'Zeal and Common-wealth infest / My Land again' (37). Mercury advises that Albanius be sent abroad, to which Albion agrees, lamenting the loss of a brother and friend: James left England for the continent in 1679 to allow tempers to cool. Apollo descends to assure them of eventual victory, when they will be 'In Lustre equal to the God of Day' (40). Neptune rises with a train of rivers, Tritons and sea-nymphs, and Dryden relaxes with a fine song in celebration of the ocean. Neptune had long been considered the special patron of the island of Britain, and Camden says that Albion was the son of Neptune.[18]

Act III is set at Dover, which had seen the landing of Charles II on his return from exile in 1660, and that of James in 1679. Albion enters with 'Acacia or Innocence', and laments that he has been uncrowned and bound by his people. But Acacia reminds him:

> Empire o'er the Land and Main,
> Heav'n that gave can take again;
> But a mind that's truly brave,
> Stands despising,
> Storms arising,
> And can ne'er be made a Slave. (43)

Albion replies that he has discovered that it is fatal to try to rule by love, which recalls the one criticism of Charles I which we hear in the Restoration period, that he had been too mild in dealing with his opponents. At this point Nereids and Tritons appear to console Albion, but soon there enter 'Tyranny, Democracy, *represented by Men, attended by* Asebia [Impiety], Zelota, *Women*' (44). Zelota says that their business was 'to please the throng, / And Court their wild applause'; Tyranny and Democracy have trammelled Albion:

> To make him safe, we made his Friends our Prey;
> To make him great we scorn'd his Royal sway,
> And to confirm his Crown, we took his Heir away.
> T' encrease his store,
> We kept him poor.
> And when to wants we had betray'd him,
> To keep him low,
> Pronounc'd a Foe,
> Who e're presum'd to aid him. (45)

Though these points apply to the opposition to Charles II, the phrasing is also chillingly reminiscent of the way in which parliamentary leaders constantly claimed to be defending the true interests and rights of Charles I both before and during the Civil War. Asebia reveals their intentions: to betray the people into a new form of slavery by calling it freedom:

> Freedom is a bait alluring;
> Them betraying, us securing,
> While to Sovereign pow'r we soar. (46)

Next 'Six Sectaries begin a formal affected Dance, the two gravest whisper the other Four, and draw 'em into the Plot: They pull out and deliver Libels to 'em, which they receive'. Democracy, Tyranny and Zelota agree that Albion must be killed:

> But who shall then Command?
> The People: for the right returns to those,
> Who did the trust impose. (46)

Democracy here is using a quasi-Hobbesian argument, and Asebia invokes a quasi-Hobbesian nominalism in saying that virtue is only 'an empty Name' (46). Democracy suggests that 'Ere *Albion*'s death we'll try, / If one or many shall his room supply' (47). But the plotters fall out amongst themselves, to an optimistic analysis from Acacia: 'Factions mutually contending, / By each other fall at last' (47).

The cave of Proteus now appears, and Albion and Acacia seize him to make him foretell the future. Proteus is introduced partly as a prophet, but probably also because he was seen as an emblem of the political qualities needed in a successful king: 'wisdom, policy, and fore-know-ledge, are gifts very requisite in a Prince; and if he will govern his people well, he must change himself into many shapes, he must sometimes put on the shape of a Lamb, sometimes of a Lion ... he that cannot dissemble cannot govern; yet Princes must take heed of dishonourable and impious dissembling'.[19] Indeed, dissimulation was one of Charles's famous char-acteristics.[20] Proteus eventually greets him as '*Albion*, lov'd of Gods and Men', recalls that Heaven protected him in his exile, and assures him of its continued care.

Democracy and Zelota return; after the quarrel of their friends, the republicans are left, and they plot the death of Albion at the hands of a one-eyed archer. The archer advances, but a fire arises between him and Albion. This is a translation into simple stage terms of the Rye House Plot, an attempt by the one-eyed Richard Rumbold to kill the King on his return from Newmarket in April 1683, a design which failed when Charles left early because of a fire. Charles's deliverance is celebrated, and Venus is then seen with Albanius sitting 'in a great Scallop-shell' drawn forward by dolphins (50). This is an allusion to James's interest in the sea (as Lord

High Admiral of England from 1661 to 1673) and specifically recalls the painting on one of the coronation arches of 1661, which showed 'the Duke of YORK, habited *à l'antique*, like *Neptune*, standing on a Shell drawn by *Sea-Horses*, before which a *Triton* sounding'.[21] Apollo descends in a spectacular machine of clouds with angels, to announce that Albion must change his abode, for he has been adopted in heaven. He will be seen in the zodiac:

> Betwixt the *Balance* and the *Maid*,
> The Just,
> August,
> And peaceful shade,
> Shall shine in Heav'n with Beams display'd,
> While great *Albanius* is on Earth obey'd. (51)

This is the section which Dryden added after the death of Charles. For his material he has turned to the classical accounts of the stellification of Roman emperors. Albion is accorded the title 'August', linking Charles with the Roman emperor Augustus who restored peace to the Roman world after the civil war which followed upon the assassination of Julius Caesar. Dryden probably had a specific passage in mind, from Claudian's *Panegyric on the Third Consulship of Honorius*, lines which describe the apotheosis of the Emperor Theodosius:

> —nor more he said,
> But through the yielding Clouds his passage made,
> And reach'd the *Moon*, then *Mercury* forsakes,
> And to the milder Sphere of *Venus* makes:
> Thence to the *Sun*, and *Mars* malignant fire,
> And milder *Jove*; then mounts the highest Sphere,
> Where in a colder Circle *Saturn* lords.
> Heaven's Purple Gates ope of their own accords.
> Him to his *Northern* Car *Boötes* courts,
> *Orion* girt unlocks the *Southern Ports*,
> And the new Star invite: both him intreat
> He would vouchsafe to nominate his Seat;
> What Stars for his Associates he approv'd,
> And in which Constellation would be mov'd.[22]

Dryden would have been reminded of this passage by its appearance in Ogilby's account of the 1661 coronation, but there is another reason why it should have come into Dryden's mind at this point. Theodosius leaves behind him two sons, Arcadius and Honorius, emperors respectively of the east and the west, and Claudian celebrates these *unanimi fratres*, brothers who have a single heart, to whom fate has entrusted sea and land.

As Albion is drawn up into heaven, Venus assures us of future triumphs: 'Already are they fixt by Fate, / And only ripening Ages wait' (52). But the opera does not end with the apotheosis of Albion. The final scene shows us Windsor Castle: 'In the Air is a Vision of the Honors of the Garter, the Knights in Procession, and the King under a Canopy: Beyond this, the upper end of St. George's Hall.' Perhaps Dryden had in mind the concluding tableau of Carew's *Coelum Britannicum*: 'In the firmament ... was a troope of fifteene starres, expressing the stellifying of our British Heroes; but one more great and eminent than the rest ... figured his Majesty. And in the lower part was seene a farre off the prospect of *Windsor Castell*, the famous seat of the most honourable Order of the Garter'.[23] But then in Dryden's masque Fame rises in the middle of the stage, standing on a globe which carries the arms of England. The globe rests on a pedestal, on the front of which 'is drawn a Man with a long, lean, pale Face, with Fiends Wings, and Snakes twisted round his Body: He is incompast by several Phanatical Rebellious Heads, who suck poyson from him, which runs out of a Tap in his Side' (53). This is the most arresting of Dryden's literal translations of politics into stage imagery, for it represents the Earl of Shaftesbury, organizer of the Whig opposition, who as the result of an accident had a silver tap fitted to his side to draw off the poisonous matter. He had died abroad in 1683, but Dryden's image suggests that he remains, as it were, the fountainhead of corruption in the body politic.

A song by Fame celebrating Albion (but not, by an odd oversight in the revision, Albanius) and a full chorus of all the voices and instruments, together with two dozen dancers, brings the masque to an end.

Such, in outline, is Dryden's deployment of traditional iconography in the cause of the restored Stuart monarchy, meeting the uncertainty of a new reign with a slightly strident assertion of kingly power. Let us now ponder some of the factors which have created a distance between Dryden and the masques of the early Stuart court.

Dryden is writing in the aftermath of changes in the public language of England which occurred between 1640 and 1660. One of the most important of these changes was in the way men expressed the idea of sovereignty. Although there had been political theories which stressed other elements, it is broadly true that before the Civil War the King was both the ceremonial and the effective embodiment of national sovereignty. The artistic expressions of that consciousness tended to stress the personal interests of the individual monarchs: the ceiling of the Banqueting House adopted James I's image of himself as Solomon the wise ruler, while court masques for Charles I celebrated the chaste platonic love which he and his Queen liked to encourage. But in the years of the Interregnum the public language changed. Despite the use of quasi-monarchical images during the Protectorate, there had been a shift of emphasis to the idea of the Commonwealth of England, and this was supported both by political theory and by the realities of political power. After the Restoration, which was a negotiated rapprochement between Charles and the country, the King could no longer be seen as the embodiment of nationhood—nor, come to that, as the fountainhead of virtue.

The masque had re-enforced the monarchical perception of sovereignty by celebrating the King's attributes around his physical presence. In its use of audience and actors, masque functions almost as a liturgy, for its participants are released and redeemed from their grosser selves and made the vehicles of a divine order. Masque is acted, and one's participation in dramatic action may raise questions of identity at a depth not otherwise tapped. Plato was perhaps right to suspect drama: to him there was a danger in allowing the young members of the governing class to act, in that they would tend to grow into the roles which they played. The court masque is therefore perhaps the only form of drama (apart from the mystery plays, and the Mass itself) which relies upon a Platonic rather than an Aristotelian theory of dramatic effect. The drama in which one collaborates is thus a temporarily achieved articulation of the ideal which (were it not for the imperfections of human nature) one would act out all the time. The physical and spiritual worlds meet in man, and this art helps him to redeem the former by the latter. Dryden's masque, however, cannot use this redemptive participation of the audience in the action; the King may not be present, and the construction of the theatre imposes a physical and aesthetic distance between drama and audience. The rhetoric which now has to bridge this gap can no longer assume cooperation from its hearers, and hence takes on a propagandist tone.

In so far as there was a philosophical assumption behind the masque of the early Stuart court it was thus a neo-Platonic view of the ordering of the universe, and of the King's place in it. The masque created around the physical person of the King an image of a settled system of values; the divinely-ordained, platonically ideal harmony of the universe is repeated (or perhaps one might say that it is made incarnate) in the King and in the harmony which he creates in his court and in his country. But the Platonic system was no longer a usable philosophical justification for the restored Stuart monarchy of 1660–85.

We can, in fact, observe Dryden moving away from Platonist notions in the course of his writing. He had been familiar with these ideas as a young man, and in his poem *Upon the Death of the Lord Hastings* (1649) he used imagery which assumed a neo-Platonic hierarchical universe:

> His body was an Orb, his sublime Soul
> Did move on Vertue's and on Learning's Pole:
> Whose Reg'lar Motions better to our view,
> Then *Archimedes* Sphere, the Heavens did shew.   (ll. 27–30)

And in 1662 Dryden tried to revive this language to express the relations between Charles II and his Lord Chancellor, the Earl of Clarendon; to Clarendon he says:

> So well your Vertues do with his agree
> That though your Orbs of different greatness be,
> Yet both are for each others use dispos'd,
> His to inclose, and yours to be inclos'd.

But this conceit is itself enclosed, and limiting; it is an image in which the vehicle traps our imagination and will not allow it to enlarge our sense of kingly power and its origins:

> In open prospect nothing bounds our eye
> Until the Earth seems joyn'd unto the Sky:
> So in this Hemisphaer our utmost view
> Is only bounded by our King and you:
> Our sight is limited where you are joyn'd
> And beyond that no farther Heav'n can find.[24]

This elaborate compliment to Clarendon remains sterile because Dryden has already begun to think about politics in terms of how events are actually managed. When he writes of Cromwell that he 'own'd a soul above / The highest Acts it could produce to show', there is a Platonist shape to the idea: Cromwell's actions only imperfectly reveal his soul, as the sublunary world is but an imperfect copy of the Platonic Idea. Yet if we complete the stanza—'Thus poor *Mechanique Arts* in publique moove / Whilst the deep Secrets beyond practice goe'[25]—we find that Dryden is also brooding upon the Machiavellian origins of political action in political calculations (one meaning of 'practice' is 'calculation') which are not assessable by the observer. Similarly, when describing how the Restoration came about, Dryden says that we 'Th' effect did feel but scarce the manner see'[26]; yet he knows that events are only produced by intricate political manoeuvring, and he makes this plain in an image which, as it were, takes us backstage in the masque:

> The blessed Saints that watch'd this turning Scene
> Did from their Stars with joyful wonder leane,
> To see small clues [*threads*] draw vastest weights along,
> Not in their bulk but in their order strong.[27]

Dryden has seen that there is an art to politics which resembles the manipulation of a complex system of pulleys.

Perhaps we are now in a position to assess why *Albion and Albanius* is an unsatisfactory work. To begin with, it is mythologically decadent. It mixes personifications from different sources without establishing any differentiation between their activities. Charles as Albion moves through a play in which he is essentially passive in the face of the personified hostility of the London opposition. He does not act, either as a politician or as a monarch with kingly power and sacred aura, and there is little encompassing imagery to supplement the meaning of his role. Instead, a wholly predictable group of gods and goddesses reassures him of his safety while doing little to achieve it, and the opposition is left to confound itself. In the masques of the early Stuart court, political challenges to the establishment were understated, and generally confined to the comic or grotesque antimasque, where they could be safely contained. 'The antimasque world', says Stephen Orgel, 'was a world of particularity and mutability—of accidents; the masque world was one of ideal abstractions and eternal verities.'[28] Dryden has mixed the two, making his hero vulnerable to direct challenge; he offers a satisfying rendering neither of the worlds of mutability nor of eternity, and has botched their moments of interpenetration.

In some respects this is curious, seeing that Dryden is acutely aware of this meeting of worlds, and elsewhere handles it with brilliance. In *Annus Mirabilis* (1667) he portrays God's intervention in the Fire of London with a totally resolute wit:

> An hollow chrystal Pyramid he takes,
> In firmamental waters dipt above;
> Of it a brode Extinguisher he makes,
> And hoods the flames that to their quarry strove.   (ll. 1121-4)

But Dryden's baroque imagination here offended his readers, and even if one accepts the image in a poem, one can hardly entertain the possibility of a comparable stage image being taken seriously; or rather, being taken with a humour which relished and did not destroy it. If Dryden's exactitude of wit in *Absalom and Achitophel* (1681) is again an *ad hoc* success, it is also the case that his more solemn passages there on the relation between eternal and contingent worlds are likewise impatient of translation into visual terms for the stage. In that poem he suggests that the leaders of the opposition are momentary incarnations of an eternal principle of chaos and volatility, and invites us to see the Exclusion Crisis as a further example of the dangerous misuse of human freedom which had previously been manifest in the Civil War, in the reign of King David, and in the Garden of Eden. And it is clear that, more generally, Dryden was deeply absorbed by the idea of change, and found in the Lucretian and Ovidian depictions of mutability a profound spiritual challenge and consolation.[29] But this tends to happen only when Dryden is pushed to his limits, and forced to confront the ultimate values and processes of life. Naturally, he cannot always afford to do this, and much of his work quite properly operates at a lower pressure. *Absalom and Achitophel* is an extraordinary example of Dryden's ability to link depth and surface, but in *Albion and Albanius* the pressure is off.

When the crisis was still dangerous, Dryden had written thus in his preface to *The Duke of Guise* (1683): 'since this glorious Work is yet unfinish'd, and though we have reason to hope well of the success, yet the Event depends on the unsearchable Providence of Almighty God, 'tis no time to raise Trophees, while the Victory is in dispute' (A2v). But a year or so later the crisis has passed, and the King's party is ready to stage a triumph. This is how Dryden later remembered the circumstances of *Albion and Albanius:* 'It was indeed a Time, which was proper for a Triumph, when he had overcome all those Difficulties which for some Years had perplex'd His Peaceful Reign: ... when He had just restor'd His People to their Senses, and made the latter End of His Government, of a Piece with the Happy Beginning of it'.[30] So *Albion and Albanius* is an assertion of triumph. It is under no compulsion to persuade its audience by unlocking some of the archetypal power latent in particular images, or by engaging in argument; hence it can use its mythology scrappily and guy its victims with cliché.

It may be appropriate to conclude by recalling Jonas Barish's summary of the social function of the early Stuart masque: '[it] represents a society not so much aspiring after as joyfully contemplating its own well-being, the possession of the blessings it considers itself to have achieved. The compliments to the king ... are one expression of this self-congratulation on the part of the community.'[31] By contrast, Dryden's masque is too much of a factional piece to embody the values of a community. In contemplating the blessings of the reign of Charles II it manages to suggest no more than that Charles muddled through; for it seems to have no real faith in the King's political skills or in the hand of Providence. It is in the end rather appropriate that a mistimed triumph should so rapidly have been buried by changing circumstances which it had failed either to deflect or to transmute into the eternity of true art.

NOTES

1 *Collected Poems of Sidney Godolphin*, ed. William Dighton (Oxford, 1931), p. 13.

2 Line 26.

3 Richard Luckett, 'Music', in *The Diary of Samuel Pepys*, ed. Robert Latham and William Matthews, 11 vols (London 1970–83), 10, pp. 258–82, p. 263.

4 See Richard Luckett, 'Exotick but Rational Entertainments: The English Dramatick Operas', in *English Drama: Forms and Development*, ed. Marie Axton and Raymond Williams (Cambridge, 1977), pp. 123–141.

5 *Works of John Dryden*, volume 15, edited by Earl Miner and George R. Guffey (Berkeley, 1976), p. 12. Quotations are from this edition, with page references given in parentheses.

6 Either Dryden and Davenant's revision of Shakespeare's play (1670), or, more probably, Shadwell's operatic version of that revision (1674).

7 *For the Honour of Wales*, l. 373.

8 See David M. Bergeron, *English Civic Pageantry 1558–1642* (London, 1971), Chapters 1–2.

9 See John Ogilby, *The Entertainment of His Most Excellent Majestie Charles II, In his Passage through the City of London to his Coronation* (London, 1662).

10 For the origin of the name, see William Camden, *Britain* (London, 1610), p. 80; and cf. Edmund Bolton, *London, King Charles, his Augusta* (London, 1648).

11 See Richard Luckett, 'The Fabric of Dryden's Verse', *Proceedings of the British Academy*, 67 (1981), 289–305.

12 Roy Strong, *Britannia Triumphans: Inigo Jones and Whitehall Palace* (London, 1980), pp. 42–4.

13 Stage direction after line 211.

14 See Frances Yates, *Astraea: The Imperial Theme in the Sixteenth Century* (London, 1975).

15 Ogilby, *The Entertainment of . . . Charles II*, p. 37.

16 Benjamin Boyce, 'News from Hell', *PMLA*, 58 (1943), pp. 402–37.

17 Ogilby, p. 41.

18 Camden, *Britain*, p. 24; cf. Ogilby, pp. 53, 103–5.

19 Alexander Ross, *Mystagogus Poeticus, or The Muses Interpreter* (London, 1648), p. 371.

20 See Halifax, *The Character of King Charles the Second*, Chapter 2.

21 Ogilby, p. 93.

22 Quoted from the translation in Ogilby, pp. 34–5; lines 162–74 in the Latin.

23 *The Poems of Thomas Carew*, ed. Rhodes Dunlap (Oxford, 1949), pp. 182–3.

24 *To My Lord Chancellor*, ll. 37–40, 31–6.

25 *Heroique Stanza's, Consecrated to the Glorious Memory of his most Serene and Renowned Highnesse OLIVER Late LORD PROTECTOR of this Common-Wealth*, ll. 125–8.

26 *Astraea Redux*, l. 130.

27 *Astraea Redux*, ll. 153–6.

28 *The Jonsonian Masque* (Cambridge, Mass., 1965), p. 73.

29 As I have argued in 'The Integrity of Dryden's Lucretius', *MLR*, 78 (1983), pp. 1–23.

30 *King Arthur: or, The British Worthy* (London, 1695), A2r.

31 *Ben Jonson and the Language of Prose Comedy* (Cambridge, Mass., 1960), p. 244.

Since David Bergeron's bibliography (listed below) is comprehensive, the selection of items published after 1970-1 is rather more generous than those of earlier date. The sections on Milton and on Masque and Drama include all the material referred to in the essays in this volume, but are necessarily highly selective. To attempt to cover all the work on Milton, or on Shakespeare's late plays, would extend this bibliography much too far. The bibliography is subdivided as follows: A, Bibliographies and Reference Books; B, Texts; C, Surveys; D, Ben Jonson; E, Milton; F, General; G, Scene; H, Music; I, Masque and Drama.

A. BIBLIOGRAPHIES AND REFERENCE WORKS

G.E. Bentley, *The Jacobean and Caroline Stage*, 7 vols (Oxford, 1941-68).
David M. Bergeron, ed., *Twentieth Century Criticism of English Masques, Pageants and Entertainments 1558-1642* (San Antonio, 1972).
E.K. Chambers, *The Elizabethan Stage*, 4 vols (Oxford, 1923).
Inga-Stina Ewbank, '"The Eloquence of Masques": A Retrospective View of Masque Criticism', *Renaissance Drama*, N.S. 1 (1968), pp. 307-28.
W.W. Greg, *A List of Masques, Pageants etc., Supplementary to a List of English Plays* (London, 1902).
Alfred Harbage, *Annals of English Drama 975-1700*, rev. S. Schoenbaum (London, 1964).
K.M. Lea, 'The Court Masque', in *English Drama, Select Bibliographical Guides*, ed. Stanley Wells (Oxford, 1975).
Mary Susan Steele, *Plays and Masques at Court during the Reigns of Elizbeth, James and Charles* (New Haven and London, 1926).

B. TEXTS

(a) ANTHOLOGIES
Richard Dutton, ed., *Jacobean and Caroline Masques*, Vol. 1 (Nottingham, 1981). (Contains masques by Jonson and Daniel; a seond volume is promised.)
H.A. Evans, ed., *English Masques* (London, 1909). (The largest anthology.)
Murray Lefkowitz, *Trois Masques à la Cour de Charles Ier d'Angleterre* (Paris, 1970). (Contains *The Triumph of Peace, The Triumphs of the Prince d'Amour, Britannia Triumphans*.)
John Nichols, *The Progresses of Queen Elizabeth*, 3 vols (London, 1823).
—— *The Progresses of James the First*, 4 vols (London, 1828).
T.J.B. Spencer and Stanley Wells, eds., *A Book of Masques in Honour of Allardyce Nicoll* (Cambridge, 1967). (The widest range of masques currently in print.)
Jean Wilson, ed., *Entertainments for Elizabeth I* (Woodbridge, 1980).

(b) SINGLE AUTHORS AND TEXTS

Francis Beaumont, *The Masque of the Inner Temple*, in *Beaumont and Fletcher: Dramatic Works*, 1, general editor Fredson Bowers (Cambridge, 1966).

Thomas Campion, *The Works*, ed. Walter R. Davis (London, 1969).

Thomas Carew, *Collected Poems*, ed. Rhodes Dunlap (Oxford, 1949).

George Chapman, *The Plays of George Chapman: The Comedies*, ed. Allan Holaday and Michael Kiernana (Urbana, Ill., 1970).

A. Cokayne, *Dramatic Works*, ed. J. Maidment and W.H. Logan (Edinburgh, 1874).

Samuel Daniel, *Works*, ed. A. B. Grosart, Vol. 3 (London, 1885) —— *Vision of Twelve Goddesses*, ed. Ernest Law (London, 1880).

William Davenant, *The Dramatic Works*, ed. J. Maidment and W.H. Logan (Edinburgh and London, 1872-4).

Thomas Dekker, *Dramatic Works*, ed. Fredson Bowers, 4 vols (Cambridge, 1955-70). *Introduction, Notes and Commentary* ed. Cyrus Hoy (Cambridge, 1980).

George Gascoigne, *Complete Works*, ed. J.W. Cunliffe (Cambridge, 1907-10).

Gesta Grayorum, ed. D. Bland (Liverpool, 1968).

Ben Jonson, *Ben Jonson*, eds. C.H. Herford and Percy and Evelyn Simpson, 11 vols (Oxford, 1925-52).

—— *The Complete Masques*, ed. Stephen Orgel (New Haven, Conn., and London, 1969).

——*Selected Masques*, ed. Stephen Orgel (New Haven and London, 1970).

——*Jonson's Masque of Gipsies*, ed. W.W. Greg (London, 1952).

Robert Laneham's Letter, ed. F. J. Furnivall (London, 1907).

John Lyly, *The Complete Works*, ed. R.W. Bond, 3 vols (London, 1902).

The Lord Mayor's Show of 1590, ed. John C. Meagher, *English Literary Renaissance*, 3 (1973), pp. 94-104.

The Masque of Truth, ed. David Norbrook, *Paideia*, Renaissance Issue (forthcoming).

Thomas Middleton, *The Works*, ed. A. H. Bullen 8 vols (London 1885-6).

Thomas Nashe, *The Works*, ed. R.B. McKerrow, rev. F.P. Wilson (Oxford, 1958).

Sir Philip Sidney, *Miscellaneous Prose*, ed. Katherine Duncan-Jones and Jan van Dorsten (Oxford, 1973).

Aurelian Townshend, *The Poems and Masques*, ed. Cedric C. Brown (Reading, 1983).

C. SURVEYS

Rudolf Brotanek, *Die Englischen Maskenspiele* (Vienna and Leipzig, 1902).

Stephen Orgel, *The Illusion of Power* (Berkeley, Los Angeles and London, 1975).

—— *The Jonsonian Masque* (Cambridge, Mass., 1965).

Paul Reyher, *Les Masques anglais* (Paris, 1909).

Mary Sullivan, *The Court Masque of James I* (Lincoln, 1913).

Enid Welsford, *The Court Masque* (Cambridge, 1927).

D. BEN JONSON

Don Cameron Allen, 'Ben Jonson and the Hieroglyphics', *Philological Quarterly*, 18 (1939), pp. 290–300.

Jonas A. Barish, 'Jonson and the Loathèd Stage', in *A Celebration of Ben Jonson*, ed. William Blisset, Julian Patrick and R. W. van Fossen (Toronto, 1973), pp. 27–53.

—— *Ben Jonson and the Language of Prose Comedy* (Cambridge, Mass., 1960).

M. C. Bradbrook, 'Social Change and the Evolution of Ben Jonson's Court Masques', *Studies in the Literary Imagination*, 6 (1973), pp. 103–38.

Norman Council, 'Ben Jonson, Inigo Jones, and the Transformation of Tudor Chivalry', *ELH*, 47 (1980), pp. 259–75.

Dolora Cunningham, 'The Jonsonian Masque as a Literary Form', *ELH*, 22 (1955), pp. 108–24.

Edgar Hill Duncan, 'The Alchemy in Jonson's *Mercury Vindicated*', *Studies in Philology*, 39 (1942), pp. 625–37.

Philip Edwards, *Threshold of a Nation* (London, 1979).

Jeffrey Fischer, '*Love Restored*: A Defense of Masquing', *Renaissance Drama*, N. S. 8 (1977), pp. 231–44.

W. Todd Furniss, 'Ben Jonson's Masques', in *Three Studies in the Renaissance* (New Haven, Conn., 1958).

A. H. Gilbert, 'The Function of the Masques in *Cynthia's Revels*', *Philological Quarterly*, 22 (1943), pp. 211–30.

—— *The Symbolic Persons in the Masques of Ben Jonson* (Durham, N. C., 1948).

D. J. Gordon, *The Renaissance Imagination*, ed. Stephen Orgel (Berkeley, Los Angeles and London, 1975). Reprints Gordon's articles on *Blackness and Beauty, Hymenaei, Haddington Masque*.

W. W. Greg, 'Jonson's Masques: Points of Editorial Principle and Practice', *Review of English Studies*, 18 (1942), pp. 144–66.

Irena Janicka, 'The Popular Background of Ben Jonson's Masques', *Shakespeare Jahrbuch*, 105 (1969), pp. 183–208.

Bruce Louis Jay, 'The Role of Verse and the Dynamics of Form in Jonson's Masques', *Etudes anglaises*, 29 (1976), pp. 129–43.

Ann Clive Kelly, 'The Challenge of the Impossible: Ben Jonson's *Masque of Blackness*', *College Language Association Journal*, 20 (1977), pp. 341–55.

Leah Sinanoglou Marcus, 'Present Occasions and the Shaping of Ben Jonson's Masques', *ELH*, 45 (1978) pp. 201–25.

—— 'The Occasion of Jonson's *Pleasure Reconciled to Virtue*', *Studies in English Literature*, 19 (1979), pp. 271–93.

John C. Meagher, *Method and Meaning in Jonson's Masques* (Notre Dame, Ind., 1966).

John Orrell, 'The Musical Canon of Proportion in Jonson's *Hymenaei*', *English Language Notes*, 15 (1978), pp. 171–8.

Richard S. Peterson, 'The Iconography of Jonson's *Pleasure Reconciled to Virtue*', *Journal of Medieval and Renaissance Studies*, 5 (1975), pp. 123–54.

Dale B. J. Randall, *Jonson's Gypsies Unmasked* (Durham, N. C., 1975).

Catherine M. Shaw, 'The Masques of Ben Jonson: Editions and Editorial Criticism', *Genre*, 3 (1970), pp. 272–88.

Ernest W. Talbert, 'Current Scholarly Works and the "Erudition" of Jonson's *Masque of Augurs*', *Studies in Philology*, 44 (1947), pp. 605–24.

Ernest W. Talbert, 'The Interpretation of Jonson's Courtly Spectacles', *PMLA*, 61 (1946), pp. 454–73.

Eugene M. Waith, 'Things as they are and the world of absolutes in Jonson's plays and masques', *Elizabethan Theatre*, 4 (1974), pp. 106–26.

Albert Wertheim, 'James Shirley and the Caroline Masques of Ben Jonson', *Theatre Notebook*, 27 (1973), pp. 9–14.

C.F. Wheeler, *Classical Mythology in the Plays, Masques and Poems of Ben Jonson* (Princeton, N.J., 1938).

Mary C. Williams, 'Merlin and the Prince: The Speeches at Prince Henry's Barriers', *Renaissance Drama*, N.S. 8 (1977), pp. 221–30.

E. MILTON

Robert M. Adams, 'Reading *Comus*', *Modern Philology*, 51 (1953), reprinted in his *Milton and the Modern Critics* (New York, 1955), and in Diekhoff volume.

C. L. Barber, 'A Mask Presented at Ludlow Castle: The Masque as a Masque' in *The Lyric and Dramatic Milton*, ed. Joseph Summers (New York and London, 1965), pp. 35–63.

Barbara Breasted, '*Comus* and the Castlehaven Scandal', *Milton Studies*, 3 (1971), pp. 201–24.

Philip Brockbank, 'The Measure of *Comus*', *Essays and Studies*, 21 (1968), pp. 46–61.

Cedric C. Brown, 'The Chirk Castle Entertainment of 1634', *Milton Quarterly*, 11 (1977), pp. 76–86.

—— 'Milton's *Arcades*: Context, Form and Function', *Renaissance Drama*, N. S. 8 (1977), pp. 245–74.

Archie Burnett, *Milton's Style* (London, 1981).

John D. Cox, 'Poetry and History in Milton's Country Masque', *ELH*, 44 (1977), pp. 622–40.

John G. Demaray, '*Arcades* as a Literary Entertainment', *Papers on Language and Literature*, 8 (1972), pp. 15–26.

—— *Milton and the Masque Tradition* (Cambridge, Mass., 1968).

John S. Diekhoff, ed., *A Maske at Ludlow: Essays on Milton's Comus* (Cleveland, Ohio, 1968).

A.E. Dyson, 'The Interpretation of *Comus*', *Essays and Studies*, N.S. 8 (1955), pp. 89–114. (Revised in *Between Two Worlds* (London, 1972) pp. 15–40.)

Stanley E. Fish, 'Problem Solving in *Comus*', in *Illustrious Evidence*, ed. Earl Miner (London, 1975).

Angus Fletcher, *The Transcendental Masque* (Ithaca, N.Y., 1971).

S.L. Goldberg, 'The Word, The Flesh and *Comus*', *Melbourne Critical Review*, 6 (1963), 56–68.

Eugene Haun, 'An Inquiry into the Genre of *Comus*', in *Essays in Honor of W.C. Curry* (Nashville, Texas., 1954), pp. 221–39.

William B. Hunter, Jr., 'The Liturgical Context of *Comus*', *English Language Notes*, 10 (1972), pp. pp. 11–15.

—— 'The Date and Occasion of *Arcades*', *English Language Notes*, 11 (1973), pp. 46–7.

Sears Jayne, 'The Subject of Milton's Ludlow *Mask*', *PMLA*, 74 (1959), pp. 533–43. (Reprinted in Arthur E. Barker, ed., *Milton: Modern Essays in Criticism* (London, 1965), and in Diekhoff volume.)

Terry Kidner Kohn, 'Landscape in the Transcendent Masque', *Milton Studies*, 6 (1974), pp. 143–64.

Julian Lovelock, ed., *Milton: Comus and Samson Agonistes*, Casebook series (London, 1975).

Mary Ann McGuire, 'Milton's *Arcades* and the Entertainment Tradition', *Studies in Philology*, 75 (1978), pp. 451–71.

Jeanne S. Martin, 'Transformation in Genre in Milton's *Comus*', *Genre*, 10 (1977), pp. 195–213.

Louis B. Martz, *Poet of Exile: A Study of Milton's Poetry* (London, 1980).

Richard Neuse, 'Metamorphosis and Symbolic Action in *Comus*', *ELH*, 34 (1967), pp. 49–64.

Balachandra Rajan, *The Lofty Rhyme* (London, 1970).

Alice-Lyle Scoufos, 'The Mysteries in Milton's *Masque*', *Milton Studies*, 4 (1974), pp. 113–42.

James G. Taaffe, 'Michaelmas, the "Lawless Hour", and the Occasion of Milton's *Comus*', *English Language Notes*, 6 (1969), pp. 257–62.

John Malcolm Wallace, 'Milton's *Arcades*', *Journal of English and Germanic Philogy*, 58 (1959), pp. 627–36.

A.S.P. Woodhouse, *The Heavenly Muse: A Preface to Milton* (Toronto, 1972).

F. GENERAL

Sydney Anglo, 'The Evolution of the Early Tudor Disguising, Pageant and Mask', *Renaissance Drama*, N.S. 1 (1968), pp. 3–44.

—— *Spectacle, Pageants and Early Tudor Policy* (Oxford, 1969).

Marie Axton, *The Queen's Two Bodies* (London, 1977).

David M. Bergeron, *English Civic Pageantry* (London, 1971).

——'Civic Pageants and Historical Drama', *Journal of Medieval and Renaissance Studies*, 5 (1975), pp. 89–105.

——'Elizabeth's Coronation Entry (1559): New Manuscript Evidence', *English Literary Renaissance*, 8 (1978), pp. 3–8.

Harry H. Boyle, 'Elizabeth's Entertainment at Elvetham: War Policy in Pageantry', *Studies in Philology*, 68 (1971), pp. 146–66.

M.C. Bradbrook, 'Drama as Offering: The Princely Pleasures at Kenelworth', *Rice Institute Pamphlet*, 46 (1960), No. 4, 57–70.

—— 'The Politics of Pageantry: Social Implications in Jacobean London', in *Poetry and Drama 1500–1700: Essays in Honour of Harold F. Brooks*, ed. Antony Coleman and Antony Hammond (London, 1981), pp. 60–75.

Ernest Brenneke, 'The Entertainment at Elvetham, 1591', in *Music in English Renaissance Drama*, ed. John H. Long (Lexington, Ky., 1968), pp. 32–56.

R. J. Broadbent, 'The Masque at Knowsley', *Transactions of the Historical Society of Lancashire and Cheshire*, 41 (1925), pp. 9–16.

Helen Cooper, *Pastoral: Medieval into Renaissance* (Ipswich, 1977).

Norman Council, 'O *Dea Certe:* The Allegory of *The Fortress of Perfect Beauty*', *Huntington Library Quarterly*, 34 (1975–6), pp. 329–42.

Geoffrey Creigh, 'Samuel Daniel's Masque *The Vision of Twelve Goddesses*', *Essays and Studies*, 24 (1971), pp. 22–35.

J.W. Cunliffe, 'The Queenes Majesties Entertainment at Woodstocke', *PMLA*, 26 (1911), pp. 92–141.

Margaret Dean-Smith, 'Folk-Play Origins of the English Masque', *Folklore*, 65 (1954), pp. 74–86.

Richard L. DeMolen, 'Richard Mulcaster and Elizabethan Pageantry', *Studies in English Literature*, 14 (1974), pp. 209–21.

A. Leigh DeNeef, 'Structure and Theme in Campion's *Lords' Maske*', *Studies in English Literature*, 18 (1977), pp. 95–103.

J.A. van Dorsten, 'Garter Knights and Familists', *Journal of European Studies*, 4 (1974), pp. 178–88.

Rhodes Dunlap, 'King James's Own Masque', *Philological Quarterly*, 41 (1962), pp. 249–256.

Leonard Forster, 'Die Festlichkeiten bei der Trauung Friedrichs von der Pfalz 1612–13', *Anglia*, 62 (1938), pp. 362–7.

——'Two Drafts by Weckherlin for a Masque for the Queen of England', *German Life and Letters*, 18 (1964–5), pp. 258–63.

Jonathan Goldberg, 'James I and the Theatre of Conscience', *ELH*, 46 (1979), pp. 379–98.

D.J. Gordon, *The Renaissance Imagination*, ed. Stephen Orgel (Berkeley, Los Angeles, and London, 1975), reprints articles on 'Roles and Mysteries' and 'Chapman's *Memorable Masque*'.

J. Jacquot, ed., *Les Fêtes de la Renaissance* (Paris, 1956).

Paula Johnson, 'Jacobean Ephemera and the Immortal World', *Renaissance Drama*, N.S. 8 (1977), pp. 151–72.

Gordon Kipling, 'Triumphal Drama: Form in English Civic Pageantry', *Renaissance Drama*, N.S. 8 (1977), pp. 37–56.

David Lindley, *Thomas Campion* (Leiden, forthcoming 1984).

——'Who paid for Campion's *Lord Hay's Masque*?', *Notes and Queries*, N.S. 26 (1979), pp. 144–5.

——'Campion's Lord Hay's Masque and Anglo-Scottish Union', *Huntington Library Quarterly*, 43 (1979), pp. 1–11.

Leah Sinanoglou Marcus, 'Masquing Occasion and Masque Structure', *Research Opportunities in Renaissance Drama*, 24 (1981), pp. 7–16.

Louis Adrian Montrose, 'Celebration and Insinuation: Sir Philip Sidney and the Motives of Elizabethan Courtship', *Renaissance Drama*, N.S. 8 (1977), pp. 3–35.

——' "Eliza Queen of Shepherds" and the Pastoral of Power', *English Literary Renaissance*, 10 (1980), pp. 153–82.

Graham Parry, *The Golden Age Restor'd: The Culture of the Stuart Court* (Manchester, 1981).

T.M. Parrott, 'Comedy in the Court Masques: A Study of Jonson's Contribution', *Philological Quarterly*, 20 (1941), pp. 428–41.

Wayne H. Phelps, 'The Second Night of Davenant's *Salmacida Spolia*', *Notes and Queries*, N.S. 26 (1979), pp. 512–3.

Lois Potter, '*The Triumph of Peace* and *The Cruel War*, Masque and Parody', *Notes and Queries*, 27 (1980), pp. 345–8.

Jack E. Reese, 'Unity in Chapman's *Masque of the Middle Temple and Lincoln's Inn*', *Studies in English Literature*, 4 (1964), pp. 291–305.

Raymond C. Shady, 'Thomas Heywood's Masque at Court', *The Elizabethan Theatre*, 7 (1981), pp. 147–66.

Bruce R. Smith, 'Landscape with Figures: The Three Realms of Queen Elizabeth's Country-House Revels', *Renaissance Drama*, N.S. 8 (1977), pp. 57-115.

Ian Spink, 'Campion's Entertainment at Brougham Castle, 1617', in *Music in English Renaissance Drama*, ed. John H. Long (Lexington and London, 1968), pp. 57-74.

DeWitt T. Starnes and E.W. Talbert, *Classical Myth and Legend in Renaissance Dictionaries* (Chapel Hill, N.C., 1955).

Roy Strong, *The Cult of Elizabeth* (London, 1977).

——and J.A. van Dorsten, *Leicester's Triumph* (Leiden and Oxford, 1964).

Dick Taylor, 'The Masque and the Lance: The Earl of Pembroke in Jacobean Court Entertainments', *Tulane Studies in English*, 8 (1958), pp. 21-53.

Eugene Waith, 'Spectacles of State', *Studies in English Literature*, 13 (1973), pp. 317-330.

C.V. Wedgwood, 'The Last Masque', in *Truth and Opinion* (London, 1960).

Glynne Wickham, 'The Stuart Mask', in *Shakespeare's Dramatic Heritage* (London, 1969), pp. 103-18.

Jerry Williamson, *Myth of the Conqueror: Prince Henry Stuart. A Study of Seventh-Century Personation* (New York, 1978).

Robert Withington, *English Pagentry: An Historical Outline*, 2 Vols (Cambridge, Mass., 1918).

Fraces Yates, *Astraea: The Imperial Theme in The Sixteenth Century* (London, 1975).

G. SCENE

Lily B. Campbell, *Scenes and Machines on the English Stage* (Cambridge, Mass., 1923).

John P. Cutts, 'Seventeenth-century Illustrations of Three Masques by Jonson', *Comparative Drama*, 36 (1972), pp. 125-34.

John Harris, Stephen Orgel, and Roy Strong, *The King's Arcadia: Inigo Jones and the Stuart Court* (London, 1973).

Allardyce Nicoll, *The Development of the Theatre* (London, 1927).

——*Stuart Masques and the Renaissance Stage* (London, 1937).

Stephen Orgel and Roy Strong, *Inigo Jones: The Theatre of the Stuart Court*, 2 vols (New York and London, 1973).

Stephen Orgel, 'The Renaissance Artist as Plagiarist', *ELH*, 48 (1981), pp. 476-95.

John Orrell, 'The Agent of Savoy at *The Somerset Masque*', *Review of English Studies*, 28 (1977), pp. 301-4.

—— 'Antonio Galli's Description of *The Masque of Beauty*', *Huntington Library Quaterly*, 43 (1979), pp. 13-23.

——'Inigo Jones and Amerigo Salvetti: A Note on the Later Masque Designs', *Theatre Notebook*, 30 (1976), pp. 109-14.

—— 'The London Stage in the Florentine Correspondence, 1604-1618', *Theatre Research International*, 3 (1978), pp. 157-75.

Per Palme, *The Triumph of Peace: A Study of Whitehall Banqueting House* (London, 1957).

John Peacock, 'Inigo Jones and the *Livre de le Conqueste de la Toison d'Or*', *Gazette de Beaux Arts* (forthcoming).

—— 'Inigo Jones's Stage Architecture and its Sources', *Art Bulletin*, 64 (1982).

—— 'New Sources for the Masque Designs of Inigo Jones', *Apollo*, 107 (1978).

Select bibliography

Richard Southern, *Changeable Scenery* (London, 1952).
Roy Strong, *Britannia Triumphans: Inigo Jones, Rubens and Whitehall Palace* (London, 1980).
—— *Festival Designs by Inigo Jones* (Washington, D.C., 1967).
—— *Splendour at Court: Renaissance Spectacle and Illusion* (London, 1973).
John Summerson, *Ingio Jones* (Harmondsworth, 1966).
Glynne Wickham, *Early English Stages, 1300–1600*, 4 vols (London, 1959–1981).

H. MUSIC

Mary Chan, *Music in the Theatre of Ben Jonson* (Oxford, 1980).
John P. Cutts, 'Ben Jonson's Masque *The Vision of Delight*', *Notes and Queries*, N.S. 3 (1956), pp. 64–7.
—— 'Jacobean Masque and Stage Music', *Music and Letters*, 35 (1954), pp. 185–200.
—— 'Le Role de la musique dans les masques de Ben Jonson', in Jacquot volume, pp. 285–302.
—— 'Robert Johnson and the Stuart Masque', *Music and Letters*, 41 (1960), pp. 11–26.
Edward J. Dent, *Foundations of English Opera* (Cambridge, 1928).
John Duffy, *The Songs and Motets of Alfonso Ferrabosco the Younger* (Ann Arbor, Mich., 1980).
MacDonald Emslie, 'Nicholas Lanier's Innovations in English Song', *Music and Letters*, 41 (1960), pp. 13–27.
Willa McClung Evans, *Ben Jonson and Elizabethan Music* (Lancaster, Pa., 1929)
—— *Henry Lawes* (New York and London, 1941).
David Fuller, 'The Jonsonian Masque and its Music', *Music and Letters*, 54 (1973), pp. 440–52. (Corrections and additions offered by Peter Holman in *Music and Letters*, 55 (1974), pp. 250–2.)
Otto Gombosi, 'Some Musical Aspects of the English Court Masque', *Journal of the American Musicological Society*, 1 (1948), p. 3.
Murray Lefkowitz, *William Lawes* (London, 1960).
—— 'The Longleat Papers of Bulstrode Whitelocke; New Light on Shirley's *Triumph of Peace*', *Journal of the American Musicological Society*, 18 (1965), pp. 42–60.
Richard Luckett, 'Exotick but Rational Entertainments: the English Dramatic Operas', in *English Drama: Forms and Development*, ed. Marie Axton and Raymond Williams (Cambridge, 1977), pp. 123–41.
John C. Meagher, 'The Dance and the Masque of Ben Jonson', *Journal of the Warburg and Courtauld Institutes*, 25 (1962), pp. 258–77.
Wilfred Mellers, *Harmonious Meeting* (London, 1965).
Andrew J. Sabol, *Four Hundred Songs and Dances for the Stuart Masque* (Providence, R.I., 1978).
—— *Songs and Dances for the Stuart Masque* (Providence, R.I., 1959).
—— 'New Documents on Shirley's Masque *The Triumph of Peace*', *Music and Letters*, 47 (1966), pp. 10–26.
Ian Spink, *English Song, Dowland to Purcell* (London, 1974).
P.J. Willetts, 'Sir Nicholas Le Strange's Collection of Masque Music', *British Museum Quarterly*, 29 (1965), pp. 79–81.

I. MASQUE AND DRAMA

Marie Axton, 'The Tudor Mask and Elizabethan Court Drama', in *English Drama: Forms and Development*, ed. Marie Axton and Raymond Williams (Cambridge, 1977), pp. 24-47.

Daniel C. Boughner, 'Jonsonian Structure in *The Tempest*', *Shakespeare Quarterly*, 21 (1970), pp. 3-10.

John B. Bender, 'Affinities between Jacobean Masques and Plays', *Research Opportunities in Renaissance Drama*, 17 (1974), pp. 9-12.

David M. Bergeron, 'The Restoration of Hermione in *The Winter's Tale*', in *Shakespeare's Romances Reconsidered*, ed. Carol McGinnis Kay and Henry F. Jacobs (Lincoln, Nebraska, and London, 1978), pp. 125-33.

Edward I. Berry, '*Henry VIII* and the Dynamics of Spectacle', *Shakespeare Studies*, 12 (1979), pp. 229-46.

Ralph Berry, 'Masques and Dumb Shows in Webster's Plays', *The Elizabethan Theatre*, 7 (1981), pp. 124-46.

M.C. Bradbrook, *The Living Monument: Shakespeare and the Theatre of His Time* (Cambridge, 1976).

Inga-Stina Ewbank, '"These Pretty Devices": A Study of Masques in Plays', in *A Book of Masques* (see 'Anthologies'), pp. 405-48.

Northrop Frye, 'Romance as Masque' in *Shakespeare's Romances Reconsidered*, pp. 11-39.

Ernest B. Gilman, '"All eyes": Prospero's Inverted Masque', *Renaissance Quarterly*, 33 (1980), pp. 214-30.

M.R. Golding, 'Variations in the Use of the Masque in English Revenge Tragedy', *Yearbook of English Studies*, 3 (1973), pp. 44-54.

Suzanne Gossett, 'Masque Influence on the Dramaturgy of Beaumont and Fletcher', *Modern Philology*, 69 (1972), pp. 199-208.

—— 'The term "Masque" in Shakespeare and Fletcher and "The Coxcomb"'. *Studies in English Literature*, 14 (1974), pp. 285-95.

Marianne Hallar, *The English Court-Masque and its Influence upon Shakespearean Dramaturgy* (Copenhagen, 1968).

Cyrus Hoy, 'Masques and the Artifice of Tragedy', *The Elizabethan Theatre*, 7 (1981), pp. 111-23.

Jean Jacquot, 'The Last Plays and the Masque', in *Shakespeare 1971*, ed. Clifford Leech and J.M.R. Margeson (Toronto, 1972), pp. 156-73.

George R. Kernodle, *From Art to Theatre* (Chicago, Ill., 1944).

Jacqueline M. Latham, '*The Tempest* and *The Masque of Queenes*', *Notes and Queries*, N.S. 23 (1976), pp. 162-3.

Clifford Leech, 'Masking and Unmasking in the Last Plays', in *Shakespeare's Romances Reconsidered*, pp. 40-59.

Michael Neill, '"The Simetry, which Gives a Poem Grace": Masque, Imagery, and the Fancy of *The Maids Tragedy*', *Renaissance Drama* N.S. 3 (1970), pp. 111-35.

Allardyce Nicoll, 'Shakespeare and the Court Masque', *Shakespeare Jahrbuch*, 94 (1958), pp. 51-62.

Gary Schmidgall, *Shakespeare and the Courtly Aesthetic* (Berkeley, Los Angeles, and London, 1981).

Irwin Smith, 'Ariel and the Masque in *The Tempest*', *Shakespeare Quarterly*, 21 (1970), pp. 213-22.

Select bibliography

Richard Studing, 'Spectacle and Masque in *The Winter's Tale*', *English Miscellany*, 21 (1970), pp. 56–80.

A.H. Thorndike, 'The Influence of the Court-Masques on the Drama, 1608–1615', *PMLA*, 15 (1900), pp. 114–20.

Alice Venezky, *Pageantry on the Shakespearean Stage* (New York, 1951).

Glynne Wickham 'Masque and Anti-Masque in *The Tempest*', *Essays and Studies*, 28 (1975), pp. 1–14.

Of authors and titles of masques and plays
discussed in the body of the text